Inland Marine Insurance

Volume I

Inland Marine Insurance

Volume I

RODERICK McNAMARA
Vice President
Marine Office of America Corporation

ROBERT A. LAURENCE
Manager
Sponsored Automobile and Homeowners Operations
Aetna Life and Casualty Company

GLENN L. WOOD, Ph.D, CPCU, CLU
Professor of Finance
California State College

First Edition • 1987

INSURANCE INSTITUTE OF AMERICA
720 Providence Road, Malvern, Pennsylvania 19355-0770

Second Printing • December 1991

Library of Congress Catalog Number 87-82150
International Standard Book Number 0-89462-042-8

Printed in the United States of America

Foreword

Over the years, the American Institute for Property and Liability Underwriters and the Insurance Institute of America have responded to the educational needs of the property and liability insurance industry by developing courses and administering national examinations specifically for insurance personnel. These companion nonprofit educational organizations receive the support of the insurance industry in fulfilling this need.

The American Institute maintains and administers the program leading to the Chartered Property Casualty Underwriter (CPCU®) professional designation.

The Insurance Institute of America offers a wide range of associate designation and certificate programs in the following technical and managerial disciplines:

Accredited Adviser in Insurance (AAI®)
Associate in Claims (AIC)
Associate in Underwriting (AU)
Associate in Risk Management (ARM)
Associate in Loss Control Management (ALCM®)
Associate in Premium Auditing (APA®)
Associate in Management (AIM)
Associate in Research and Planning (ARP®)
Associate in Insurance Accounting and Finance (AIAF)
Associate in Automation Management (AAM®)
Associate in Marine Insurance Management (AMIM)
Associate in Reinsurance (ARe)
Certificate in General Insurance
Certificate in Supervisory Management
Certificate in Introduction to Claims
Certificate in Introduction to Property and Liability Insurance

The Institutes developed the Associate in Marine Insurance Management program at the behest of the American Institute of Marine Underwriters and the Inland Marine Underwriters Association as well as many other representatives of the industry who recognized the need to address professional education in the marine field. The Associate in Marine Insurance Management program has two basic objectives: to provide in-depth knowledge of the marine field, both ocean and inland, and to broaden the student's understanding of insurance and risk management principles, insurance company operations, the legal environment of insurance, and management.

As with all Institute publications, this text has been extensively reviewed by a group of industry experts, and they are recognized in the authors' preface. Throughout the development of this series of texts, it has been—and will continue to be—necessary to draw on the knowledge and skills of Institute personnel. These individuals receive no royalties on texts sold; their writing responsibilities are seen as an integral part of their professional duties. We have proceeded in this way to avoid any possibility of conflict of interests.

We invite and welcome any criticisms of our publications. It is only with such comments that we can provide high quality study materials. Comments should be directed to the Curriculum Department of the Institutes.

Norman A. Baglini, Ph.D., CPCU, CLU, AU
President

Preface

This book has been prepared as the text for AMIM 122, one of six courses in the Associate in Marine Insurance Management program. The other courses consist of AMIM 121 (Ocean Marine Insurance) and CPCU courses in insurance principles, insurance company operations, law, and management. The AMIM program provides a means for those involved in the marine field to enhance their professional skills and increase their technical proficiency.

The objectives of AMIM 122 are to enable the student to identify inland marine loss exposures, select and analyze appropriate insurance coverages, and describe the underwriting criteria applicable to those coverages. Chapter 1 describes the various classes of inland marine business, the general characteristics of inland marine loss exposures, and the principles of inland marine underwriting. Chapter 2 examines the commercial inland marine program of the Insurance Services Office as a frame of reference for describing the many forms discussed in other chapters of the text. Chapters 3 through 11 describe specific categories of *commercial* loss exposures and insurance, along with applicable underwriting criteria and loss control measures. Chapters 12 and 13 provide the same treatment for the *personal* classes of inland marine insurance.

The original manuscript for this text was produced by the Inland Marine Underwriters Association (IMUA) and graciously donated to the Insurance Institute of America. The portions of the manuscript describing commercial coverages were written by Roderick McNamara, Vice President, Marine Office of America Corporation. The portions of the manuscript on personal inland marine insurance were written by Robert A. Laurence, Manager of Sponsored Automobile and Homeowners Operations, Aetna Life and Casualty Company.

After the original manuscript was delivered to the Institute, Glenn

L. Wood, Ph.D., CPCU, CLU, Professor of Finance, California State College, served as coordinating author. In that capacity, Dr. Wood reorganized and supplemented the manuscript to conform to the educational objectives and course outline developed by the Institute.

Arthur L. Flitner, CPCU, Assistant Director of Curriculum, Insurance Institute of America, served as technical editor of the final manuscript. He also wrote Chapter 2 and updated various sections of the manuscript dealing with forms that had become obsolete with the Insurance Services Office's revision of inland marine forms in 1986.

Besides the authors, many persons lent their time and efforts to this text. While a diligent effort has been made to list all reviewers and contributers below, the authors extend their sincere thanks to all who assisted them in any way, even though they may not be listed here.

In his work on the commercial lines portion of the manuscript, Mr. McNamara was assisted by the members of the IMUA Educational Seminars Committee, each of whom reviewed or otherwise contributed to one or more chapters of the manuscript. These members are Francis X. Brewi, Vice President, GRE-Talbot Bird; Alwin E. Bulau, Assistant Vice President, Crum & Forster Insurance Companies; Timothy S. Clark, Marine Underwriting Operations Director, The Hartford Insurance Group; Laura A. Frisch, Senior Marine Underwriter, Aetna Life and Casualty Company; Timothy J. Guiltinan, Assistant Secretary, Wm. H. McGee & Co., Inc.; Harry R. Hanson, Vice President, American Home Assurance Company; William G. Heaphy, Inland Marine Manager, Commercial Union Insurance Companies; Edward C. Leber, Jr., CPCU, Assistant Vice President, United States Fidelity and Guaranty Company; David T. Lind, Assistant Vice President, Chubb Group of Insurance Companies; Paul D. Ranieri, CPCU, Underwriter, Seneca Insurance Company; John W. Screeden, Regional Underwriting Director, St. Paul Fire and Marine Insurance Company; Kathleen M. Stearns, Senior Underwriting Officer, Chubb Group of Insurance Companies; William E. Tap, Secretary, The Home Insurance Company; and Kevin J. Wolfe, President, Wolfe Associates, Inc.

In his work on the personal lines portion, Mr. Laurence received review and other assistance from the following members of the IMUA Personal Lines Committee: Gary W. Cross, First Vice President, American Hardware Insurance Group; William B. Finnerty, Manager of Commercial Lines Underwriting, National Grange Mutual Insurance Company; Doris K. Freyland, Assistant Vice President, Wm. H. McGee & Co., Inc.; and Milton M. Joye, Product Consultant, Royal Insurance Companies.

All chapters of the text were reviewed by two men whose writings have informed the minds of inland marine practitioners for many years:

William H. Rodda, CPCU; and James D. Youd, CPCU. Mr. Rodda's additional role as a contributing author is acknowledged on the separate Contributing Authors page of this book.

The following persons reviewed one or more chapters of the text: Lawrence E. Brown, Jr., Assistant Manager, Commercial Property Division, Insurance Services Office; Robert J. Gibbons, Ph.D., CPCU, CLU, Vice President, Insurance Institute of America; Robert Montgomery, Vice President, Communications, American Association of Insurance Services; Maurice E. Southwell, CPCU, CLU, ChFC, ARM, Assistant Manager, Commercial Property Division, Insurance Services Office; and Eric A. Wiening, M.S., CPCU, ARM, AU, Director of Curriculum Development, Insurance Institute of America.

Contributions to the overall text or to particular chapters were made by Hylan Cooper, LL.B., LL.M., M.B.A., Partner, Schindel, Cooper, Farman & Sorkin; John C. Herman, Vice President, IMUA; James E. Mooney, CPCU, ARM, Assistant Vice President, IMUA; Michael A. Pero, P.E., Second Vice President, General Reinsurance Corporation; William F. Warm, (Retired) President, Hull & Cargo Surveyors, Inc.; and William T. Wildprett (Retired), The Atlantic Companies.

Although we have strived to create a correct and complete book, we realize that this book may contain inadvertent errors, for which we accept responsibility. We will be grateful for any corrections or suggestions, which may be addressed to the Curriculum Department of the Institute.

Roderick McNamara
Robert A. Laurence
Glenn L. Wood

Contributing Authors

The Insurance Institute of America and the authors acknowledge, with deep appreciation, the work of the following contributing authors:

Arthur L. Flitner, CPCU
Assistant Director of Curriculum
Insurance Institute of America

William H. Rodda, CPCU
Consultant

Table of Contents

CHAPTER 1

Fundamentals of Inland Marine Insurance

INTRODUCTION

The purpose of inland marine insurance is to protect against the financial consequences resulting from loss of or damage to property. Thus, inland marine insurance has the same basic purpose as "commercial property," "dwelling," and other types of property insurance. Despite this commonality of purpose, inland marine insurance is treated as a separate line of coverage by both insurance companies and insurance regulators.

The principal difference between inland marine insurance and other types of property insurance is in the *kinds of property* insured. An informal guiding principle, though there are exceptions to it, is that inland marine insurance covers property while being transported, property of a movable, or "floating," nature, and property instrumental in transportation or communication. Often, these criteria include unique property (for example, a traveling Rembrandt exhibition) that does not lend itself to being insured under a "standard" insurance policy and charged a "manual" rate. Consequently, inland marine insurance on many types of property (like ocean marine insurance generally) is not subject to the usual regulations requiring insurance rates and forms to be submitted to state insurance departments for their inspection or approval. Thus, inland marine insurance often entails greater flexibility than other property lines in determining policy provisions and premiums.

Some common examples of property covered by inland marine insurance are cargo being moved by train, truck, or airplane; bulldozers, cranes, and other types of mobile equipment; bridges, tunnels, and viaducts; radio and television transmitting equipment; personal jewelry and furs; musical instruments; art collections; livestock and other animals; doctors' and dentists' instruments; and theatrical equipment. This sampling, while by no means exhaustive, illustrates the breadth of properties eligible for inland marine coverage.

The initial concern of this chapter is to describe the types of property that have come to be subjects of inland marine insurance. That is accomplished by reviewing the history of inland marine insurance, with emphasis on the development of the Nation-Wide Marine Definition, a document that defines the various classes of inland (and ocean) marine insurance. From there, the chapter analyzes inland marine loss exposures in terms of property subject to loss, causes of loss, types of financial loss, and the parties who may sustain financial loss. Finally, Chapter 1 examines the principles of inland marine underwriting, the process by which insurance companies decide which risks are acceptable, what premium will be charged, and what policy provisions will be used.

HISTORICAL DEVELOPMENT OF INLAND MARINE INSURANCE

The term "inland marine" came into being in the 1920s. Someone not familiar with the term might make a logical, though erroneous, deduction that it relates to the insurance of cargo and vessels on inland waterways. The name is an anomaly that provides no clues as to the true nature of the class. This is not an indictment of the name, as no two words, or three, or four, can accurately depict the multiplicity of coverages, many of them seemingly unrelated, that can be written as inland marine. To understand why these various coverages coalesced under one banner requires some understanding of how inland marine insurance developed.

Extension of Marine Insurance to Inland Transportation

Prior to World War I, the railroads and inland waterways were the principal means of transporting goods from one place to another in the United States. The trucking industry was still in its infancy. The railroads were fair and prompt in their settlement of claims, and there was little need for insurance on property in transit. During World War I, the government enlisted the use of the railroads in the war effort and placed a heavy load on the rail system. This resulted in certain gaps in the railroads' protection of freight and a deterioration in claims service, which in turn gave rise to a new market for insurance protection. After the war, the trucking industry began to grow. Hampered by a lack of capital, the new industry's response to shippers' claims was unsatisfactory. This reinforced the need for insurance of goods in inland transit.

Who could fill that need? The "fire" companies writing property insurance were regulated as to the type of coverage they provided and the rates they charged. Their policy forms were designed for fixed location exposures and not property moving from place to place. Nor could they provide theft coverage, which was a principal hazard to goods in transit. Companies writing casualty insurance were of no assistance. They were similarly regulated, and the automobile coverage they wrote pertained to the vehicle, not the cargo.

Companies writing marine insurance enjoyed an advantage over their fire and casualty counterparts. Marine insurance, due to its international flavor, was not regulated as to rate or form. In addition, marine insurers were already accustomed to writing insurance on property in inland transit. A "warehouse-to-warehouse" clause attached to the ocean marine policy provided coverage for the land portion of an ocean shipment. An ocean cargo policy containing this clause could insure the property from the time it left London until it reached Chicago. As the ocean cargo policy was designed to cover all perils of the seas, the warehouse-to-warehouse clause emerged as coverage against "all risks" of loss in transit. Providing insurance for domestic shippers was a natural next step for marine insurers.

Extension to Other Classes of Property

In the years following World War I, people began to amass some wealth. How could one obtain broad insurance coverage on a valuable ring? Fire insurers could provide coverage against certain named perils, principally fire and windstorm, but normally only while the property was at the fixed location described in the policy. Casualty companies provided burglary insurance, which covered loss due to breaking and entering the building named in the policy. Conventional sources could not provide coverage for the loss of a ring left in the washroom of a theater, or the loss of a gem that dropped out of its setting. Nor did they have any great desire to provide such insurance.

The time was right for the entry of the marine underwriter, the adventurer with the "all-risks" form and the frontier spirit. Marine insurers were willing to underwrite this new class of business, and the jewelry floater was born. (Inland marine policies that cover property of a "floating" nature are often called *floaters*.) Coverage on fur coats, fine arts, cameras, and musical instruments followed, as did coverage on the stocks in trade of jewelers. Bridges and tunnels also came into the fold. Conventional sources could not provide coverage for collapse of a bridge or tunnel, and so the marine underwriter's "all-risks" form satisfied the need for such coverage. Insurance for many other classes of business followed the same pattern. The marriage of the necessity of the times and the adventurous spirit of the marine insurers produced a growing line of insurance that came to be called inland marine.

During the 1920s, inland marine insurance flourished. Due to the lack of rate restrictions and regulations regarding the coverage that could be written, there was intense competition among marine companies that resulted in inadequate rate levels. To establish some order within the industry, over 140 insurance companies organized the Inland Marine Underwriters Association (IMUA). The purpose of the group, formed on January 1, 1931, was to stabilize the new line with respect to agency commissions, to control rebating and unfair discrimination, to devise uniform forms and clauses, and to establish rating methods for those classes that then lent themselves to class (or manual) rating.

From its inception until 1945, IMUA functioned as both a rating bureau and a trade association. The South-Eastern Underwriters Association (SEUA) decision, in 1944, had the effect of forcing the separation of bureau and trade association functions. IMUA has continued as a trade association since 1948, when the last of the rate, form, and rule functions were transferred to Inland Marine Insurance Bureau, which has since become a part of Insurance Services Office (ISO). Today IMUA serves more than 350 member companies and pursues a number of definitive purposes:

1. to provide a forum for the discussion of general problems of common concern to companies doing inland marine insurance business;
2. to develop insurance policy language that is clear, simple, and adequate for the protection of the public;
3. to advise with respect to legislation affecting the business;
4. to promote cooperation with state insurance departments and other public officials and with other organizations; and
5. to conserve and promote the interests of its members and their policyholders in every legitimate manner consistent with the public welfare.

The Nation-Wide Marine Definition[1]

As inland marine premiums grew during the 1920s and into the 1930s, the fire and casualty companies became increasingly aware of the business they were losing: fire premiums on the property side and burglary premiums on the casualty side. The marine companies, proceeding full speed ahead, were writing business—such as the merchandise of department stores—that had theretofore been the province of fire and casualty insurers.

Such unhampered activity, however, was short-lived. In 1932, New York State defined what was eligible for insurance under a marine policy. Following New York's lead, the National Convention of Insurance Commissioners (NCIC) at a meeting later that year proposed that a nationwide definition of marine insurance be adopted. In 1933, a "Nation-Wide Definition and Interpretation of the Insuring Powers of Marine and Transportation Underwriters" was adopted by the NCIC and recommended to the individual states for adoption as a ruling or regulation. Eventually, a majority of the states did adopt this definition. As can be inferred from its title, the Definition was not designed as a permissive document, but rather as one that limited the insuring powers of marine insurers. It specified in some detail what were considered to be marine exposures and what could not be covered by marine insurance.

In general, exposures that could not be covered by marine insurers were insured by fire or casualty insurers. Although conservatism left many uninsured gaps, the fire and casualty insurers were somewhat successful in limiting the further expansion of marine underwriters. A committee of insurance company representatives was empowered by regulations in many states and by agreements among insurance companies to penalize insurers writing business as marine insurance that was outside the Definition.

Effect of the SEUA Decision and Multiple-Line Legislation The South-Eastern Underwriters Association (SEUA) decision in 1944 brought insurance business within the scope of the federal antitrust laws. This made it undesirable or impossible for associations of insurance company representatives to penalize insurance companies for their actions. The development of multiple-line insurance around 1950 also made archaic the Nation-Wide Marine Definition as a definition of insuring powers. Insurance companies generally acquired expanded insuring powers that covered the entire scope of property and liability insurance. The era of "compartmentalization" into fire insurers, casualty insurers, and marine insurers was officially ended.

1953 Revision of the Definition All this led to a revised concept of the Nation-Wide Marine Definition. The 1953 convention of the National Association of Insurance Commissioners (formerly the NCIC) adopted a revised Nation-Wide Marine Definition, which includes this statement:

> This instrument shall not be construed to restrict or limit in any way the exercise of any insuring powers granted under charters and license whether used separately, in combination or otherwise.

The Definition thus became a document for classification purposes rather than a definition of underwriting powers. Its principal function since the 1953 revision has been to determine how an insurer is to report for statistical and annual statement purposes the premiums and losses written as marine business. It has a collateral effect in setting out various forms of insurance policies. The Definition has also been used by rating organizations and state insurance departments in determining what classes of inland marine insurance are subject to rate filing requirements. (Rate filing requirements are discussed in more detail later in this chapter.)

1976 Revision of the Definition The Nation-Wide Marine Definition was again amended by the NAIC in 1976. The result was an expansion of the definition to classify a wider range of property as inland marine. For example, the 1976 Definition added electronic data processing equipment and builders risk policies. Other differences between the 1953 and 1976 Definitions are noted as appropriate in later chapters of this book.

Principles of the Definition The starting point of the Definition is the principle that there should be an element of transportation present if property is to be eligible for insurance under an inland marine policy. Of course, bridges and tunnels are not intended to be moved, but they are held to be insurable under an inland marine policy because they are "instrumentalities of transportation." Some of the dealer or "block" policies described later in this book are clearly coverages on stocks of merchandise. Such stocks of merchandise as those in jewelry stores had been insured by marine insurers for many years before any effort was made to define marine insurance. The drafters of the original Definition had no practical choice but to include jewelers block insurance as a marine coverage because the bulk of jewelry stocks were then being insured with marine policies. The same justification was accepted for insurance on bridges and tunnels. Thus, because of historical developments, it became customary to expand marine insurance beyond the arbitrary standard of "transportability."

The Marine Definition covers both ocean and inland marine insurance. However, the principal effect of the Definition is on inland marine insurance. Ocean marine coverages are so clearly established that questions seldom arise regarding classification of such exposures.

General Effect of the Definition In many cases, an insurer will write an inland marine policy to cover a situation that is not specifically within the Definition. Providing some kind of coverage is entirely legal as long as the insurer has multiple-line insuring powers. There may be a technical violation of regulations if an insurer writes as inland marine coverage a policy that would be under rate regulatory requirements of some other form of insurance. However, the Definition and the practices of the business are so fluid that there is seldom criticism of an insurer for handling a borderline case according to whatever procedures seem to fit the situation.

At the same time, many "commercial property" insurance policies include some coverage for property away from the insured's premises, and many provide a small amount of transit insurance. So, nonmarine policies also include some coverages that technically could qualify for marine insurance.

Text of the Definition The Definition is of such importance in the writing of inland marine insurance in the United States that the student must be familiar with its terms. The text of the 1976 version is presented here. This version has been adopted by a majority of states. The 1953 version is still in effect in a small number of states. Texas has its own definition, and other states have not formally adopted a marine definition.

1976 NATION-WIDE MARINE DEFINITION

The purpose of this instrument is to describe the kinds of risks and coverages which may be classified or identified under State Insurance Laws as Marine, Inland Marine or Transportation insurance, but does not include all of the kinds of risks and coverages which may be written, classified or identified under Marine, Inland Marine or Transportation insuring powers, nor shall it be construed to mean that the kinds of risks and coverages are solely Marine, Inland Marine or Transportation insurance in all instances.

This instrument shall not be construed to restrict or limit in any way the exercise of any insuring powers granted under charters and license whether used separately, in combination or otherwise.

I. Marine and/or transportation policies may cover under the following conditions:

A. Imports

Imports may be covered wherever the property may be and without restriction as to time, provided the coverage of the issuing companies includes hazards of transportation.

An import, as a proper subject of marine or transportation insurance, shall be deemed to maintain its character as such, so long as the property remains segregated in such a way that it can be identified and has not become incorporated and mixed with the general mass of property in the United States, and shall be deemed to have been completed when such property has been:

(a) sold and delivered by the importer, factor or consignee; or

(b) removed from place of storage and placed on sale as part of importer's stock in trade at a point of sale-distribution; or

(c) delivered for manufacture, processing or change in form to premises of the importer or of another used for any purposes.

B. Exports

Exports may be covered wherever the property may be without restriction as to time, provided the coverage of the issuing companies includes hazards of transportation.

An export, as a proper subject of marine or transportation insurance, shall be deemed to acquire its character as such when designated or while being prepared for export and retain that character unless diverted for domestic trade, and when so diverted, the provisions of this Ruling respecting domestic shipments shall apply, provided, however, that this provision shall not apply to long established methods of insuring certain commodities, e.g., cotton.

C. Domestic Shipments

1. Domestic shipments on consignment, [provided the coverage of the issuing companies includes hazards of transportation] for sale or distribution, exhibit, or trial, or approval or auction, while in transit, while in the custody of others and while being returned, provided that in no event shall the policy cover on premises owned, leased or operated by the consignor.

2. Domestic shipments not on consignment, provided the coverage of the issuing companies includes hazards of transportation, beginning and ending within the United States, provided that such shipments shall not be covered

at manufacturing premises nor after arrival at premises owned, leased or operated by Assured or purchaser.

D. Bridges, Tunnels and Other Instrumentalities of Transportation and Communication (excluding buildings, their improvements and betterments, furniture and furnishings, fixed contents and supplies held in storage)

The foregoing includes:

1. Bridges, tunnels, other similar instrumentalities, including auxiliary facilities and equipment attendant thereto.
2. Piers, wharves, docks, slips, dry docks and marine railways.
3. Pipelines, including on-line propulsion, regulating and other equipment appurtenant to such pipelines, but excluding all property at manufacturing, producing, refining, converting, treating or conditioning plants.
4. Power transmission and Telephone and Telegraph lines, excluding all property at generating, converting or transforming stations, substations and exchanges.
5. Radio and Television Communication Equipment in use as such including towers and antennae with auxiliary equipment, and appurtenant electrical operating and control apparatus.
6. Outdoor cranes, loading bridges and similar equipment used to load, unload and transport.

E. Personal Property Floater Risks covering individuals and/or generally

1. Personal Effects Floater Policies.
2. The Personal Property Floater.
3. Government Service Floaters.
4. Personal Fur Floaters.
5. Personal Jewelry Floaters.
6. Wedding Presents Floaters for not exceeding 90 (ninety) days after the day of the wedding.
7. Silverware Floaters.

8. Fine Arts Floaters covering paintings, etchings, pictures, tapestries, art glass windows, and other bonafide works of art of rarity, historical value or artistic merit.

9. Stamp and Coin Floaters.

10. Musical Instrument Floaters. Radios, televisions, record players and combinations thereof are not deemed musical instruments.

11. Mobile Articles, Machinery and Equipment Floaters (excluding motor vehicles designed for highway use and auto homes, trailers and semitrailers except when hauled by tractors not designed for highway use) covering identified property of a mobile or floating nature pertaining to or usual to a household. Such policies shall not cover furniture and fixtures not customarily used away from premises where such property is usually kept.

12. Installment Sales and Leased Property Policies covering property pertaining to a household and sold under conditional contract of sale, partial payment contract or installment sales contract or leased, but excluding motor vehicles designed for highway use. Such policies must cover in transit but shall not extend beyond the termination of the seller's or lessor's interest.

13. Live Animal Floaters.

F. Commercial Property Floater Risks covering property pertaining to a business, profession or occupation.

1. Radium Floaters.

2. Physicians' and Surgeons' Instrument Floaters. Such policies may include coverage of such furniture fixtures and tenant Assured's interest in such improvements and betterments of buildings as are located in that portion of the premises occupied by the assured in the practice of his profession.

3. Pattern and Die Floaters.

4. Theatrical Floaters, excluding buildings and their improvements and betterments, and furniture and fixtures that do not travel about with theatrical troupes.

5. Film Floaters, including builders' risk during the production and coverage on completed negatives and positives and sound records.

6. Salesmen's Samples Floaters.

7. Exhibition Policies on property while on exhibition and in transit to or from such exhibitions.

8. Live Animal Floaters.

9. Builders' Risks and/or Installation Risks covering interest of owner, seller or contractor, against loss or damage to machinery, equipment, building materials or supplies, being used with and during the course of installation, testing, building, renovating or repairing. Such policies may cover at points or places where work is being performed, while in transit and during temporary storage or deposit, of property designated for and awaiting specific installation, building, renovating or repairing.

   Such coverage shall be limited to Builders' Risks or Installation Risks where Perils in addition to Fire and Extended Coverage are to be insured.

   If written for account of owner, the coverage shall cease upon completion and acceptance thereof; or if written for account of a seller or contractor the coverage shall terminate when the interest of the seller or contractor ceases.

10. Mobile Articles, Machinery and Equipment Floaters (excluding motor vehicles designed for highway use and auto homes, trailers and semitrailers except when hauled by tractors not designed for highway use and snow plows constructed exclusively for highway use), covering identified property of a mobile or floating nature, not on sale or consignment, or in course of manufacture, which has come into custody or control of parties who intend to use such property for the purpose for which it was manufactured or created. Such policies shall not cover furniture and fixtures not customarily used away from premises where such property is usually kept.

11. Property in transit to or from and in custody of bailees (not owned, controlled or operated by the bailor). Such policies shall not cover bailee's property at his premises.

12. Installment Sales and Leased Property. Policies covering property sold under conditional contract of sale, partial payment contract, installment sales contract, or leased but excluding motor vehicles designed for highway use. Such policies must cover in transit but shall not extend beyond the termination of the seller's or lessor's interest. This section is not intended to include machinery and equipment under certain "leaseback" contracts.

13. Garment Contractors Floaters.

14. Furriers or Fur Storer's Customer's Policies (i.e., policies under which certificates or receipts are issued by furriers or fur storers) covering specified articles the property of customers.

15. Accounts Receivable Policies, Valuable Papers and Records Policies.

16. Floor Plan Policies, covering property for sale while in possession of dealers under a Floor Plan or any similar plan under which the dealer borrows money from a bank or lending institution with which to pay the manufacturer, provided:

    1. Such merchandise is specifically identifiable as encumbered to the bank or lending institution.

    2. The dealer's right to sell or otherwise dispose of such merchandise is conditioned upon its being released from encumbrance by the bank or lending institution.

    3. That such policies cover in transit and do not extend beyond the termination of the dealer's interest.

    Provided that such policies shall not cover automobiles or motor vehicles; merchandise for which the dealer's collateral is the stock or inventory as distinguished from merchandise specifically identifiable as encumbered to the lending institution.

17. Sign and Street Clock Policies, including neon signs, automatic or mechanical signs, street clocks, while in use as such.

18. Fine Arts Policies covering paintings, etchings, pictures, tapestries, art glass windows, and other bonafide works of art of rarity, historical value or artistic merit, for account

of museums, galleries, universities, businesses, municipalities and other similar interests.

19. Policies covering personal property which, when sold to the ultimate purchaser, may be covered specifically, by the owner, under Inland Marine Policies including:

   (a) Musical Instrument Dealers Policies, covering property consisting principally of musical instruments and their accessories. Radios, televisions, record players and combinations thereof are not deemed musical instruments.

   (b) Camera Dealers Policies, covering property consisting principally of cameras and their accessories.

   (c) Furrier's Dealers Policies, covering property consisting principally of furs and fur garments.

   (d) Equipment Dealers Policies, covering mobile equipment consisting of binders, reapers, tractors, harvesters, harrows, tedders and other similar agricultural equipment and accessories therefor; construction equipment consisting of bulldozers, road scrapers, tractors, compressors, pneumatic tools and similar equipment and accessories therefor; but excluding motor vehicles designed for highway use.

   (e) Stamp and Coin Dealers covering property of philatelic and numismatic nature.

   (f) Jewelers' Block Policies.

   (g) Fine Arts Dealers

   Such policies may include coverage of money in locked safes or vaults on the Assured's premises. Such policies also may include coverage of furniture, fixtures, tools, machinery, patterns, molds, dies and tenant insureds interest in improvements of buildings.

20. Wool Growers Floaters.

21. Domestic Bulk Liquids Policies, covering tanks and domestic bulk liquids stored therein.

22. Difference in Conditions Coverage excluding fire and extended coverage perils.

23. Electronic Data Processing Policies.

II. Unless otherwise permitted, nothing in the foregoing shall be construed to permit Marine or Transportation Policies to Cover:

A. Storage of Assured's merchandise, except as hereinbefore provided.

B. Merchandise in course of manufacture, the property of and on the premises of the manufacturer.

C. Furniture and fixtures and improvements and betterments to buildings.

D. Monies and/or securities in safes, vaults, safety deposit vaults, bank or Assured's premises, except while in the course of transportation.

FILED AND NONFILED FORMS AND RATES

The classes of business written as inland marine can be placed into two categories—*filed* and *nonfiled* (sometimes referred to as *controlled* and *noncontrolled*).

Filed classes are those for which forms or rates or both must be filed with the insurance regulatory officials of a particular state in order for the insurer to write policies for that class of business in that state. Generally, the filed classes are those for which a large number of insureds with similar exposures exist. Jewelry, furs, and coin collections are common examples of filed classes of business.

Filing requirements are not entirely consistent from state to state. Some states publish detailed bulletins showing which classes of business are filed. Other states take a more flexible approach. For instance, the filing law or regulation of a particular state may merely contain a provision to the effect that "inland marine risks which by general custom of the business are not written according to manual rates or rating plans" need not be filed.

Under the latter approach, the key to whether a class of business is considered filed or nonfiled depends on whether forms, rules, and rates for the class are filed by the two major insurance rating and advisory organizations on behalf of their member insurance companies. If these organizations make filings for a class, it is presumably a filed class. If they do not make filings for a class, it is presumably nonfiled.

From the underwriter's viewpoint, the significance of whether a particular class of business is filed or nonfiled is that there is more flexibility in the underwriting of the nonfiled classes. The underwriter is free to determine policy provisions and rates, which can be arranged to fit the specific situation for the most appropriate cost. More than one-half of all inland marine insurance is written on nonfiled classes.

With filed classes, underwriters are less able to deviate from the filed forms and rates. The rules for some filed coverages do, however, permit the underwriter to make certain modifications at his or her discretion, such as adding or deleting an exclusion or expanding or contracting the coverage territory. Otherwise, filed forms and rates cannot be modified unless the underwriter obtains the insured's written consent and files the consent form with regulatory officials.

The Role of Rating Organizations

The two rating and advisory organizations referred to above are the Insurance Services Office, Inc. (ISO), headquartered in New York City; and the American Association of Insurance Services (AAIS), headquartered in Bensenville, Illinois. Both organizations provide services to their member companies in other property and liability fields, but attention here is focused on their inland marine services. The differences that exist between ISO and AAIS filings are principally editorial rather than substantive. The classes of business filed by both organizations are shown in Exhibit 1-1.

The obligation to make rate and form filings is placed on the insurance companies. Having the rating organizations make these filings on behalf of many insurers is an economical arrangement, but it is not used by all insurers. An insurance company makes its own decision whether to use a rating organization or to make independent filings, after determining which approach appears more advantageous. Independent filings often bear a close resemblance to the "standard forms" filed by ISO or AAIS.

INLAND MARINE LOSS EXPOSURES[2]

Inland marine insurance exists because businesses and individuals face certain *loss exposures.* A loss exposure has been defined as a condition of susceptibility or vulnerability to loss, that is, the possibility of financial loss. Every loss exposure has three elements:

- the item subject to loss,
- the perils or forces that may cause the loss, and
- the potential financial impact of the loss.[3]

For example, a manufacturer that ships its stereo sets by truck faces a loss exposure because all three elements are present. During the course of their transit, the stereo sets are subject to loss by various

Exhibit 1-1
Classes Filed by AAIS and ISO*

PERSONAL CLASSES

Bicycles	Livestock (AAIS)[1]
Cameras[3]	Musical Instruments
Coin Collections	Outboard Motors & Boats[2]
Farm Equipment (AAIS)[1]	Personal Articles Floater
Fine Arts	Personal Effects Floater
Furs	Personal Property Floater
Golfers Equipment	Silverware
Jewelry	Stamp Collections

COMMERCIAL CLASSES

Accounts Receivable	Jewelers Block (Jewelry Dealers)
Camera and Musical Inst. Dlrs.	Mail Coverage
Commercial Articles [3]	Physicians & Surgeons Equipment
Equipment Dealers (ISO)[4]	Radioactive Contamination (AAIS)[4]
Film (ISO)[4]	Radium(AAIS)[4]
Floor Plan	Signs
Fur Dealers (AAIS)[4]	Theatrical Property
Furriers Customers (AAIS)[4]	Valuable Papers
Implement Dealers (AAIS)[4]	

NOTES:

[1] ISO rules and rates for mobile agricultural machinery and livestock are no longer included in the Inland Marine Division of the ISO Commercial Lines manual. The Farm Division should be referred to for rates and rules for these classes.

[2] Outboard motor and boat rates, rules, and forms apply in just a few states for boats 16 feet in length or less.

[3] The Commercial Articles class includes cameras, musical instruments, and (AAIS only) fine arts.

[4] Only the rating organization in the parenthesis has filed the class. For example, furriers customers is a filed class for AAIS companies, but not a filed class for ISO companies.

*Adapted with permission from *Inland Marine Handbook* (Bensenville, IL: Inland Marine Handbook Inc., December 1986), p. 81.

perils, including collision or overturn of the truck carrying them, theft, windstorm, and earthquake. If such an event were to occur, the cost of replacing the stereo sets would be a financial loss to the owner.

The same shipments could create an additional loss exposure for the operator of the truck, if the operator were a party different from the owner of the property being shipped. For example, if the stereo sets were destroyed in a highway accident caused by the negligent operation of the truck, the operator could become legally obligated to pay the owner for the loss of the stereo sets. Thus, an additional element of loss exposures can be said to be the parties that may be affected when property is lost or damaged. Inland marine insurance often involves property whose loss or damage can pose a loss exposure to more than one party.

The sections that follow describe the four elements of loss exposures: types of property exposed to loss; perils, or causes of loss; parties that may be affected; and potential financial consequences.

Types of Property

At the outset of this chapter, it was said that the principal difference between inland marine insurance and other property insurance is in the types of property eligible for inland marine coverage. Accordingly, the scope of property generally considered as eligible for inland marine coverage was surveyed earlier in this chapter by means of the Nation-Wide Marine Definition.

Perils Affecting Property

A *peril* is a cause of loss. Some inland marine policies even use the phrase "cause of loss" in place of the word "peril."

Which perils are covered and which are excluded in an inland marine policy depend on the needs of the insured, the willingness of the insurer to cover certain perils, and the extent to which it is commercially feasible to insure certain perils. For example, coverage against "cratering" and "blowout" may be essential to the owner of an oil rig but will not be needed by other insureds. Whether an underwriter is willing to extend coverage for a certain peril, such as theft, may largely depend on how the underwriter views the insured's loss history and loss control practices. And some perils, such as war and nuclear reaction, pose the likelihood of such widespread and severe losses that virtually no insurer will cover them.

Insurers use two basic methods of expressing which perils are covered: the *"all-risks" approach* and the *named perils* (or specified perils) *approach.*

"All-Risks" Approach The "all-risks" approach is more commonly used in inland marine policies than the named perils approach. An "all-risks" policy does not name specific perils as being covered. It merely states which causes of loss are *not* covered through the use of various exclusions. Thus, a covered peril is any accidental, or "fortuitous," cause of loss or damage that is not specifically excluded in the policy. The concept of "all-risks" coverage underscores the inland marine underwriter's broad-based approach to insuring many perils.

The name "all-risks" is derived from traditional policy wordings that express the insurer's promise to pay for loss to covered property "by all risks of direct physical loss or damage," subject to policy exclusions and conditions. For reasons that will be discussed in Chapter 2, the wording "all-risks" is falling into disuse in insurance contracts themselves. However, the concept remains the same, and insurance people continue to use "all-risks" to describe an inclusive approach to perils covered in which the scope of the insurance provided is determined largely by the exclusions and conditions rather than by any specific listing of covered perils.

An important practical effect of "all-risks" coverage is that it places the burden of proof on the insurer in the event of a loss. If the insurer cannot prove that the loss is specifically excluded, it must be paid.

Named Perils Approach When an insurance policy uses the named perils approach, only those perils specifically named in the policy are covered. For example, a policy might state that it insures against direct loss or damage by:

1. fire,
2. windstorm,
3. explosion,
4. hail,
5. riot including riot attending a strike,
6. civil commotion,
7. vehicles not owned or operated by the insured,
8. aircraft,
9. smoke,
10. accident to conveyance, and
11. burglary.

The mere listing of the perils does not mean that the policy is intended to cover every loss associated with one or more of the perils. To the contrary, policy exclusions, definitions, and other provisions invariably restrict the scope of the coverage by narrowing the meaning of some or all of the perils. For example, the named peril of "burglary" may be defined by the policy as "the taking of property from inside the premises by a person unlawfully entering or leaving the premises as evidenced by marks of forcible entry or exit." Consequently, if burglars took property without leaving evidence of forcible entry or exit, the burglary peril would not provide coverage for the stolen property.

In contrast with the "all-risks" approach, the named perils approach has the practical effect of placing the burden of proof on the insured. To obtain coverage, the insured must be able to prove that the loss was caused by a covered peril. If such proof cannot be provided by the insured, the insurer is not legally obligated to pay the loss.

Although less widely used than "all-risks" coverage in inland marine insurance, the named perils approach is used frequently for certain classes of inland marine business.

Doctrine of Proximate Cause[4] The *doctrine of proximate cause* is a traditional rule of insurance policy interpretation developed by courts of law. According to this doctrine, loss or damage is not covered in an insurance policy unless a covered peril is the *proximate cause of loss.* A covered peril is the proximate cause if it is the cause that initiates an unbroken chain of events contributing to the loss. Or, as stated in one court decision:

> The proximate cause of any result is the active, efficient cause that sets in motion a train of events which brings about the result without the intervention of any force started and working actively from a new and independent source.[5]

In the case from which this quotation is taken, machinery in a factory was insured against loss by fire. A fire ignited an electrical tower on the insured's premises, some distance from the building in which the insured machinery was located. As a result of the fire, there was an electrical short circuit, which in turn caused a sudden increase in the pressure on a belt driving a flywheel. The flywheel disintegrated, and its flying fragments damaged the machinery in question. By the standard given in the above quotation, the damage to the machinery was ruled to have been proximately caused by fire. Since the insurance policy covered direct damage by fire, the insurer had to pay for the damaged machinery, even though collision with flywheel fragments was not a covered peril. The fire unleashed an unbroken chain of events that resulted in the loss. Fire was the proximate cause of the loss, and fire was a covered peril.

Through the application of the proximate cause doctrine to specific sets of facts, the courts have significantly broadened the coverage scope of many property insurance policies. For example, when food stored under refrigeration was insured against "direct loss by windstorm," wind damage to power lines located off the insured's premises caused a failure of refrigeration and consequent spoilage of the food. This spoilage was ruled to be a covered loss proximately caused by windstorm.[6] Similarly, when cattle being transported by truck were insured against "direct loss by overturning of the vehicle," cattle tracks leading from the overturned truck went directly to a quicksand bog into which the cattle presumably wandered. The death of the cattle was ruled an insured event. Their carcasses were never found.[7] In this situation, the available evidence suggested an unbroken chain of events originating in the peril of overturning, a covered peril under the policy.

In spite of the difficulty of forecasting how a court might interpret the proximate cause doctrine in the light of a given set of facts, understanding the requirement of proximate cause is important to what constitutes "covered perils." An insured loss must not only involve a covered cause; a covered cause must also be the proximate cause of the loss.

Parties Affected When Property Is Damaged or Destroyed

The party most often affected when property is lost, damaged, or destroyed is the owner. Other parties also affected may include:

- common carriers and bailees,
- users of property, and
- lenders of money to the owner of property.

Property Owners If property has some value and is lost, damaged, or destroyed, the owner of the property incurs a financial loss because of the cost of repairing or replacing the property. For example, if contractor Smith's bulldozer is destroyed in a fire, Smith will have to replace the destroyed bulldozer in order to continue his business.

Bailees and Common Carriers A *bailee* is a person to whom property is entrusted for storage, repair, processing, transportation, or other purpose. Dry cleaners, television repair shops, and trucking companies are examples of commercial bailees. A *common carrier* is a special type of bailee that offers its transportation services to the general public.

Depending on the circumstances, bailees and common carriers can become legally responsible to pay for loss or damage to property in their care, custody, or control. Moreover, even if bailees are not legally liable for loss to customers' property, they may suffer loss of their good reputation if they are unable to pay customers' losses after a fire or other accident.

Users of Property Persons or organizations that use property they do not own may also face loss exposures with respect to that property. For example, a retailer that leases a computer or a contractor that rents a front-end loader may have agreed to pay for any accidental damage to the equipment. And, if the leased or rented property is damaged, the user's business may be disrupted or actually come to a standstill, with a corresponding loss of business income.

A similar situation exists when a tenant rents a building and installs certain equipment or other property as *improvements or betterments* to the building. These improvements and betterments become part of the building and therefore the property of the building owner. However, the tenant retains an insurable "use interest" in the property for the remainder of the rental period. If the improvements are destroyed, the tenant will need to replace them in order to continue operations.

Lenders When money is borrowed to finance the purchase of property, the lender may acquire some conditional rights to the property, such as the right to repossess the property if the borrower fails to make loan payments. This right gives the lender security. Such a lender is called a *secured lender* or a *secured creditor*. When an individual or business borrows money to buy a home or a building and the property serves as security for the loan, the secured lender is called a *mortgagee* and the borrower is a *mortgagor*.

Both the property owner and the lender are exposed to loss when property is used to secure a loan. If, for example, a fire destroys contractor Smith's bulldozer and Smith has no money to pay off the loan, the lender would have only the scorched remains of the bulldozer to repossess. Often, a lender protects its interest by requiring the borrower to cover the property with an insurance policy that names the lender as a *loss payee* or mortgagee. For example, a policy covering Smith's bulldozer could include a *loss payable endorsement* stating that the lender will be paid for a covered loss to the extent of its interest in the property.

Another approach is for the lender to purchase its own insurance on the property. Installment sales policies and floor plan policies are two types of inland marine insurance that can be used to insure lenders' interests.

Potential Financial Consequences

The loss of property or damage to it may have undesirable financial consequences. The adverse financial impact may occur in any one of three ways. A property loss may:

- reduce the value of the property,
- cause an increase in the owner's (or other party's) expenses, or
- reduce the owner's (or other party's) income.

Reduction in Value of Property When property is lost or damaged, the property is reduced in value. The actual amount of the reduction in value can be measured in different ways, sometimes with differing results. If the property can be repaired or restored, one measure of the reduction in value is the cost of the repair or restoration. Property that must be completely replaced has no remaining worth, unless some salvageable items can be sold as junk.

- A sign worth $5,000 is damaged by vandals, and the owner has to pay $1,000 to have the damage repaired. The accident—a *partial loss*—has reduced the value of the sign by $1,000.
- A camera worth $200 is run over by a truck. The value of the now worthless camera has been reduced by $200. The camera is a *total loss.*

If an item is lost, stolen, or otherwise disappears, its value *to the owner* is reduced just as though it had been completely destroyed and retained no salvage value.

A further reduction in value may occur if repaired property is worth less than it would be worth had it never been damaged. This is true for collectors' items, such as fine paintings and other art objects. Many collectibles are valuable largely because they are in "original condition," "mint condition," or "perfect condition." An object that has been repaired after damage from a tear, scratch, or fire is no longer in that unspoiled condition and its value will decline. The owner faces loss in the form of the cost to repair the object, as well as a further reduction in value because of the changed condition.

An article of property may have a number of different "values," depending on the method by which the value is determined. For purposes of inland marine insurance, the most common measures of value are *actual cash value, invoice cost,* and *agreed value.* These and other methods of valuing property insured under inland marine policies are discussed along with other policy provisions in Chapter 2.

Increased Expenses When property is damaged, the property itself declines in value and the owner, or other affected party, suffers a corresponding loss. In addition, the owner or other user of that property may have to incur extraordinary expenses in acquiring a temporary substitute or in temporarily maintaining the property in usable condition.

- A business whose computer is damaged may have to rent other equipment or facilities in order to continue its operations.
- A coal company whose conveyor system is destroyed may be obligated to fulfill its contracts with public utilities by buying coal on the open market at a cost considerably higher than its regular production costs.
- Following collapse of its transmitting antenna, a radio station whose broadcasts must continue in order to fulfill advertising

contracts may have to rent additional facilities and, at the same time, pay contractors overtime wages to rebuild the antenna.

Because so many variables are involved, it is difficult to estimate the extra expenses that might be required to stay in business following damage to business property. Determining the extent of a property loss exposure involves giving consideration to the extra expenses required in the event of the loss of property.

Lost Income Many of the types of property insured under inland marine policies are used to produce income. When such property is damaged, income may be lost because the income-producing capacity of the property is reduced or terminated entirely until the property is repaired, restored, or replaced.

- A toll bridge that must be closed for repairs will produce no income while repairs are being made.
- The destruction of an apartment building under construction, to the extent that it delays completion, will reduce the projected rental income that its owner would have earned.
- The loss of a one-of-a-kind machine tool during its transit from California to its new owner in Maine will result in a loss of production and probably a corresponding loss of income while a replacement is being made and shipped.

Determining the dollars of business income that might be lost due to a property loss requires estimating the future level of activity of a firm and doing a "what if" analysis. "What if the business could not operate for six months because it would take six months to rebuild after a fire? How much income would be lost?" This analysis involves projections of the firm's revenues and expenses (1) in normal circumstances and (2) in the event a property loss disrupts normal operations. The comparison of these two projections reveals the potential loss of income.

TREATMENT OF INLAND MARINE LOSS EXPOSURES

When an individual or a business discovers and analyzes its loss exposures, it must decide how these loss exposures will be treated. The major techniques for treating loss exposures are:

- avoidance,
- loss control,
- retention,
- transfer other than insurance, and

- insurance.

It is common for individuals and businesses to use more than one technique for each identified loss exposure. Insurance policies often incorporate a form of retention as well as insurance. An example is the deductible that applies to each loss under a camera dealers policy. Also, insurance company underwriters sometimes require insureds to adopt safety measures as a condition of an insurance policy. Such safety measures are a form of loss control.

Avoidance

When feasible, avoidance is the most effective technique for treating loss exposures. *Avoidance* means an individual or a business avoids potential losses by choosing not to own certain property or engage in certain activities. To avoid an exposure to vandalism, a museum might choose not to erect an outdoor sculpture garden.

Loss Control

Losses can be controlled through:

- *loss prevention* (lowering the frequency of loss),
- *loss reduction* (lowering the severity of the loss that occurs), or
- a combination of loss prevention and loss reduction.

Loss frequency refers to how often a loss occurs or how many losses occur during a given time period. *Loss severity* refers to the size of the losses that have occurred or might occur in the future.

The installation of deadbolt locks on doors and iron bars on windows is an example of loss prevention—it can lower the number of break-ins that occur. Installing a sprinkler system is an example of loss reduction—it cannot prevent a fire, but if a fire does start, the sprinklers can reduce the extent of damage that would have occurred in the absence of the system.

Unlike avoidance, loss control does not eliminate the possibility of loss. Some chance of loss remains although it may be minimized. In this regard, insureds and their insurance companies and agents share a common goal: prevention or reduction of losses and, consequently, the total cost of losses.

Retention

Retention means keeping or absorbing all or part of the financial impact of a loss. Examples of retention are a $500 deductible on a jewelers block policy, or the planned noninsurance of flood or earthquake losses. If a loss exposure is not avoided, controlled, transferred, or insured, it is retained, consciously or not.

Retention is not merely a last resort. It can be the most cost effective way to deal with high frequency (occurring often), low severity (not large) losses.

For example, a shipper such as a large department store making frequent deliveries may decide to insure only packages with an invoice value of over $200. If instances of damage and nondelivery (however caused) consistently amount to less than 5 percent of annual shipments, and packages valued at $200 or less comprise 60 percent of all deliveries, the store can retain these loss exposures and budget the expected losses as a cost of doing business.

Transfer Other Than Insurance

Transfer other than insurance occurs when the loss exposure of one person or organization is assumed by another, usually through a contract. To continue the department store example, after a review of costs and exposures the store could well decide to eliminate its own delivery vehicles, personnel, and insurance and transfer these loss exposures to a regional transporter such as UPS or a similar parcel delivery service.

Such transfers shift responsibility for the financial consequences of a loss exposure to another party.

Insurance

Insurance is a system that enables an individual or an organization to transfer a loss exposure to an insurance company for an amount of money called the insurance premium. In return for this premium, the insurance company will pay the insured's losses as agreed in the insurance policy.

Inland marine insurance provides the means of insuring the scope of loss exposures described in this chapter. Other chapters of this book describe these exposures in more detail and examine the appropriate insurance coverages and underwriting criteria for the various classes of inland marine business. Before the various classes are separately examined, however, it is essential to gain a general knowledge of inland marine underwriting and policy provisions. The final portion of this chapter examines the role of underwriting in inland marine insurance, and Chapter 2 introduces inland marine policy provisions.

INLAND MARINE UNDERWRITING[8]

As used in this book, *underwriting* means deciding which risks are acceptable, determining the premium to be charged and the terms and conditions of the insurance contract, and monitoring these decisions. While ultimate underwriting responsibility and the determination of underwriting policy rest with top management, the day-to-day activities of risk selection are performed by people who specialize in the various kinds of insurance the insurance company offers. There are many persons involved in underwriting. They may range from an agent or a broker at the initial stage all the way up through a senior vice president of underwriting for the insurer.

A specialist in the types of insurance with which he or she comes in frequent contact, the inland marine underwriter deals with many different kinds of property in a variety of situations—in a finished state, in the course of manufacture or construction, and while undergoing repairs. While inland marine insurance is concerned with numerous types of property at fixed locations, the underwriter is also involved with providing coverage on property that may be in transit frequently or occasionally or otherwise in irregular or unusual situations such as temporary exhibition, storage, and in use in a multitude of ways. In order to provide coverage that meets the needs of insured owners or other individuals, the underwriter must evaluate *risk* in many different settings.

Inland marine underwriting is especially challenging because it requires broad-based interest and inquiry and involves diverse knowledge and expertise. Successful inland marine underwriters must inform themselves and stay up to date on a wide variety of business disciplines, procedures, practices, and hazards. These include inter-industry applications of management, accounting, law and government regulation, economics, and human relations. A basic knowledge of transport rules and practices is essential. Beyond shippers and carriers, the inland marine underwriter's world includes builders, contractors, jewelers, warehousemen, furriers, broadcasters, museums, manufacturers, dry cleaners and laundries, art dealers, highway, port, and power authorities, farmers, construction equipment dealers and operators, and individuals who own boats, furs, fine arts, jewelry, and all manner of other unique collectibles. The inland marine underwriter faces new and different challenges every day and remains a student of the world throughout a satisfying career—a calling characterized by continuing curiosity. Because of its breadth, a study of inland marine is a valuable extension of understanding for any insurance practitioner.

As with any other business or profession, insurance people

sometimes use terms that sound ordinary but nevertheless have particular meanings or connotations. One of these is the word "risk." Essentially, *risk* means chance of loss. More specifically, risk exists any time there is absence of certainty.

As used in risk management and in the context of insurance, *risk* means an exposure to potential occurrences that could result in economic loss or human suffering. Risks that offer the possibility of gain as well as loss are generally not the subject of insurance or risk management.

The word "risk" is often used by insurance people in a more general sense. When referring to a specific coverage situation an underwriter might well say, "This is a marginal risk"; or, "He or she is a good risk."

The words "peril" and "loss exposure," discussed earlier in this chapter, are also widely used by underwriters when they assess risk. Another key term is "hazard." A *hazard* is anything that tends to increase the probable frequency or severity of losses. The hazards that concern underwriters are those related to losses that may be caused by the perils to be insured.

Sometimes the terms *peril* and *hazard* are used interchangeably. For example, property stored in a building is subject to the *peril* of fire. The practice of storing gasoline in or near that building is a *hazard:* a practice that tends to increase the probable frequency or severity of losses caused by fire. Along the same lines, original artwork or statuary is subject to the *peril* of theft. If the artwork is small enough to be stashed in either a briefcase or a shopping bag and if the artwork is frequently on exhibition to the public, there exist two *hazardous* conditions that increase the probable frequency of theft.

Underwriting Objectives

The major goal of underwriting is the selection and maintenance of a profitable, growing book of business. An insurance company can fulfill its commitments to its insureds, stockholders, employees, and the community at large only if it is financially sound. Underwriting, a major department of any insurance company, plays a central role in seeing that the insurer meets its survival, security, and financial goals.

There are several underwriting objectives related to this major goal: (1) to provide proper coverage; (2) to maintain selection standards; (3) to maintain pricing standards; and (4) to maintain high standards of professional competence.

Provide Proper Coverage A primary underwriting objective, providing proper coverage means furnishing insurance protection at a profit while meeting the wants and needs of the insurance-buying public. Frequently, these needs can be met by using a standard form of coverage. However, the inland marine underwriter must remain continually flexible in order to meet the needs of insureds with unique hazards. Insurance coverage is the underwriter's product—his or her stock in trade. The underwriter needs to be creative in finding ways to accept business.

Proper coverage must also be provided "at the right price," and underwriters must constantly be aware of the changes in the economy, the environment, and in ordinary business practices to be sure that the coverages offered reflect current needs and circumstances. For example, widely fluctuating gold prices affect the values and prices of jewelry. Micro-technology continues to give rise to new hazards and susceptibilities.

Maintain Selection Standards It is up to the underwriter to accept or reject all submissions, and to maintain selection standards to help assure financial integrity and profit for the insurer. This does not mean that underwriters should accept only "perfect" risks. If the insurance product is priced properly, the "average" risk will also generate a profit for the insurer in the long run.

Maintaining selection standards also helps an insurer avoid the consequences of adverse selection. *Adverse selection* means there is a disproportionately large share of applicants for insurance who have an above-average probability of loss. Adverse selection tends to occur when demand for the insurance exists primarily among those who are most likely to have a loss. For example, celebrities are far more subject to jewelry theft than relatively anonymous ordinary people, and if the demand for insurance on jewelry came only from celebrities, it would be almost impossible to underwrite successfully. So it is important to be able to write a sizable and varied book of business priced appropriately to the hazards involved.

Maintain Pricing Standards Although some inland marine rates are established by a rating organization, underwriters have much to do with determining rates and with applying those rates properly. A *rate* is the price per exposure unit for an insurance coverage. The exposure unit is the fundamental measure of the possibility of loss. Thus, a rate usually applies per $100 of insurance, or per $1,000 of insurance—or per item.

It is up to the inland marine underwriter to determine whether "standard" or "average" rates are adequate or excessive insofar as any particular risk is concerned and to adjust the rate upward or downward accordingly. This is especially important as respects nonfiled classes in which rates are influenced heavily by the underwriter's judgment.

Maintain a High Level of Professional Competence A business endeavor may be characterized as a "profession" if it requires a commitment to high ethical standards, formal educational preparation, training and measurement of that training, mandatory continuing education and, to some extent, public recognition as a profession.

In this context, underwriters should strive at all times to be professional in their activities by staying current on insurance topics, continuing their education, conducting their duties and handling problems in a professional manner, approaching the job with a professional attitude, and by accomplishing their objectives.

Underwriters must "service what they sell." The underwriter's service begins the moment an application is completed, and it continues as long as the insurance remains in force. Professionalism in this service includes prompt action on the application, accurate and prompt policy issuance, responsive and accurate answers to questions, and an attitude of earnest inquiry to discover the risks faced by a prospective insured and to seek all reasonable means to meet the insured's requirements at a reasonable price.

Underwriting Activities

The activities performed by underwriters to meet these objectives are many, but they can be grouped into the following categories: (1) hazard identification and evaluation; (2) pricing; (3) determination of policy terms and conditions; (4) risk selection decision; and (5) monitoring and servicing the account.

Hazard Identification and Evaluation Underwriters must identify and evaluate the hazards associated with the loss exposures of applicants. What conditions exist that will increase the frequency or severity of losses? A dealer in gold, for example, worries little about damage to bullion while in transit. Gold is virtually indestructible by perils such as fire, collision, or flood. On the other hand, it is a highly tempting target for thieves since it can be easily transformed and sold at market rates anywhere in the world. An egg farmer, on the other hand, worries considerably about transport, but very little about theft. Even a minor collision or upset could result in the loss of an entire truckload of eggs both because they may be easily destroyed and, because, as a foodstuff, they are subject to condemnation by health authorities. The egg farmer is equally concerned with delays in shipment since eggs are highly perishable. Once hazards are identified, the underwriter must determine how dangerous they are and what precautions can be taken to prevent or minimize loss.

The underwriter must evaluate the entire situation and determine whether all the hazards, alone or in combination, raise the probability of loss to an unacceptable level. What is unacceptable? Once the hazards are identified and evaluated, the underwriter must compare these hazards with similar risks. How do the exposures of this gold dealer differ from the exposures of other gold dealers? Is this egg farmer able to get eggs to market more safely than others? These comparisons determine whether the risk is above or below average—one indication of acceptability.

An underwriter must also consider the positive steps that can be taken to try to control these hazards. An applicant for insurance may be considered "above average" if he or she has implemented a constructive loss control program which works both to reduce the incidence of loss as well as to minimize its financial impact.

Financial strength and sound reputation are also indicators of "above average" risks. Conversely, a similar risk may be considered "below average" because the owners have not undertaken any loss prevention measures, have lost money for the past five years, and have questionable reputations.

Pricing A below average risk can often be made acceptable and profitable with appropriate premium increases. On the other hand, many filed forms of insurance rates are controlled, and there may be no pricing flexibility at all. If the premium is adequate only for average or better risks, below average risks are not likely to be insured.

Frequently, pricing involves the proper classification of the applicants' exposures and the application of rates to exposure units (rating). The premium is the product of the rate times the number of exposure units (for example, a rate times each $100 of value for a musical instrument). Proper classification is of utmost importance. For instance, the trumpet belonging to a professional musician is far more exposed to loss than a trumpet belonging to a high school student who takes perhaps one lesson a week and plays in the high school band during the football season.

A second aspect of pricing is the proper application of rates to the exposure units. Exposure units must be accurately determined and the proper rate applied to these units. Often volume affects rate levels. The shipper who sends out 100 packages worth $200 each during the course of the year must be charged a higher rate than the shipper who sends out 10,000 of the same types of package per year. The risks to the lower-volume shipper are far more concentrated and rates, therefore, are higher.

Many classes of inland marine business are nonfiled; that is, coverage forms and rates need not be filed with or approved by insurance departments. This means that the underwriter, in addition to being conversant with all the hazards and exposures associated with the insurance in question, must have a sense of how to price competitively in order to have a fair opportunity of obtaining the business in an open market.

Determination of Policy Terms and Conditions Closely intertwined with the pricing and risk selection decision is the determination of policy terms and conditions. In some cases, this is simply a matter of providing the requested coverage through use of a standard form with no modifying endorsements or conditions. In other cases, extensive negotiations with the applicant over policy coverages, conditions, requirements, deductibles, exclusions, and endorsements might be involved. The final result may be coverage very different from that offered by any standard policy. As respects nonfiled classes of inland marine business, the underwriter is frequently involved in such negotiations and needs to be highly knowledgeable about coverage conditions and the means of modifying them.

Risk Selection Decision At some point the underwriter must make a decision. Yes or no are obviously two choices, but often the underwriter will say, "No, unless..." or "Yes, if...." Can some loss control device or loss prevention measure make the risk acceptable? Could risk improvement coupled with increased deductibles or perhaps increased premium also contribute toward making the risk acceptable? In such cases, the underwriter is saying, in effect, "If you do this, the coverage will be provided."

Monitoring and Servicing the Account Acceptance of a risk does not complete the underwriter's task. The policy(ies) must be issued properly and the account must be serviced and monitored. Servicing might include issuing endorsements, making required filings with the state, explaining coverages, and so on. At renewal time, the account must sometimes be underwritten again to see if there have been any changes in exposures or hazards or changes in the coverage provided that would affect the acceptability of the account.

The underwriter must also keep an eye on the loss experience both at renewal and during the year. If at any time the experience deteriorates or the exposures have increased measurably, the underwriter must suggest corrective action. If reunderwriting is indicated at renewal, the underwriter repeats the entire underwriting process that was performed when the account was first submitted.

The Producer as Underwriter

The agent or broker is truly on the front lines of an insurance company's effort to underwrite large volumes of business and thereby spread its risks. It is the insurance producer who has the primary contacts with insureds and prospective insureds and whose job it is to know which insurers provide what kinds of insurance and which of them does it best. Since there are so many insurers competing for business, keeping abreast of this vast market is no easy task.

Still, it is the producer who must first review the risks presented by a prospective insured, analyze the insurance needs, and interpret these risks to the insurance marketplace. In this role, the producer must be a broad-based generalist of professional quality. If the agent or broker is uninformed or careless, risks will not be presented in the proper markets and information relating to risks will tend to be sketchy and incomplete. The result is that a prospective insured may fail to obtain appropriate coverage or any coverage at all or receive an unrealistically high premium quotation.

The more producers know about the services they sell, the better served will be the insurance-buying public and the entire insurance mechanism.

The Decision-Making Process

A process is a series of actions or operations directed toward a particular result. Decision making can be viewed as a creative process combining knowledge, experience, and thought. Because the underwriter is constantly involved in decision making relative to acceptance, rejection, and modification of new and renewal business, it is important to understand this process in order to improve the results of decision making.

The underwriting decision-making process involves the following steps:

1. recognition of a situation that calls for a decision about what action should be taken;
2. gathering, organizing, and analyzing information pertinent to the decision;
3. identification and development of alternative courses of action;
4. evaluation of the alternatives;
5. choosing one of the alternatives; and
6. implementing and monitoring the selected course of action.

Underwriting has been referred to as an art that cannot be taught. The decision-making process that the experienced underwriter applies to the task of risk selection involves the application of his or her knowledge and experience in a manner that has long ago become habitual (unconscious). Thus, to the observer, and perhaps even to the underwriter, it appears that the selection of a proper alternative is arrived at by intuition. What is actually taking place is not so much intuition as an internalization of the decision-making process, which includes all these steps.

Recognition of the Need for a Decision and Information Development Recognition of a situation calling for a decision is often quite simple. When an application for insurance reaches an underwriter's desk, the need for a decision is obvious. The situation is more complex with respect to underwriting management, such as the need to determine when the underwriting manual requires rewriting.

The first activity that takes place when the need for a decision has been recognized is the gathering of information. The underwriter's initial task in decision making, then, is to collect the information needed to make a decision.

Information Efficiency. Information gathering, regardless of the source, always has some cost attached to it in terms of time, money, or both. The time and money allocated and the accuracy required in a decision should be appropriate to its importance. The choice of a restaurant for lunch does not justify a staff study of the food service industry. An inland marine underwriter considering participation on the George Washington Bridge does not send out an engineering firm to inspect it. An underwriter considering a large jewelry schedule would not hire a detective agency to observe the prospective insured in order to find information on moral character and reputation in the community. The premium involved clearly would not justify such an expenditure in any of the above instances. Even more to the point, the information obtained would likely add very little to the quality of the decision reached.

This concept is referred to as *information efficiency.* The underwriter must constantly ask the question, "What will this added information really tell me?" Underwriting decisions are made under conditions of uncertainty. No underwriter can ever find out all there is to know about a given risk. And, at the point in time where the underwriter has developed sufficient practical information, sound underwriting judgment must come into play.

Sources of Information. Because the only purpose of information gathering is to enable the underwriter to improve decision making, it is important that the underwriter weigh the improvement in the decision that will be made possible by the gaining of additional information against the cost in time and money in obtaining that information. This is not an easy task.

The major sources of information, both internal and external, available to insurers include the following.

The Application/Underwriting File. The basic source of information for new business is the application itself. For renewal and mid-term underwriting, the major source of information is the underwriting file, which usually contains the application, loss information, and all other inspection and financial reports on the insured.

Because there are so many classes of inland marine insurance, there are few standard application forms, and most of the ones that do exist serve merely to collect basic information, leaving it up to the underwriter and the producer to identify and evaluate the specific hazards involved and coverage to be obtained.

Only in a few cases is the application a formal one that becomes part of the contract. The most familiar of these is the jewelers block application, which is extremely detailed and provides underwriting and rating information as well as the data needed to complete the declarations page of the policy. In fact, the jewelers block application clearly states that it is warranted to be a part of the policy.

The Producer. The producer is a continuing source of supporting and supplemental information on the new submission or existing business. As the person on the scene and closest both to the insured and to the community and environment in which the insured operates, the producer is in the best position to provide an objective general appraisal of the information submitted.

Government Records. Occasionally useful for the inland marine underwriter, the records of many federal, state, and local departments or courts may contain a wealth of information. Most mortgages and liens are recorded locally. Business licenses and records such as bankruptcy filings are not difficult to obtain. Criminal records also are largely a matter of public information.

Financial Rating Services. Financial rating services such as Standard & Poor's, Dun & Bradstreet, and others provide data on credit ratings and industry averages for purposes of comparison. These services provide a great deal of financial information regarding the strength and stability of business enterprises that use commercial credit.

Financial information regarding the motor carrier industry is generally available through the Central Analysis Bureau (CAB), which also serves as a clearinghouse for motor carrier legislation and regulatory activities.

Additional sources of information are the financial statements and accounting records of the insured. These records often provide more detailed information on the insured's financial strength than reports from financial rating services. However, the reliability of such information is only as good as the person who prepared the report and the firm that audited it.

Consumer Investigation Reports. Individual consumer investigation reports obtained from such firms as Equifax, Inc., may provide some corroborative background information concerning applicants for personal lines insurance.

However, these reports are limited in their usefulness. Federal privacy laws and credit reporting regulations have reduced the information that can be obtained by the reporting firm and severely curtailed their use by underwriters. Adverse information developed in such reports should always be checked out through another source if possible.

Previous Insurers. Occasionally, the inland marine underwriter has access to the previous insurance carrier. And occasionally the previous insurer may be willing to comment in general terms on its experience with a given risk. Because of privacy laws and potential liabilities, however, this source is extremely limited in value.

Inspection Reports. Many insurers are staffed with competent technical personnel who are able to provide objective data and evaluation of physical and other characteristics of the risk under consideration. In addition to objective information, the impression obtained by technical representatives (loss control representatives, engineers, and so on) about the insured's attitude, cooperativeness, and moral tone are helpful to the underwriter.

In most cases, inspection reports on commercial risks result in a list of mandatory recommendations followed by a list of suggested recommendations. The willingness of the insured to follow the suggested recommendations provides a useful insight into the degree of cooperation that can be expected.

Field Sales Personnel. Field sales personnel (also referred to as special agents, marketing representatives, or similar names) can provide both specific and general information.

Often field sales personnel can be helpful to the underwriter in determining how familiar the producer is with the type of insurance that is being submitted. This is frequently an area of concern as respects inland marine submissions, especially in some commercial lines that a producer rarely sees.

Claims Department. Review of a claim file can sometimes provide insights into the character and moral tone of the insured. A questionable claim or a hostile and uncooperative attitude on the part of the insured would be of interest to the underwriter.

On the other hand, a risk that appears below average on paper may be more than offset by a claim adjuster's report of a highly competent management and a responsive and businesslike attitude.

Production Records. It is usually possible for the underwriter to check out internal records on the producer with respect to loss ratio, volume of business, length of service, mix of business, and supporting business if there is any. This information tends to indicate the experience and familiarity of the producer with the type of business under consideration. The quality of a producer's prior submissions and existing book of business is generally a good indicator of the quality of risks submitted. A producer who maintains a good book of business will be very reluctant to expose it unnecessarily to below-average loss prospects.

Insurer Underwriting Manuals and Guides. Underwriting manuals and guides may be helpful when writing a new or unfamiliar line of business. Most insurers have some form of underwriting manual that provides basic information on the loss exposures of many types of businesses. In addition, the manual states the insurer's position on the class of business in general and any deviation from company policy that may be allowed.

Other Underwriting Manuals. While not frequent with respect to inland marine business, underwriting manuals of a more general nature are sometimes available from commercial publishers.

Other Underwriters. Chances are another underwriter of the same insurer has had experience with a particular type of risk. Senior underwriters frequently have had equivalent or parallel experience and can be most helpful.

In the inland marine field, other underwriters may often be accessed through membership in the Inland Marine Underwriters Association, which publishes various special hazard reports and seminar transcripts dealing with specific technical subjects.

Informal Information Sources. Most informal information can only be considered as "filler" at best. This is largely the "general education" that underwriters receive through their daily contacts in the business world, keeping up to date on business and technological developments, and keeping current with the activities of local trade organizations. At best, such information can tip off the underwriter to check further into a particular aspect of the risk.

Hazard Evaluation. A hazard has been defined as a fact or condition that tends to increase the probable frequency and severity of a loss due to an insured peril. Hazards can be classified as physical, moral, and morale hazards.

Physical Hazards. Physical hazards are the tangible characteristics of the insured property, persons, or operations that affect the likelihood of severity of loss due to one or more perils. They can be characteristics of the risk itself, or characteristics of the environment in which the risk is located. Examples of physical hazards considered here are:

- occupancy and operations on premises;
- the means by which goods are transported from one point to another;
- geography, terrain, and climate; and
- attractiveness to thieves.

Occupancy and operations on premises. Occupancy hazards arise from the use to which a structure has been employed. A frame building used as an office presents quite different hazards with respect to the peril of fire than an identical building occupied by a garment manufacturer. Inherent in the garment manufacturer's premises are large stocks of combustible inventories all of which are subject to water and smoke damage. Also part of such a manufacturing operation is the presence of machinery used for cutting, dyeing, folding, and packing. Such machinery almost invariably requires petroleum lubricants and typically generates substantial heat and often sparks. Obviously the chance for extreme losses due to fire, water, and smoke are much greater than for an office occupancy.

Means of transportation. Various modes of transport present different hazards. The perils of collision, fire, and theft are frequently uppermost in the underwriter's mind in dealing with motor transport, whether the vehicle is a long-haul trailer, a semitrailer, or a local delivery van. Rail transport, by contrast, often presents the primary hazards of delay, exposure, and misrouting. By further contrast, air transport may present a total loss exposure whereas transport by other means may result in only partial damage.

Beyond the actual mode of transportation, the underwriter must consider the nature of the goods themselves, the way they are packed, their susceptibility to spoilage, and the risks involved in handling and transshipping.

Geography, terrain, and climate. Location is frequently a controlling factor. Property located on the San Andreas Fault in California, or in the Mississippi Delta, or at the foot of Mount St. Helens presents catastrophic exposures not present with many kinds of property located elsewhere.

Underwriters might be quite concerned about shipping fresh lettuce by truck during the summer across the Mojave Desert bound for New York City. If bulldozers, cranes, and draglines are doing their work up in the Alaska tundra, the underwriter could face a situation in the case of overturn or disablement where because of the difficulty of access it would be far more costly to repair the equipment than to pay a total loss.

Attractiveness to thieves. An underwriter would not be inclined to worry about a railway car loaded with pig iron moving between Cincinnati and Pittsburgh. Neither would most thieves. On the other hand a jewelry salesperson's sample case is very attractive indeed whether being carried by the salesperson or left in a private car.

Many motor cargoes are particularly susceptible to theft. Apparel and electronic equipment and appliances are among the leaders. Beyond the basic attraction of the property itself are such contributing factors as:

- *Location.* Thieves generally go where the action is. Thus, virtually anything at Kennedy Airport or elsewhere in the port of New York is more susceptible than if it were sitting on a loading dock in Hannibal, Missouri. The same is true for other major ports and transportation hubs in the country. Similarly, a burglar is much more likely to "patronize" Park Avenue in New York City than Park Avenue in Salem, Oregon.
- *Disposability.* Thieves flourish in areas where property is relatively liquid. Thieves need to convert their "proceeds" to cash very quickly. Again the major population centers and metropolitan corridors contribute to making theft more liquid and profitable.
- *Convertibility of Property.* Many items of jewelry and manufactured goods are susceptible to theft because their raw materials or parts are highly marketable. Gold is an obvious example. It can be melted down or converted and sold in any form. Microchips, stereo and other electronic components are also valuable as parts and by no means solely when they are installed as part of an appliance.

Moral Hazards. *Moral hazard* can be defined as a subjective characteristic of the insured that tends to increase the probable frequency or severity of a loss due to an insured peril. The hazard arises from the possibility that the insured may intentionally cause a loss. Moral hazard is not amenable to prediction by any statistical techniques; therefore, the existence of moral hazard cannot be compensated for by increasing the rate.

In general, moral hazard may be inferred from such evidence as previous questionable losses, a police record, and other evidence of moral laxity. More inferences may derive from a poor reputation in the community or a record of unethical or illegal business practices. In addition, undesirable associates of the insured would also be of concern to the underwriter.

More specifically, the financial condition of the insured or the insured's business may indicate a possibility of intentionally caused losses. A weak, failing, or volatile financial condition may cause postponement of essential maintenance or vital services and may even prompt intentional destruction or conversion of property.

Morale Hazards. *Morale hazard* arises out of carelessness or indifference to loss. It is the "Why worry, I'm insured!" attitude. Morale hazard is usually subtle and difficult to detect, but its presence does tend to increase the frequency or severity of loss. Two major indications of morale hazard are personality traits and poor management. People who thoughtlessly leave valuables about and evidence no pride of ownership suggest morale hazard. Similarly, poor housekeeping and slipshod bookkeeping are overt indications of an undesirable management attitude suggesting that similar negligence may extend to other critical areas of business operations. In these cases, there is no apparent attempt to cause actual loss; it is simply that there is no interest in the prevention or reduction of loss, with such an attitude abetted by the existence of insurance.

Alternative Courses of Action As suggested earlier, the essence of the underwriter's job is decision. Specifically these decisions boil down to (1) accept the risk as submitted; (2) accept the risk subject to modification; or (3) reject the risk.

Accept Without Alteration. One option as respects either a new submission or a renewal is to accept the business without alteration in rate, form, or engineering (loss control). This happens often on renewals where experience has been favorable. With new submissions, this alternative depends entirely on the quality of the business.

Accept Subject to Modification. When a risk is unacceptable as submitted, often modifications can be suggested by the underwriter to make it acceptable. The more complex the submission, the greater the variety in changes that can be made. Here are some possible courses of action:

- *Reduce Hazards.* Examples of hazard reduction through loss control include such things as alarm systems or security guard service, adoption of damage-resistant packaging materials, the removal or isolation of flammable or combustible materials, installation of auxiliary power supplies, and control of access to sensitive areas. The economic feasibility of the suggested changes and the willingness of management to institute them will often be governing factors.
- *Modify Rate.* A change in the rate or premium may make the risk acceptable. A rate surcharge or modification may be

required. As respects filed classes of inland marine where rates are subject to regulatory approval, this can often be done through "consent to rate" laws in which the insured acknowledges and accepts the agreed-upon surcharge. As respects nonfiled classes of inland marine insurance, risks tend to be less comparable to a theoretical "average," and rates are entirely negotiable between the underwriter and the insured. Rate increases in these classes are relative to what premiums were paid in the past rather than to any standard rate.

- *Modify Coverage.* A change in coverage from that originally requested or presently provided may make the risk acceptable. A policy on which renewal is doubtful under the existing contract may be retained if the coverage is modified to remove or limit the peril causing problem losses. The degree of freedom to do this depends on whether the class is filed or nonfiled.

  A contractors equipment floater that is presently unacceptable as written on an "all-risks" form may become much more attractive when converted to a named perils basis. Risks that have a poor loss history due to a large number of small losses may be greatly improved by the introduction of or increase in the deductible. By and large, as the size and complexity of the risk increases, it may be necessary to change all three variables—coverage, rate, and hazards—in order to make the risk acceptable.
- *Modify Retention.* This is an internal option available to the underwriter. If exposures are perceived by the underwriter as "higher than normal," he or she may suggest that the insurer retain less than its customary percentage for its own account and perhaps "split the line" (share the business) with other insurers, obtaining reinsurance on a facultative basis, or obtaining other types of reinsurance arrangements. On many nonfiled classes, participation with other underwriters on a risk is common. These changes in retention generally offer a method of dealing with a risk that is otherwise acceptable except for its size or unique characteristics.

Reject. With some submissions, no alternative remains but rejection. This should be considered as a last resort because it is costly to reject business. A submission the underwriter has considered and analyzed represents an expenditure of underwriting time at the very least. In addition, there may be information gathering expenses and clerical expenses such as telephone calls and letters regarding the submission and possibly even the expense of on-site inspection. It is an obvious but important fact that the rejected risk generates no premium.

This does not mean that an unacceptable risk should be written, but that every effort should be expended to find a way in which a risk can be made acceptable before it is rejected. No amount of loss control or coverage modification will remove moral hazard, but risks with other types of deficiencies frequently can be modified to make them acceptable.

The Evaluation of Alternatives Once the alternative courses of action have been identified and developed, the relative merits of each course of action must be evaluated.

In those cases when the risk is clearly much better or much worse than the average in its class, the evaluation process is relatively easy. On a jewelers block submission, for example, assume that the underwriter determines that the risk is far below the average in its class due to the physical condition of the jeweler's premises. If the condition is such that loss control engineering is not feasible as a means of improving the risk, and the modifications in rate and coverage that are possible will not, in the underwriter's judgment, improve the risk materially, the rejection alternative appears to be the best course of action.

In addition to the evaluation of the risk itself, certain other factors impinge upon the decision process. These factors include:

- the degree of underwriting authority required for the decision,
- the presence of supporting business,
- mix of business, and
- producer pressure.

Underwriters must decide if they have the authority to make the final decision with respect to the submission under consideration or whether their task is to develop the underwriting file for referral to higher authority. Underwriters can waste a good deal of time evaluating alternatives in those cases when the choice of the course of action is going to be or should be made by someone else.

Supporting business may make a marginal submission acceptable. Underwriters should consider the desirability of the entire account. For example, a marginal personal lines submission may become acceptable when considered together with a sizable commercial account for the same insured.

The mix of business in the underwriting book must be considered. The *mix of business* refers to the distribution of individual risks among the various lines or classifications within a certain line. If a particular class of business is heavily over-represented in the book of business, the book is unbalanced. One exception to this situation occurs when the insurer, because of its expertise in the area or because of an attractive class rate, has a program to emphasize a particular class of business.

Particularly when marketing through independent agents and brokers, pressure from producers must be weighed in the decision. Producer pressure typically occurs on marginal submissions. A marginal submission from a highly professional producer with a large volume of profitable business usually merits a "second look."

Choice of Alternatives This is the decision itself. After carefully weighing all the alternatives that have been identified and developed, the underwriter chooses one of them. One of the keys to efficient decision making is to determine when sufficient information has been gathered, when the proper amount of analysis has been performed, and when the decision should be made. There is a natural tendency, which should be resisted, to postpone difficult decisions. Perfect information is not attainable in an underwriting situation; therefore, the decision must be made on the basis of information that can be reasonably obtained. Insurance underwriting consists of the taking of calculated risks by selection of the best course of action from the set of available alternatives.

Implementing and Monitoring the Decision When the decision has been made, the underwriter's task is not completed. The decision must be implemented by communication to the producer and then monitored to determine its outcome.

In many cases, it is necessary for the underwriter to telephone or write the producer to pass along the decision. In other cases, particularly when a policy is going to be issued on the same terms as requested, no communication is required and the implementation of the decision is the issuance of the policy.

When the decision is to accept the submission subject to a modification of the rate, deductible, or other policy provision, the first step in implementation of the decision is to inform the producer. If the rate is to be increased, for example, the underwriter should tell the producer the reason for the increase. If the producer understands the reasoning behind the requested modification, the underwriter is more likely to obtain the business.

With a rejection, the underwriter has the task of selling the negative result. The underwriter should effectively communicate not only the rejection of a risk but also the reasons that led to the rejection. This provides the producer with a guide for future submissions and contributes to his or her education as a field underwriter.

One aspect of monitoring underwriting decisions involves the evaluation of the results of those decisions. The premium volume and the loss ratio indicate the results of underwriting decisions. The second aspect of monitoring deals with periodic review of the risks underwritten to determine that recommendations have been implemented and that hazards have not increased.

Rates and Ratemaking

Two terms that often enter into discussions of the pricing of insurance are "rate" and "ratemaking." A *rate,* as noted earlier, is the price per exposure unit for insurance coverage. For example, the rate that an insurer charges for personal jewelry coverage in a particular territory may be $1 per $100 of jewelry insured. *Ratemaking* is the process by which rates are determined. The different types of rates used in pricing inland marine insurance are discussed below, along with the different methods that insurers use to make these rates.

There are three basic types of rates: class or manual rates, individual rates, and judgment rates.

Class or Manual Rates Class or manual rates are average rates applied to all members of a group. These rates are developed by grouping together insureds having similar characteristics into a single "class." Typical of class rates in inland marine insurance are rates for personal jewelry. In some states, a set of graduated rates applies statewide. In others, experience may dictate that classes be subdivided by county or other territories.

Since an essential feature of class rates is uniformity within a given class, rates tend to reflect average costs across the board: average losses, average loss adjustment expenses, average administrative expenses, and overhead.

Individual Rates Individual rates are essentially a modification of class rates and have been developed to take into account relative differences in insured risks. If insureds having dissimilar loss characteristics are placed in a class having a single rate, then the insureds having better-than-average loss characteristics will be charged a rate that is too high, while insureds having below average loss characteristics will receive what is, in effect, a subsidy.

The distinction between class and specific fire rates offers an illustration. Brick buildings within a given zone of fire protection may all be charged the same rate if they are used for residential purposes. A similar brick building, perhaps larger, used for commercial or manufacturing purposes will be subject to specific rating which, in essence, modifies the class rates up or down based on occupancy, protection, and exposure, meaning adjacent properties or hazards.

In addition to hazard differentials, individual rates can be based on differences in expected expenses. It costs quite a bit more to handle a monthly reporting policy on goods in transit than to issue an annual policy for a maximum limit that will not likely generate any premium or endorsement activity until the next renewal.

Judgment Rates Rates are made by judgment in three situations. First, there are certain types of risk for which there are no distinguishable classes or individual rate systems that can be used. This is the case with most of the nonfiled inland marine classes. In this situation, the underwriter must develop a rate based on available statistical information and an estimate of the probable frequency and severity of the loss exposure. The estimate of the underwriter generally is predicated on information derived from comparable or near-comparable exposures but may be based on purely subjective or nonquantitative estimates.

The second situation in which judgment plays a key role in developing rates is when an underwriter recognizes important and distinctive hazard differentials among highly distinctive risks. In this situation, the underwriter can evaluate the loss characteristics of the loss exposure by applying various judgment debits and credits to the base rate. An example is the potential "credit" given to a manual-rated jewelry policy when a vault warranty is included.

A third common situation exists when a new coverage is being developed and little, if any, pertinent statistical data are available to establish the initial rates. This would be the case when a brand new type of insurance is being introduced. An example is the broad form coverages developed to respond to electronic data processing risks in recent years.

The primary characteristics of all judgment rates is a lack of rating information concerning a particular loss exposure. As a substitute for this information, the subjective judgment or analysis of the underwriter must be used. While a judgment rate may not be precisely representative of the expected value of possible future losses, the underwriter's past experience, training, and knowledge, plus competition in the marketplace, interact to determine the judgment rate. In some cases, however, competition may cloud the judgment of the underwriter.

Ratemaking Many filed classes of inland marine insurance lend themselves to some semblance of scientific ratemaking: jewelry, furs, musical instruments, and so on. In these classes, there is a sufficiently large number of exposure units and detailed records of loss and loss adjustment expenses to arrive at a so-called "pure premium," with adjustments for inflation and other trends and for some practical differences in exposures and expenses and, of course, with additions for operational and selling overhead.

Risks primarily at a fixed location and at which the building and its occupancy constitute the primary hazards are often rated using the fire contents rate as a starting point and then increasing this with "loadings" to reflect other perils to be insured. Fire contents rates tend to be either class rates if the property is residential or specific rates if the property is commercial or manufacturing. Specific fire rates are, in effect, individual rates that have been modified to take into account the hazards of the particular occupancy (a mattress factory being much more exposed to loss than a jewelry store), the protection provided (whether public or private), and the hazards of management, which comprise the attitudes and habits of the firms occupying the premises.

Risks involving property primarily or frequently in transit or temporarily at locations other than the premises of the insured are usually judgment rated, with the underwriter having to consider both the perils insured and the fact that the property is outside the insured's control. In judgment rating, the underwriter also must consider the characteristics of those individuals or businesses who *will* have custody or control of the property, their loss records if available, and the frequency with which the property is worked upon, transported, stored, put on public exhibit, or in whatever situation in which insurance is required.

Probable Maximum Loss and Reinsurance

Two interrelated concepts of frequent concern to inland marine underwriters are "probable maximum loss" and reinsurance. The need for reinsurance greatly depends on the probable maximum loss to which the insurer is exposed.

Probable Maximum Loss (PML) Regardless of amounts of insurance, the underwriter will almost always seek to estimate PML from any peril or combination of perils insured. The limit or amount insured may not always be the amount subject to any single loss—either from a particular peril or due to an aggregation of values at a single point, either in transit or at a location that may be subject to general catastrophic perils. Limits or amounts of insurance may be peak or maximum values, or they may reflect a collection of values perhaps at different locations or in transit by various means or otherwise dispersed.

On a contractors equipment floater, for example, the total schedule may be $1,000,000, but the highest valued single item is $150,000 in a mobile derrick that works often in conjunction with a bulldozer and a loader valued at $75,000 and $35,000 respectively. Thus, the underwriter would consider the PML to be $260,000.

The underwriter seeks to estimate the PML for a single loss both to evaluate the true loss exposure and to determine what percentage of the total risk he or she wishes to retain for the direct account of the insurer and what percentage will be "ceded" to reinsurers—in other words, how much will be shared among other insurers by various means.

Reinsurance Reinsurance is insurance on insurance. While reinsurance has many legitimate uses and purposes (and indeed is a study in itself), the underwriter's use of it is primarily as a mechanism to (1) spread risk, (2) limit probable maximum loss (PML) to the insurance company, and (3) enable an insured to purchase adequate limits of insurance on high-valued property subject to a catastrophic loss. In these contexts, reinsurance is the insurance industry's way of avoiding shock losses by dispersing concentrations of risk throughout the national and international insurance system.

Spreading Risk. In general, a concentration of risk exists whenever one or more loss exposures present the possibility of actual loss beyond the ability of a single individual, business, institution, city, town, or political subdivision to withstand.

If an individual, family, firm, or county can assume and pay for losses as they occur, it has little need of insurance. By extension, if an insurer underwrites a sufficiently large book of business in a particular class, such as mail order shipments, and enough premium is pooled to pay all the expected losses and expenses, the insurer has little need of reinsurance support.

But, for many risks there is too much exposure to a single large loss or multiple losses in a disaster to be absorbed either by the insured or by the pooling mechanism of a single insurance company. Therefore, the insurer must reach out to other insurance companies to share the premium and the risk so that should serious loss occur, it can be paid without impairing the financial stability of the insured or of any single insurance company.

Limit Probable Maximum Loss. To guard their own financial strength and stability, insurers must establish how much of a loss they can absorb in any one class and in any single risk within a class of business. They must also guard against the possibility of a catastrophe loss occurring as a result of an event that may affect several classes of business such as a hurricane, a flood, or an earthquake.

The actuarial and financial considerations compel the insurer to "set a net line"; in other words, to establish how much of any given risk or combination of risks or how much of the PML in any one catastrophe the insurer is able to retain and pay out of its own account without impairing its own solvency. These thresholds are also called *net retentions.*

Whenever the risks of a single insured or a group of insureds in the same class and facing the same catastrophic loss exposure *exceed* the limits of the insurer's net retention, the insurer must seek reinsurance from other insurers.

Provide Adequate Limits to a Single Risk. An insured with high values or high combinations of values wants to be able to deal with one or two primary sources in purchasing insurance. The insured does not want to approach every name in the Yellow Pages to find enough insurance companies whose net retentions, taken together, combine to meet its needs. And there are many such risks which the inland marine underwriter confronts—bridge, tunnel, and highway authorities; regional and national air and ground transportation firms such as UPS and Federal Express; pipeline companies and railroads, to name a few. In such situations, the primary insurance underwriter will generally seek to create the capacity the customer needs by enlisting other insurers as participating reinsurers on the risk.

Facultative Reinsurance vs. Treaty Reinsurance. Reinsurance may be categorized in several ways. The most basic categorization is between *facultative* and *treaty* reinsurance.

In facultative reinsurance, the primary (or ceding) insurer negotiates a separate reinsurance agreement for each policy it wishes to reinsure. The ceding company is not under any obligation to purchase reinsurance on anything it does not wish to reinsure, and the reinsurer is not obligated to accept any business it does not want.

In treaty reinsurance, the ceding company agrees in advance to cede certain classes of business to the reinsurer in accordance with the terms and conditions of the treaty, and the reinsurer agrees to accept the business to be ceded.

SUMMARY

The principal difference between inland marine and other types of property insurance is in the kinds of property insured. Although there are exceptions, basically inland marine insurance covers property in the course of transit, property of a movable, or "floating," nature, and property instrumental to transportation or communication. Examples of property covered by inland marine insurance include cargo being moved by train, truck, or airplane; bulldozers, cranes, and other types of mobile equipment; bridges, tunnels, and viaducts; radio and television transmitting equipment; personal jewelry and furs; musical instruments; art collections; livestock and other animals; doctors' and dentists' instruments; and theatrical equipment.

Heavy use of the rail system during World War I and the growth of the trucking industry after the war reinforced the need for insurance of goods in transit. Companies writing marine insurance, which was not regulated as to rate or form, began providing such coverage. In the years following World War I, people began to amass some wealth and required coverage for items such as valuable jewelry. Marine insurers developed the jewelry floater, which was followed by floaters designed to cover fur coats, fine arts, cameras, and musical instruments. Bridges and tunnels also came into the fold.

In 1931 over 140 insurance companies organized the Inland Marine Underwriters Association (IMUA) to stabilize the new line with respect to agency commissions, to control rebating and unfair discrimination, to devise uniform forms and clauses, and to establish rating methods for those classes that lent themselves to class (or manual) rating. In 1933, a "Nation-Wide Definition and Interpretation of the Insuring Powers of Marine and Transportation Underwriters" was adopted by the NCIC and eventually by the majority of the states. It specified in detail what were considered to be marine exposures and what could not be covered by marine insurance. The SEUA decision and new multiple-line legislation led to a revision of the Definition in 1953. In 1976, the NAIC again amended the Definition to classify a wider range of property as inland marine.

The classes of business written as inland marine can be placed into two categories—filed and nonfiled (sometimes referred to as controlled and noncontrolled). From an underwriting standpoint, there is more flexibility in the writing of the nonfiled classes. Two rating and advisory organizations—Insurance Services Office (ISO) and American Association of Insurance Services (AAIS)—file forms, rules, and rates for inland marine coverages on behalf of their member insurance companies.

Inland marine insurance exists because businesses and individuals face certain loss exposures. Types of property exposed to loss, perils or causes of loss, parties affected by loss, and potential financial consequences of loss are all elements of loss exposures. Once loss exposures have been identified and analyzed, they may be treated by one or more techniques: avoidance, loss control, retention, transfer other than insurance, and insurance.

Inland marine underwriting is especially challenging because it requires broad-based interest and inquiry and involves diverse knowledge and expertise. The inland marine underwriter deals with many different kinds of property in a variety of situations—in a finished state, in the course of manufacture or construction, and while undergoing repairs. Further, the underwriter is involved with providing coverage on property that may be in transit in irregular or unusual situations. Underwriting activities can be grouped into the categories of hazard identification and evaluation, pricing, determination of policy terms and conditions, risk selection decision, and monitoring and servicing the account. Two interrelated concepts of frequent concern to inland marine underwriters are probable maximum loss and reinsurance.

Chapter Notes

1. Portions of this section are based on the manuscript that will appear as Chapter 9 in William H. Rodda, James S. Trieschmann, Eric A. Wiening, and Bob A. Hedges, *Commercial Property Risk Management and Insurance,* Vol. I, 3rd. ed. (Malvern, PA: American Institute for Property and Liability Underwriters, 1988).
2. Portions of the discussion of inland marine loss exposures and their treatment are adapted from Barry D. Smith, James S. Trieschmann, and Eric A. Wiening, *Property and Liability Insurance Principles* (Malvern, PA: Insurance Institute of America, 1987), pp. 4-6 and 20-40.
3. C. Arthur Williams, Jr., George L. Head, Ronald C. Horn, and G. William Glendenning, *Principles of Risk Management and Insurance,* Vol. I, 2nd ed. (Malvern, PA: American Institute for Property and Liability Underwriters, 1981), p. 2.
4. The discussion of proximate cause is adapted from *Principles of Risk Management and Insurance,* Vol. II, pp. 86-88.
5. Lynn Gas and Electric Company v. Meriden Fire Insurance Company, 158 Mass. 570, 33 N.E. 690 (1893).
6. Fred Meyer, Inc. v. Central Mutual Insurance Company, 235 F. Supp. 540 (1964).
7. Providence Washington Insurance Company v. Weaver, 242 Miss. 141, 113 So.2d 635 (1961).
8. The discussion of inland marine underwriting is based on excerpts from J.J. Launie, J. Finley Lee, and Norman A. Baglini, *Principles of Property and Liability Underwriting,* 3rd ed. (Malvern, PA: Insurance Institute of America, 1986).

CHAPTER 2

Inland Marine Policy Provisions

INTRODUCTION

This chapter examines the basic provisions likely to be found in many inland marine policies. Accordingly, it serves as an introduction to the more specific and detailed study of inland marine policy provisions in later chapters of this book. The policy provisions examined in this chapter are those of the commercial inland marine forms filed by Insurance Services Office (ISO) and the American Association of Insurance Services (AAIS), the two rating organizations described in Chapter 1.

While a great deal of commercial inland marine insurance is issued using nonfiled forms, the forms described here are the industry standards that nonfiled policies often resemble. This resemblance may be particularly strong when nonfiled coverages are added to a commercial package policy that otherwise contains filed forms only. In other cases, nonfiled policies are one-of-a-kind contracts that bear little resemblance to the filed forms. Accordingly, the chapter concludes with a brief discussion of the different approaches that insurers may take in drafting nonfiled forms. The actual provisions found in nonfiled policies are described in other chapters of this text.

ISO COMMERCIAL INLAND MARINE PROGRAM

The ISO commercial inland marine program provides forms and endorsements that can be used as either a *monoline inland marine policy* or as the inland marine portion of a *commercial package policy.*

Rules and rating procedures are contained in the ISO Commercial Lines Manual.

ISO defines a monoline inland marine policy as a policy that provides only inland marine coverage. A commercial package policy (CPP) provides two or more lines of coverage, the available lines being commercial property, commercial general liability, business auto, commercial crime, boiler and machinery, farm, and commercial inland marine.

Each line of coverage is contained in a *coverage part.* An ISO commercial inland marine coverage part consists of four distinct documents:

1. One or more *coverage forms.* Each coverage form contains the provisions that apply specifically to the class of property insured by that form.
2. A *declarations page* for each coverage form. This shows the limits of insurance, premium, deductible, and other pertinent information applying to the coverage form.
3. The *commercial inland marine conditions form.* This form contains provisions that generally apply to all of the inland marine coverage forms.
4. Any *applicable endorsements.* Endorsements are added to the coverage part to amend policy provisions to fit the needs of a particular insured or make the coverage acceptable to the insurance company.

If an inland marine coverage part is to be issued as a monoline policy, it is combined with two additional documents:

1. *Common policy declarations,* showing the insured's name and address, the effective date and expiration date of the policy, the description of the business insured, the policy premium, and a list of all the coverage parts included in the policy. The common policy declarations may be combined with the declarations applying to the coverage form(s).
2. The *common policy conditions form.* These conditions relate to matters such as cancellation, changes, and payment of premium, that affect any type of coverage, whether inland marine or other.

If inland marine coverage is to be issued as part of a commercial package policy, the above ingredients are simply combined with one or more additional coverage parts. These elements are depicted in Exhibit 2-1.

Exhibit 2-1
Contents of the ISO Commercial Package Policy (CPP)

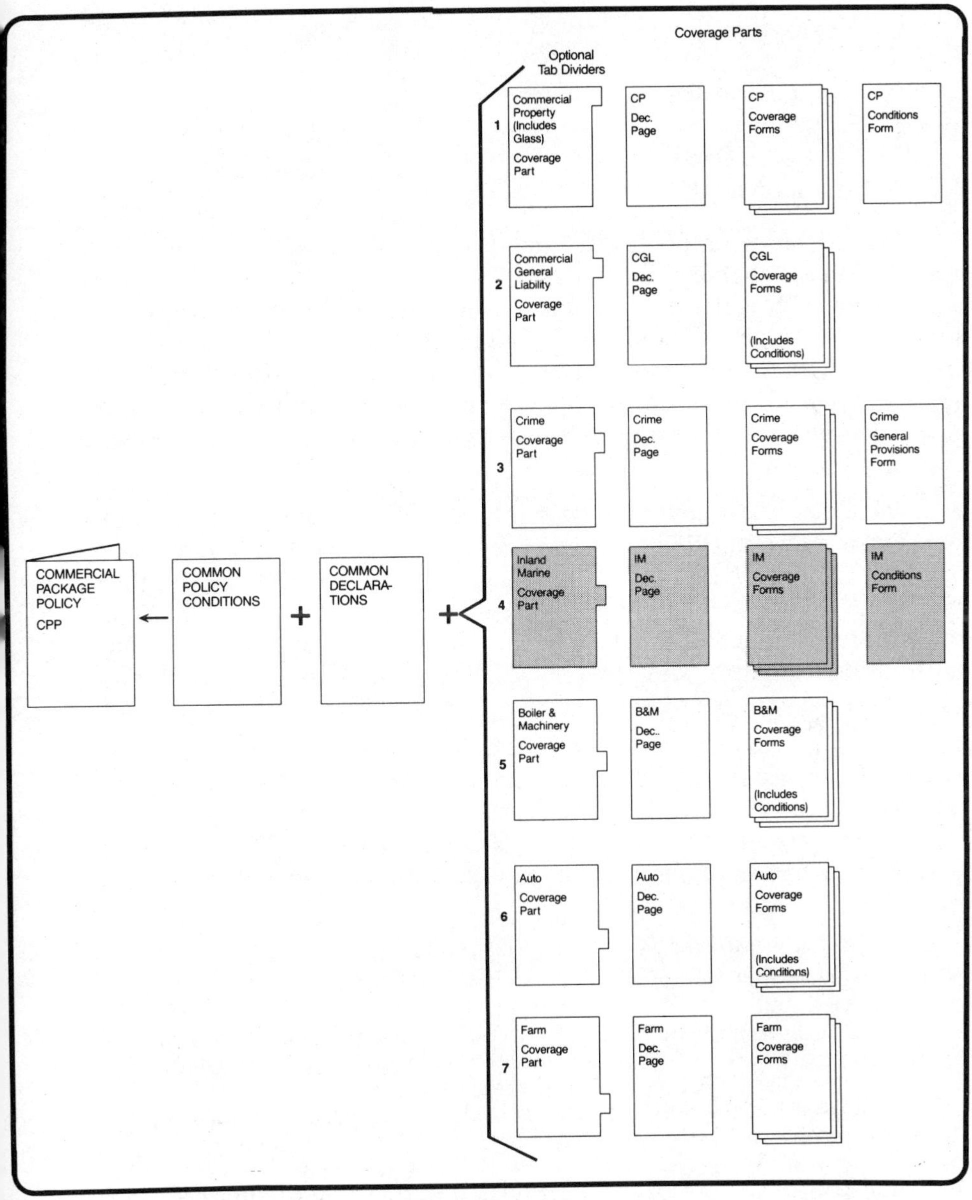

ISO Coverage Forms

The ISO commercial inland marine coverage forms follow a standard format, the major headings of which are shown below.

A. Coverage
B. Exclusions
C. Limits of Insurance
D. Deductible
E. Additional Conditions
F. Definitions

The provisions usually found under each of these headings are described in the sections that follow.

Incidentally, both the ISO and the AAIS inland marine forms are written in "simplified language" to make them easier to read and understand than previous forms. One element of the simplified approach, which will become apparent in certain quotations of policy language below, is reference to the insured as "you" and the insurance company as "we."

Coverage The coverage section ordinarily contains at least four major provisions, entitled "covered property," "property not covered," "covered causes of loss," and "additional coverage—collapse." Other provisions that appear in some coverage forms are coverage extensions and coverage options. The lead-in language of the coverage section states that the insurer will pay for "loss" to covered property from any of the covered causes of loss.

Covered Property and Property Not Covered. The "covered property" provision describes the type of property covered by the particular form. No two coverage forms are alike in this section, since each form relates to a different class of property. The "covered property" provision of the ISO film coverage form is quoted here as an example.

> COVERED PROPERTY, as used in this Coverage Form, means:
> a. Exposed motion picture film and its sound track or other sound record; and
> b. Properly recorded magnetic or video tape and its sound track or other sound record. Tape is considered to be properly recorded if it has been replayed and checked after recording;
>
> when used in the production shown in the Declarations and that you own or have in your care, custody or control.

The "property not covered" provision states any qualifications or exceptions to what is covered property. The "property not covered" provision of the film coverage form is as follows:

Covered Property does not include:
a. Cut-outs;
b. Unused footage;
c. Positive prints or films;
d. Library stock; or
e. Contraband, or property in the course of illegal transportation or trade.

Together, the two parts are intended to tell the insured exactly what property is covered and what is not. The reference to "contraband, or property in the course of illegal transportation or trade" appears in the "property not covered" provision in all of the ISO coverage forms.

Covered Causes of Loss. The "covered causes of loss" provision found in most of the coverage forms states that:

> Covered Causes of Loss means RISKS OF DIRECT PHYSICAL "LOSS" to Covered Property except those causes of "loss" listed in the Exclusions.

This clause provides the "all-risks" coverage that has been a characteristic of most inland marine policies since inland marine insurance began. Even though the word "all" is no longer used in connection with "risks" in the ISO insuring agreement, the underlying concept remains the same: the insurance covers direct physical loss by any fortuitous cause other than those that the policy specifically excludes.

The word "loss," as used above and elsewhere in ISO coverage forms, means "accidental loss or damage." The requirement that, to be associated with a covered cause, the loss be "direct" and "physical" underscores the fact that ISO commercial inland marine forms do not cover time element losses. Examples of time element losses are (1) loss of income resulting from shutdown and (2) extra expense incurred to continue operations, due to damage or destruction of covered property.

Time element coverages *are* provided by some nonfiled inland marine coverage forms, as discussed in later chapters. When an inland marine form does not provide time element coverage, the coverage can often be provided through "commercial property" forms such as the ISO business income coverage form.

Additional Coverage—Collapse. The commercial inland marine coverage forms exclude "collapse except as provided in the Additional Coverage—Collapse section of this Coverage Form." The effect is that loss resulting from collapse of a building or part of a building is covered only if the collapse is due to a cause of loss specified in the "additional coverage—collapse" provision. These covered causes of loss are:

a. fire; lightning; windstorm; hail; explosion; smoke; aircraft; vehicles; riot; civil commotion; vandalism; breakage of glass; falling objects; weight of snow, ice or sleet; water damage; all only as covered in this Coverage Form;
b. Hidden decay;
c. Hidden insect or vermin damage;
d. Weight of people or personal property;
e. Weight of rain that collects on a roof;
f. Use of defective materials or methods in construction, remodeling or renovation if the collapse occurs during the course of the construction, remodeling or renovation.

This approach was developed in reaction to the legal doctrine of *concurrent causation,* which the courts of some states have adopted in interpreting property insurance. Briefly stated, the doctrine of concurrent causation allows an insured to collect for loss jointly caused by an excluded peril and a peril that is not specifically excluded. As the concurrent causation doctrine developed, insurers became concerned that many losses caused by an excluded peril, such as earthquake, might be held covered if the insured building or the building containing insured property collapsed, since collapse was not specifically excluded. The "additional coverage—collapse" feature was devised to counter this possibility by stating that collapse is covered only if it results from one of the listed perils, which do not include earthquake, war, flood, or any of the other perils that are ordinarily excluded.

Coverage Extensions and Coverage Options. Some forms contain coverage extensions and coverage options, and others do not. No attempt is made here to describe all of the extensions and options, since they are described in later chapters of this text along with the particular forms to which they belong. However, it is important to understand the difference between a coverage extension and a coverage option.

A *coverage extension* provides insurance for a usually incidental exposure that would not otherwise be covered by the particular form. For example, the jewelers block coverage form, which otherwise does not cover damage to buildings, has a coverage extension stating that the insurer will pay for damage by thieves to a building containing covered property. The extension applies automatically, and there is no separate premium charge for it.

A *coverage option,* in contrast, is a policy provision that does not apply unless the insured chooses to have it apply, usually by paying an additional premium. For example, the jewelers block policy contains two coverage options, which allow the insured to purchase insurance for (1) theft of covered property from show windows at the insured's premises and (2) theft of money from within locked safes or vaults.

Unless the insured chooses to pay the additional premium, these exposures will not be covered.

Exclusions The next major section of an ISO commercial inland marine coverage form contains the exclusions, which play a large role in defining the scope of coverage. Recall that the "covered causes of loss" provision states that the insurance applies to risks of direct physical loss *except the causes of loss listed in the exclusions.*

The exclusions contained in coverage forms vary from one form to the next, depending largely on the kind of property insured. Still, there are a number of exclusions that are found in all or many of the ISO commercial inland marine coverage forms. These "common" exclusions are discussed here, so as to avoid repetition throughout the text as the various ISO coverage forms are described. Similar exclusions are likely to be found in nonfiled inland marine policies as well.

In contrast with the ISO coverage forms, some inland marine policies apply on a named perils basis. When that is the case, the scope of coverage is delineated largely by the perils named, and so fewer exclusions are needed. What exclusions are found in named perils policies ordinarily relate to particular aspects of a named peril that the insurer is unwilling to cover. For example, a named perils policy may list "theft" as a covered peril and then exclude employee dishonesty and mysterious disappearance.

The ISO commercial inland marine exclusions follow a three-tier format:

- The first-tier exclusions preclude coverage for loss by perils whose occurrence could cause certain types of "catastrophic" loss.
- The second-tier exclusions vary widely among the different coverage forms depending on the characteristics of the covered property. One form might have only two or three second tier exclusions while another could have ten or more.
- The third-tier exclusions address (1) the concurrent causation issue and (2) losses that are almost certain to occur with the passage of time or in the event the insured fails to maintain the covered property in good condition.

First Tier. In all, there are five first-tier exclusions, relating to earthquake, governmental action, nuclear hazard, war and military action, and water. The governmental action, nuclear hazard, and war and military action exclusions are found in *all* of the ISO coverage forms (with some amendments in the mail coverage form). The water and earthquake exclusions are found in only a few of the forms.

The first-tier exclusions for the most part eliminate coverage for perils that could result in catastrophic loss. Catastrophic loss is loss to a very large number of insureds resulting from a single event such as a flood, a hurricane, or a war. Some perils that may cause catastrophic loss are commonly insured under inland marine policies. For example, most inland marine policies do not exclude hurricanes or other types of windstorm, and they often have no exclusion of flood or earthquake. Other catastrophe perils, such as war and nuclear reaction, are ordinarily excluded in inland marine and most other property policies. Perils in this category are either considered uninsurable by commercial insurers or must be insured under special policies.

The lead-in language to the first tier of exclusions states that the insurer will not pay for loss caused directly or indirectly by any of the causes of loss listed there. Such loss is said to be excluded "regardless of any other cause or event that contributes concurrently or in any sequence to the loss." This language, like the collapse modifications discussed earlier, was drafted in reaction to the adoption by the courts of California and some other states of the concurrent causation doctrine. Thus, the lead-in language is aimed at eliminating coverage for any loss involving earthquake, flood, and so on, even though a nonexcluded peril may have contributed to the loss.

Earthquake. The earthquake exclusion applies only to property while located at the insured's premises and therefore does not exclude coverage for earthquake damage to covered property in transit or otherwise away from the insured's premises. Also, the exclusion states that loss by fire resulting from an earthquake is covered (as long as the fire is not otherwise excluded). If, for example, an earthquake causes a natural gas line to rupture and ignite, the resulting fire damage to covered property will be covered.

The earthquake exclusion is contained in only two of the ISO commercial inland marine coverage forms: the camera dealers form and the jewelers block form. ISO rules allow the earthquake exclusion to be deleted from those coverage forms at the insurer's discretion. Ordinarily, the insurer will charge an additional premium for deleting the exclusion.

Governmental Action. Each of the ISO commercial inland marine coverage forms excludes "seizure or destruction of property by order of governmental authority." The exclusion can come into play in a wide range of situations.

Sometimes, police officers or firefighters must take control of an insured's property to protect the common good of the community. For example, a governmental agency might confiscate contaminated property or might destroy property to prevent the spread of further destruction. By tradition, insurers have been willing to insure a portion of this exposure. The exclusion under discussion contains an exception stating that the insurer will pay for destruction ordered by governmental authorities at the time of a fire to prevent its spread.

Another type of loss that the exclusion would apply to is confiscation of covered property in a foreign country by authorities there as a result of political change or unrest. When insurance is desired, this type of loss can be covered by "political risk" insurance. Political risk insurance is available from limited markets as a specialty type coverage.

Nuclear Hazard. The nuclear hazard exclusion applies to loss caused by (1) any weapon employing nuclear fission or fusion or (2) nuclear reaction or radiation or radioactive contamination from any other cause. The first part of the exclusion is generally considered to be broad enough to apply to either accidental or intentional discharge of an atomic weapon in time of peace or war. The second part of the exclusion could apply to a wide range of occurrences, from low-level contamination of property by radium in a medical setting to the widespread contamination that could result from a mishap at a nuclear power plant.

This exclusion is present in all ISO commercial inland marine coverage forms except the mail form, which instead contains an exclusion of loss by atomic weapons or any mine or torpedo.

War and Military Action. The war and military action exclusion excludes loss caused by a wide range of conflicts:

(1) War, including undeclared or civil war;
(2) Warlike action by a military force, including action in hindering or defending against an actual or expected attack, by any government, sovereign or other authority using military personnel or other agents; or
(3) Insurrection, rebellion, revolution, usurped power or action taken by governmental authority in hindering or defending against any of these.

This exclusion is found in all of the ISO commercial inland marine coverage forms, although there are some minor variations in wording in the mail coverage form.

Water. The water exclusion applies to loss by "flood, surface water, waves, overflow of any body of water, or their spray, all whether driven by wind or not."

There is a notable exception to the exclusion: the insurer will pay for direct loss caused by fire, explosion, or theft that results from the excluded event. Also, the exclusion only applies to property at the insured's premises. It does not apply to property in transit or otherwise away from the insured's premises.

The water exclusion is present in only four of the ISO coverage forms—camera and musical instrument dealers, equipment dealers, jewelers block, and floor plan. Like the earthquake exclusion, the water exclusion may be deleted at the insured's request if the underwriter is satisfied that the additional exposure is acceptable.

If the insurer is unwilling to delete the water exclusion, the exposure can be covered, in eligible communities, by the purchase of flood insurance from the National Flood Insurance Program, which, although administered by the Federal Emergency Management Agency, is marketed directly by many insurance companies. Another possible source of flood insurance is difference in conditions (DIC) insurance, an inland marine coverage that extends the insured's basic property insurance to cover additional perils. While there is a great deal of variation among DIC policies, they often include flood coverage. DIC policies are discussed in more detail in Chapter 7.

Second Tier. By far, the greatest variation in exclusions among the different coverage forms occurs within the second tier of exclusions. Only the more frequently encountered of these exclusions are discussed here.

The lead-in to all second-tier exclusions is simply: "We will not pay for 'loss' caused by or resulting from any of the following:...." Because the second-tier exclusions apply to losses that are unlikely to involve concurrent causation, those exclusions are not subject to the concurrent causation language used with the first-tier exclusions.

Trick or Device. There are three exclusions that are found in every ISO commercial inland marine coverage form except the mail coverage form. The first of these, often called the *trick or device exclusion* or the *false pretense exclusion,* excludes loss caused by:

> Voluntary parting with any property by you or anyone entrusted with the property if induced to do so by any fraudulent scheme, trick, device or false pretense.

The trick or device exclusion is found not only in "all-risks" inland marine policies but also in commercial property "all-risks" policies, commercial crime policies, and garage policies that provide physical damage insurance on the merchandise of auto dealers. The effect of the exclusion is to eliminate coverage for loss due to the insured's being tricked into handing over covered property, *voluntarily,* to a swindler or "confidence man." Insurers exclude trickery losses because such losses can almost always be prevented if the insured exercises due diligence in parting with covered property.

The classic example of a trickery loss is when an auto dealer allows a supposed customer to take a new car for a solo "test drive" and the "customer" never returns with the car. This kind of trickery loss can easily be prevented if the dealership adheres to a policy of not allowing customers to test drive cars without a salesperson in attendance.

In the context of inland marine insurance, a trickery loss might occur when a camera dealer allows a phony customer to "try out" a camera and zoom lens outside the store without obtaining adequate identification or security. Or, a jeweler might voluntarily turn over to an imposter a valuable diamond ring that had been in the store for cleaning and repair.

Because the trick or device exclusion applies only to property that has been parted with *voluntarily* by fraudulent scheme, trick, and so on, the exclusion does not apply to robberies, where the wrongdoer threatens or actually uses violence to induce the insured to part with property. The exclusion also does not apply to any other type of theft loss where the insured does not voluntarily hand property over.

Note that the exclusion applies to voluntary parting with any property by "you" (the insured) *or anyone entrusted* with the property. Thus, if an employee, bailee, or carrier is tricked into voluntarily parting with the insured's property, the loss will be treated the same as if the insured had voluntarily parted with it.

Unauthorized Instructions. Another second-tier exclusion found in all coverage forms except the mail form applies to loss caused by or resulting from "unauthorized instructions to transfer property to any person or to any place."

There are numerous types of losses to which this exclusion could apply, many of which could also be subject to the trick or device exclusion. One example of loss that would be reached by the unauthorized instructions exclusion is where the insured has entrusted covered property to a repair shop and the shop, acting on an imposter's telephone message, delivers the covered property to someone other than the insured, and that person absconds with the property.

Another loss that would not be covered because of the unauthorized instructions exclusion is that which could occur if a computer "hacker" gained illegal access to the insured's computer system and entered unauthorized instructions to send covered property to a fictitious customer. If the covered property is subsequently delivered and thereby lost, the insured's policy will not cover the loss. This exposure is ordinarily insurable under the computer fraud coverage form that is a part of the ISO commercial crime program.

Consequential Loss. The third second-tier exclusion found in all ISO commercial inland marine coverage forms except the mail form eliminates coverage for delay, loss of use, loss of market, or any other consequential loss.

Dishonesty. Another second-tier exclusion relates to loss resulting from dishonest acts of the insured, employees of the insured, and other persons entrusted with covered property. The dishonesty exclusion is present in many of the ISO commercial inland marine coverage forms, particularly in the forms that cover merchandise of dealers. Insurers are generally willing to insure employee dishonesty, but by tradition employee dishonesty has been insured under separate commercial crime forms and is therefore excluded under all other policies.

The exclusion eliminates coverage for loss caused by or resulting from:

> Dishonest acts by you, anyone else with an interest in the property, your or their employees or authorized representatives or anyone entrusted with the property, whether or not acting alone or in collusion with other persons or occurring during the hours of employment. But this exclusion does not apply to a carrier for hire.

The portion of the exclusion respecting collusion with other persons means that the exclusion applies to an act of dishonesty by the insured, an employee, and so on, even if some other person not described in the exclusion is involved in the crime.

The portion respecting hours of employment makes it clear that if an employee steals property of the insured *after the employee's hours of employment,* there will still be no coverage. In the absence of such a clarification, it might be argued that the perpetrator was not an employee *at the time of theft* and the exclusion therefore does not apply.

Although the exclusion generally applies to dishonest acts of anyone entrusted with the covered property, the exclusion is specifically stated not to apply to property entrusted to a carrier for hire. The rationale for this exception is that the insured has little, if any, opportunity for supervising a carrier for hire. In contrast, the insured can more carefully select and supervise employees and other persons entrusted with covered property.

Other Theft-Related Exclusions. Two additional exclusions found in a number of ISO coverage forms, particularly those covering the stock in trade of dealers, eliminate coverage for loss resulting from "unexplained disappearance" and "shortage found upon taking inventory." These exclusions have essentially the same purpose: to make it clear that although theft is covered, there must be some evidence that a covered type of theft has actually occurred.

The *unexplained disappearance exclusion* addresses situations where property has disappeared without any plausible explanation or evidence of loss by a covered peril. It is understandable that inland marine underwriters may wish to exclude loss of property that disappears without explanation. An unexplained disappearance of property could actually have been caused by dishonesty, even though there is insufficient evidence to support application of the dishonesty exclusion. The *inventory shortage exclusion* addresses situations where the loss of property is discovered upon taking inventory but there is no other evidence that a covered loss has occurred. In and of itself, an inventory shortage does not prove that loss by a covered cause has occurred. For example, an inventory shortage could result from employee dishonesty, which is excluded. Unless the insured can demonstrate that the shortage is attributable to a covered cause of loss, the insurer will not pay. Once the insured has shown, independently of inventory records, that a covered loss has occurred, the insurer may allow inventory records to be used in determining the *amount* of loss.

Electric Disturbance. Many coverage forms are designed to insure property that may contain electrical components. The camera and musical instruments dealers form, the physicians and surgeons equipment form, and the signs coverage form are examples of such forms. These forms contain an exclusion of loss resulting from "artificially generated current creating a short circuit or other electric disturbance within an article covered under this Coverage Form."

Because the exclusion applies only to artificially generated current, it does not apply to similar disturbances caused by lightning, which is a *natural* source of electricity. In addition, the exclusion states that the insurer will pay for direct loss caused by fire or explosion that results from the electrical disturbance, as long as the fire or explosion would not otherwise be excluded by the coverage form. If, for example, a short circuit in a covered article starts a fire, the ensuing fire damage to covered property, including the article in which the fire originates, is not excluded.

The exclusion is also stated to apply only to loss to the article in which the disturbance occurs.

Processing or Work. Another second-tier exclusion in roughly half the ISO commercial inland marine coverage forms eliminates coverage for loss caused by or resulting from "processing or work upon the property." The exclusion contains a statement that the insurer will pay for direct loss caused by resulting fire or explosion if those causes of loss would be covered under the coverage form.

The forms that contain this exclusion cover property of a sort likely to be worked on by the insured or by others. For example, the jewelers block coverage form covers both property of the insured and property of others in the insured's care, custody, or control, either of which the insured may work upon. Traditionally, underwriters have excluded coverage for damage arising out of the insured's own work, which is generally considered to be a "business risk" assumed by the insured and beyond the scope of standard insurance coverages.

Other Exclusions. Other second-tier exclusions relate to theft from unattended vehicles; delay, or loss of market; and marring or scratching, exposure to light, and breakage of tubes, bulbs, and other glass articles. In addition, there are numerous second-tier exclusions that are found in only one coverage form, due to the peculiar qualities of the covered property. These additional exclusions are discussed in more detail in later chapters of this text in connection with the particular forms to which they relate.

Third Tier. The third tier of exclusions is introduced by a statement that the insurer will not pay for loss resulting from any of the excluded causes, but that if loss by a covered cause results from an excluded cause of loss, the resulting loss will be paid. For example, one exclusion precludes coverage for loss due to faulty design. Consequently, the insurer will not pay for the cost of remedying a design fault, but if the design fault results in a covered cause of loss, such as a fire, the fire loss will be paid.

Weather Conditions. The exclusion of "weather conditions" applies only if weather conditions contribute in any way with a cause of loss excluded in the *first tier* of exclusions. Here again, the forms are intended to preclude the possibility of an insured finding coverage through the concurrent causation doctrine. In the absence of the weather conditions exclusion, an insured might argue, for example, that although flooding and surface water are excluded, a water damage loss is nevertheless covered because rain and wind were concurrent or contributing causes of loss.

Acts or Decisions. The full exclusion relates to "acts or decisions, including the failure to act or decide, of any person, group, organization or governmental body." The purpose of this exclusion can be seen by reviewing the court case of Safeco Insurance Company of America v. Guyton.[1] In this case, policyholders sustained flood losses to their homes that resulted when heavy rains broke through flood control facilities near Palm Desert, California. The policyholders made claim for coverage under their "all-risks" homeowners policies and the insurer denied coverage, citing the flood exclusion. The policyholders then sued the insurer for coverage, contending that their losses were proximately caused by negligence of the local water authorities in maintaining flood control structures, and were therefore covered since their "all-risks" policies did not exclude third-party negligence. The Ninth Circuit Court of Appeals held in favor of the policyholders.

The acts or decisions exclusion is intended to eliminate coverage in such instances by excluding the causes of loss that might otherwise allow coverage in a concurrent causation claim.

Faulty Planning, Design, Materials, or Maintenance. Certain types of inland marine policies have traditionally excluded the cost of correcting faulty workmanship and materials. For example, such exclusions are common in builders risk policies and installation floaters, both of which insure property during the course of construction or installation, when faulty workmanship is a significant risk of loss. Until recently, faulty workmanship exclusions were not considered necessary for many inland marine classes. With the development of the concurrent causation doctrine, ISO took the precaution of adding a similar exclusion to *all* of its inland marine policies.

The case of Premier Insurance Company v. Welch demonstrates the kind of loss that prompted this action. In this case, the insured's house had been damaged by a landslide following heavy rainfall. However, the landslide was found to have resulted from the failure of a subdrain that had been damaged at the time the house was constructed. Having found a concurrent cause of loss that was not excluded in the insured's "all-risks" homeowners policy, the court held the loss to be covered, even though the policy contained an earth movement exclusion.[2]

The exclusion that ISO developed in reaction to this kind of claim is aimed at eliminating coverage for similar concurrent causation losses by excluding a variety of acts, events, processes, and so on, that might otherwise be considered covered causes of loss:

> Faulty, inadequate or defective:
> (1) Planning, zoning, development, surveying, siting;
> (2) Design, specifications, workmanship, repair, construction, renovation, remodeling, grading, compaction;
> (3) Materials used in repair, construction, renovation or remodeling; or
> (4) Maintenance; of part or all of any property wherever located.

Collapse. An earlier section of this chapter describes the "additional coverage—collapse" provision of ISO commercial inland marine coverage forms, which covers loss involving collapse, as long as the collapse is caused by one of the perils listed in that provision. The collapse exclusion, which applies to collapse "except as provided in the Additional Coverage—Collapse section of this Coverage Form," merely removes collapse from the usual scope of "all-risks" coverage and reinforces the named-perils approach of the additional coverage—collapse provision.

In the context of the present discussion, an important feature of the collapse provision is that it covers collapse resulting from use of defective materials or methods in construction, remodeling, or renovation—if the collapse occurs during the course of the construction, remodeling, or renovation. Because this aspect of coverage is contained in the separate collapse coverage, it is not subject to the faulty workmanship exclusion described above.

Nonfortuitous Losses. Most of the ISO commercial inland marine coverage forms and, for that matter, most other "all-risks" policies exclude a number of causes of loss that are deemed to be nonfortuitous, meaning that they are not accidental and are virtually certain to happen either with the passage of time or in the event the insured fails to maintain the property in good condition. In theory, such causes of loss are not "risks" of loss in the first place and are therefore not within the scope of a policy that insures against "risks of direct physical loss." However, insurers have traditionally named these causes of loss in the exclusions to "all-risks" policies in order to reinforce underwriting intent.

Although there are some variations from form to form, the exclusion that appears in most of the ISO coverage forms eliminates coverage for losses caused by:

> Wear and tear, any quality in the property that causes it to damage or destroy itself, hidden or latent defect, gradual deterioration, depreciation; mechanical breakdown; insects, vermin, rodents, corrosion, rust, dampness, cold or heat.

The lead-in language to this and the other third-tier exclusions states that the insurer will pay for resulting loss by a covered peril. If, for example, a rodent gnaws a hole in a water pipe, the damage to the water pipe will be excluded but any resulting water damage to covered property will be insured.

Limits of Insurance The limits of insurance section found in ISO commercial inland marine coverage forms is very brief. It states that the most the insurer will pay for loss in any one occurrence is the applicable limit of insurance shown in the declarations.

For example, a coverage form may have a limit of $100,000 for property at the insured's premises and a limit of $10,000 for property in transit. If the insured suffers a $12,000 loss to property in transit, the most that the insurer will pay is $10,000, the *applicable* limit of insurance.

Deductible Most of the ISO commercial inland marine coverage forms carry a mandatory minimum deductible. The deductible provision that appears in these forms is as follows:

> We will not pay for "loss" in any one occurrence until the amount of the adjusted "loss" before applying the applicable Limits of Insurance exceeds the Deductible shown in the Declarations. We will then

pay the amount of the adjusted "loss" in excess of the Deductible, up to the applicable Limit of Insurance.

This language implies that the deductible is subtracted from the amount of loss *before* the limit of insurance is applied. Consequently, in some cases the insured can collect the full amount of insurance when the amount of loss exceeds the applicable limit of insurance.

For example, say that a professional photographer insures photographic equipment under a commercial articles coverage form for $10,000, with a $100 deductible. If all of the covered property is lost in a fire and the amount of loss is determined to be $10,500, the insurer will subtract the deductible from that amount and only then apply the applicable limit of insurance, resulting in a $10,000 settlement.

Deductible clauses found in some non-ISO policies call for the deductible to be subtracted from the adjusted loss *after* application of limits, meaning that the most the insured can actually recover in a total loss is the limit of insurance less the deductible amount.

Additional Conditions Each coverage form contains one or more "additional conditions." These conditions are "additional" in that they supplement those of the commercial inland marine conditions and common policy conditions forms.

Coverage Territory. There is no provision in the commercial inland marine conditions that defines the geographical boundaries of coverage. Instead, the coverage territory is set forth in each coverage form. Several of the ISO coverage forms contain a coverage territory condition that states:

We cover property wherever located within:
a. The United States of America;
b. Puerto Rico; and
c. Canada.

Other coverage forms have essentially the same coverage territory but may specify that property located within *or between* those places or *within fifty miles of those places* is covered. These subtle differences in wording can amount to significant differences in coverage.

In contrast, some ISO coverage forms provide the broadest possible coverage territory by stating, "We cover property wherever located." And yet others may specify one territory for certain types of covered property and another territory for another type of property. For example, the mail coverage form covers first class mail, certified mail, and United States Postal Service express mail "within and between places in the United States of America, Puerto Rico, Canada, the United States Virgin Islands and other territories or possessions of the United States," but covers registered mail "between places anywhere in the world."

Many other variations in the coverage territory are found in non-ISO policies, depending largely on the nature of the property being insured and the underwriter's willingness to extend coverage.

Coinsurance. Several of the ISO coverage forms contain a coinsurance provision to encourage insureds to buy insurance to full value or to a stipulated percentage of value.

The coinsurance provision that appears in roughly half of the ISO commercial inland marine coverage forms is as follows:

> All Covered Property, except property in transit, must be insured for at least 80% of its total value as of the time of "loss" or you will incur a penalty.
> The penalty is that we will pay only the proportion of any "loss" that the Limit of Insurance shown in the Declarations for all Covered Property at all locations bears to 80% of the total value of all property at all locations as of the time of "loss." This penalty will not apply to property in transit.

To illustrate the application of this clause, assume that a musical instrument dealer with stores at two locations insures its stock of musical instruments and accessories for a total of $120,000. A fire destroys all of the stock at one of the stores, resulting in an $80,000 loss. If the value of covered property at both stores is actually $200,000 at the time of loss, the insured will not have insurance at 80 percent of value and will be able to recover only $120,000/$160,000 of the amount of loss, or $60,000.

The coinsurance provision found in many forms states that property in transit is not taken into consideration in determining the amount of insurance that should be carried. Moreover, property in transit is not subject to a coinsurance penalty resulting from underinsurance on property at the insured's premises.

The coinsurance provision in this example does not make a similar exception with respect to property of others in the care, custody, or control of the insured, a category of property that is often covered under inland marine coverage forms. Consequently, when selecting the amount of insurance on "all covered property," insureds and their advisers need to consider the maximum value of both owned *and nonowned* covered property expected to be in the insured's care at any time during the policy period. This can often be difficult as the value of property belonging to others may be hard to judge.

Some of the ISO coverage forms contain a coinsurance provision requiring that all covered property, except property in transit, be insured for its *total* value instead of 80 percent of its value. This is, in effect, a 100 percent coinsurance clause.

A variation on the 100 percent coinsurance clause is found in the commercial articles coverage form, which applies the coinsurance requirement only to "items that are covered but not individually listed and described." The coinsurance provision does not apply to individually scheduled items, since the amount of insurance shown for each item (and used for rating purposes) is ordinarily the item's full value. A similar approach to coinsurance may be taken in any inland marine policy under which some items are individually scheduled and others are covered for a blanket amount.

Reports and Premium. Coinsurance clauses as described above are not found in coverage forms that provide for coverage on a "reporting" basis. In the ISO commercial inland marine coverage forms that contain reporting arrangements, the insured's duties with respect to reporting are spelled out in an additional condition entitled "reports and premium."

While the insured's duties vary among reporting forms, the insured is generally required to report values to the insurer at a specified interval (such as every month). If the insured makes these reports on time, the insurer will pay the full amount of any loss, even if it is higher than the last report of values. However, the insured's recovery cannot exceed the limit of insurance shown in the policy. Moreover, reporting forms often contain a *full value reporting clause,* which functions somewhat like a 100 percent coinsurance clause. For example, the reports and premium condition in the ISO floor plan coverage form contains this clause:

> Reporting Less than the Total Amount Required. If your last report before any "loss" is for less than the total amount required to be reported, we will pay only that proportion of the "loss" that the amounts you reported bear to the actual total amount as of the last report.

This condition (sometimes called an "honesty clause") parallels coinsurance in that it encourages the insured to report the actual value of covered property, which, like the amount of insurance in a nonreporting form, is used in determining the insured's premium.

Many insureds and even some insurance people overlook the fact that the insured under a reporting form can recover no more than the limit of insurance, even if the insured has paid a premium based on reports of values that are actually greater than the limit. The chief benefit of reporting forms is that an insured with substantially fluctuating values pays a premium based on actual values at different times during the policy period rather than having to pay a premium for the entire policy period based on the maximum anticipated value of covered property.

Other "Additional Conditions." Other "additional conditions" relate to valuation, records and inventory, protective safeguards, and other issues that pertain only to the particular coverage form. The various approaches to valuation are discussed later in this chapter in connection with the basic valuation provision found in the commercial inland marine conditions. The remaining additional conditions are discussed in later chapters of this text in connection with the coverage forms to which they apply.

Definitions The final section of all ISO commercial inland marine coverage forms is entitled "definitions." Most coverage forms define only the word "loss," which means "accidental loss or damage." Additional definitions are contained in only a few coverage forms.

Commercial Inland Marine Conditions

The commercial inland marine conditions apply to all inland marine coverage forms except as amended by the additional conditions discussed above.

Abandonment The insured may not "abandon" property to the insurer. Insurers often take over the salvage after replacing covered property, but the insured has no right to demand that the insurer do so.

Appraisal The ISO appraisal clause, like appraisal clauses found in many other inland marine policies, outlines the procedure to be followed in the event the insurance company and the insured disagree on the value of covered property or the amount of loss and either party makes written demand for an appraisal.

Each party selects a competent and impartial appraiser, and the two appraisers select an umpire. If the appraisers cannot agree as to the value of the property and the amount of loss, their appraisals are submitted to the umpire, and an agreement by any two of the three will be binding. The insurance company and the insured each pay their own appraiser and share equally the other expenses of the appraisal and the umpire.

Although the insurance company and the insured agree to be bound by the appraisers' decision as to the value of covered property and the amount of loss, the insurance company nevertheless retains the right to deny the claim. If, for example, after appraisal of a fire loss the insured was convicted of arson, the insurer could still deny coverage for the claim.

Duties in the Event of Loss The duties that the insured must perform after loss in order to secure coverage are directly quoted below.

1. Notify the police if a law may have been broken.
2. Give us prompt notice of the "loss."

3. As soon as possible, give us a description of how, when and where the "loss" occurred.
4. Take all reasonable steps to protect the Covered Property from further damage. If feasible, set the damaged property aside and in the best possible order for examination. Also keep a record of your expenses, for consideration in the settlement of the claim.
5. Make no statement that will assume any obligation or admit any liability, for any "loss" for which we may be liable, without our consent.
6. Permit us to inspect the property and records proving "loss."
7. If requested, permit us to question you under oath, at such times as may be reasonably required, about any matter relating to this insurance or your claim, including your books and records. In such event, your answers must be signed.
8. Send us a signed, sworn statement of "loss" containing the information we request to settle the claim. You must do this within 60 days after our request. We will supply you with the necessary forms.
9. Promptly send us any legal papers or notices received concerning the "loss."
10. Cooperate with us in the investigation or settlement of the claim.

Insurance Under Two or More Coverages A fundamental principle of property and liability insurance is that it should indemnify, but not enrich, the insured. Nevertheless, a policy may contain two or more coverages that cover a particular item of property under certain circumstances. To prevent the insured from collecting more than the amount of loss in such situations, the "two or more coverages" condition states that the insurer will pay no more than the actual amount of loss, even though two or more coverages in the policy may apply to the same loss.

Loss Payment The insurer promises to pay or make good any covered loss within thirty days after (1) reaching agreement with the insured, (2) the entry of final judgment (if the insured sues the insurance company), or (3) the filing of an appraisal award.

In addition, the insurer states that it will not be liable for any part of a loss that has been paid or made good by others. If, for example, the insured recovers damages from a person who is legally responsible for damage to covered property, the insurer will not duplicate that recovery. It will, however, pay any portion of the covered loss that has not been paid or made good by the responsible party.

Other Insurance If the insured has other insurance covering the same loss, the insurer will pay only the excess over what the insured should have received from the other insurance, regardless of whether the insured collects on the other insurance.

An "excess" other insurance clause of this sort would seem to leave the insured without any coverage in the event the other insurance had the same other insurance clause. However, when insurers are confronted with such other insurance situations, they may agree to share the loss according to certain guidelines. The most common guidelines for sharing losses are contained in a document created by an all-industry committee and entitled "Guiding Principles for Overlapping Insurance Coverages."[3] No insurance company is formally bound to the Guiding Principles but most companies adhere to them.

Pair, Sets or Parts When one piece of a pair or set becomes damaged or lost, such as an irreplaceable chair in an antique dining room set, the overall value of the pair or set may be diminished beyond the individual value of the item damaged. While insurers are generally willing to pay for any resulting loss of value in a pair or set in such instances, they are unwilling to treat loss of a portion of the pair or set as a total loss. Consequently, inland marine policies (like most other property policies) customarily contain a pair or set clause to clarify underwriting intent. The pair or set clause that appears in the ISO commercial inland marine conditions is as follows:

> Pair or Set. In case of "loss" to any part of a pair or set we may:
> a. Repair or replace any part to restore the pair or set to its value before the "loss"; or
> b. Pay the difference between the value of the pair or set before and after the "loss."

Similar claims problems can develop when one part of a machine or other property consisting of multiple parts is lost or damaged. The ISO commercial inland marine conditions, as well as many other inland marine policies, therefore contain a *parts clause:*

> Parts. In case of "loss" to any part of Covered Property consisting of several parts when complete, we will only pay for the value of the lost or damaged part.

Privilege to Adjust with Owner Many inland marine policies cover property of others in the care, custody, or control of the insured. Frequently, insurance companies find it more expedient to settle claims for damage to such property directly with the owner of the property. Consequently, the commercial inland marine conditions contain a provision allowing the insurer to settle losses to such property with the owner and stating that such payment will satisfy any claim the insured might make for the same loss.

The insurer also reserves the right to provide a defense, at its own cost, for legal proceedings brought against the insured by owners of property left in the insured's care, custody, or control. Some inland marine forms cover loss to property of others in the insured's care, custody, or control only if the insured becomes *legally obligated* to pay for such loss. Consequently, insurers want the right to become involved in any such court proceedings against the insured. The insurer will have to pay if a judgment is rendered against the insured, so it is reasonable for the insurer to be allowed to handle the defense.

Transfer of Rights of Recovery Against Others to Us Sometimes a covered loss results from the carelessness of a person other than the insured. For example, property in transit may be damaged when another driver runs into the transporting vehicle. Once an insurer has paid a loss of this sort, it may assume the insured's rights of recovery against the responsible party. This assumption of the insured's rights is known as *subrogation.*

The "transfer of rights" condition sets forth the insurer's subrogation rights by stating that if any person or organization to or for whom the insurer makes payment has rights to recover damages from another, those rights are transferred to the insurer. Moreover, that person or organization must do everything necessary to secure the insurer's rights and must do nothing after loss to impair them. For example, the insurer could refuse to pay for a loss if the insured, after the loss occurred, signs a statement releasing the responsible party from liability.

Recoveries The recoveries provision makes it clear what will happen to any money or property recovered after a loss has been paid. Recovery may result from the subrogation process, as mentioned above. Money may also be recovered under the salvage process, when damaged property is sold to a salvage company that will resell the undamaged item or its salvageable parts. Recovery may also take place when stolen property is retrieved after the claim has been paid.

In any case, the recoveries provision states that any recovery or salvage is entirely to the benefit of the insurer until the recovery or salvage value equals the amount paid by the insurer. This is a departure from the practice in some lines of insurance. With personal auto coverage, for example, it is common for any recovery via subrogation to offset the insured's deductible. With commercial inland marine insurance, the form states that the insured receives no benefit of any recovery or salvage until the insurer has been reimbursed in full.

Reinstatement of Limit After Loss When an item of property insured for $10,000 sustains $5,000 of damage, the question logically arises: Does the item now have only $5,000 of coverage remaining? Although arguments can be raised on both sides of the issue, and some policies have called for reduction of the limit of losses paid, most policies today have a clause stating that the limit of insurance will not be reduced by the payment of any claim.

The ISO "reinstatement" condition provides that the limit is not reduced by payment of any claim, except for total loss of a scheduled item. The $10,000 item in the example might logically be repaired or restored to its original condition, in which case the full $10,000 of coverage would automatically be available to pay future claims. If the property were not repaired or restored, recovery for future losses would naturally be limited to the actual cash value, in the absence of another valuation provision.

When a scheduled item sustains a total loss, coverage for future claims against that item is canceled and the unearned premium is returned to the insured. Insureds would consider it unfair to be charged a premium to cover an item that is no longer exposed to loss.

Concealment, Misrepresentation, and Fraud Inland marine insurance and ocean marine insurance differ in the treatment of concealment, misrepresentation, and fraud. Any concealment on the part of an ocean marine policyholder usually has been considered to void the insurance. This is based on the usual situation where the insurer often has little or no opportunity to examine the subject of the insurance at the time coverage is written. The property may even be out at sea. With inland marine insurance, the insurer generally has an opportunity to determine the circumstances under which coverage will apply. An inspection may be made of the shipper's or the carrier's operations, or other pertinent areas.

The concealment, misrepresentation, or fraud condition of the ISO commercial inland marine conditions states that the inland marine coverage part is void in any case of fraud by the insured relating to that coverage part. The coverage part is also void if the insured intentionally conceals or misrepresents a *material* fact concerning (1) the inland marine coverage part, (2) the covered property, or (3) the insured's interest in the covered property. A material fact is one that is so important that, if the insurer were aware of it, it would alter the insurer's decision to issue coverage, settle a loss, or determine a premium.

It would be unusual for coverage to be voided under an inland marine policy by concealment or misrepresentation that was not material to the loss. The same principle would generally apply to any allegation of fraud. Fraud would have to be material to the loss before a court would be likely to sustain a voidance of coverage.

Legal Action Against Us Often referred to as the "suit" provision, this condition limits the circumstances under which the insured is permitted to sue the insurance company. Generally, a suit against the insurance company would allege that the insurer failed to honor its contractual obligation to the insured, either by refusing to pay a covered claim or by paying less than it should.

The provision in the commercial inland marine conditions stipulates that an action may be brought only within two years of the time the insured first knows of the loss. Second, the insured must have complied with all terms of the policy.

For example, if there were a dispute over the value of the property or the amount of the loss, the insured must have complied with any written demand by the insurer that the appraisal process be used. The insured must not have attempted to abandon property to the insurer (a violation of the abandonment provision), and the insured must have performed the "duties in the event of loss." Whether there has been *full* compliance in a specific situation may be a question of fact for a court to decide.

No Benefit to Bailee The "no benefit to bailee" clause addresses the situation where covered property is in the custody of someone (i.e., a bailee or carrier) other than the insured when it is lost or damaged: "No person or organization, other than you, having custody of Covered Property, will benefit from this insurance." The purpose of this clause is to preserve the insurer's right of subrogation against a bailee in possession of the insured's property at the time it is damaged. How it does so involves some explanation.

Bailees' contracts and bills of lading used by carriers may contain a provision that the bailee or carrier shall have the full benefit of any insurance on the property, so as to relieve the bailee of liability for damage to the property. Such a provision and the "no benefit to bailee" clause are in direct conflict. The provision in the bailee contract or bill of lading means that if the insured collects the amount of the loss from an insurance company, the bailee does not have to pay the claim. The insurance policy, on the other hand, provides that if the bailee is relieved from its obligation by the existence of the insurance, the insurance company pays nothing.

The "no benefit to bailee" clause generally has been held effective in preserving the right of the insurance company to pay a loss to the insured and then collect from the carrier. However, this is not universally true. When there is doubt, it is considered good practice for the insurance company to pay the insured through the use of a *loan receipt.* The insurer lends the amount of the loss to the insured, under the condition that the loan will be repaid only if the loss is recovered from the carrier or bailee. Suit is then entered against the carrier or bailee in the name of the insured. If the insured recovers the loss from the carrier or bailee, the loan is repaid to the insurance company. If the insured does not recover, the insured has no obligation to repay the insurance company.[4]

Policy Period The policy inception and expiration dates are usually stated in the declarations. Some inland marine policies cover only a specified event of limited duration, such as a single specified shipment of goods or the installation of equipment. Other policies may provide coverage that is continuous until cancelled, with no fixed expiration date. However, most policies, particularly those based on ISO forms, provide coverage for one year.

The policy period provision states that the policy covers loss *commencing* during the policy period shown in the declarations. It is not necessary that the entire loss occur before the end of the policy period. If a fire begins five minutes before the policy expires and smolders for five days, all fire damage is covered. This provision also makes it clear that a loss commencing before the beginning of the policy term is not covered by the policy.

Valuation The standard approach to determining the value of property insured under inland marine policies, as in property policies generally, is *actual cash value* (ACV). Thus it is no surprise that the valuation provision in the ISO commercial inland marine conditions form calls for actual cash value determination.

> The value of property will be the least of the following amounts:
> 1. The actual cash value of that property;
> 2. The cost of reasonably restoring that property to its condition immediately before "loss"; or
> 3. The cost of replacing that property with substantially identical property.

Insurance companies generally determine actual cash value of an item as the replacement cost of property of like kind and quality *less* accumulated depreciation on the lost or damaged item. To illustrate, assume that a medical instrument insured under the physicians and surgeons equipment coverage form is stolen. If the cost to replace the instrument with one of like kind and quality is $200 and it is determined that the instrument had suffered depreciation of 10 percent as of the time of loss, the instrument's actual cash value is $180.

When covered property is new, as in the case of merchandise insured under the various dealers forms, actual cash value is often synonymous with "replacement cost," since there is ordinarily no depreciation on unsold merchandise. For this reason, inland marine insurance is seldom written on a formal replacement cost basis.

Some of the ISO commercial inland marine coverage forms amend the usual ACV valuation provision quoted above, depending on the nature of the property being insured. For example, the jewelers block coverage form states that the value of property will be "the lowest figure put on the property in your inventories, stock books, stock papers or lists existing as of the time of loss" if that figure is less than the actual cash value or repair or replacement cost of the property. The additional language is explained by the fact that jewelry, more than most other kinds of merchandise, can rapidly increase (or decrease) in value depending on market conditions. More elaborate variations from the standard valuation condition are found in the coverage forms for film, mail, and accounts receivable, each of which presents special valuation problems.

A characteristic of inland marine insurance is that coverage of certain classes of property is ordinarily on a valued, or *agreed value,* basis. An example of valued coverage under ISO commercial inland marine forms can be found in the valuable papers and records coverage form:

> The value of each item of property that is specifically declared and described in the Declarations is the applicable Limit of Insurance shown in the Declarations for that item.

The items that are specifically declared and described are those that are considered to be difficult or impossible to replace, such as a famous author's manuscript. In such cases, underwriters prefer to establish the value at the time the policy is issued so as to avoid valuation problems at the time of a later loss.

In addition to the various valuation provisions found in the ISO coverage forms, the inland marine division of the ISO Commercial Lines Manual contains a rule stating that the valuation condition may be amended to provide for *any other basis* of valuation as agreed upon between the insurance company and the insured. For example, the underwriter and the insured may agree that property in transit will be valued at *invoice cost,* which may be easier to determine than actual cash value.

Common Policy Conditions[5]

The common policy conditions form contains the general conditions concerning such matters as cancellation and changes in the policy, which can apply to any commercial lines policy, whether inland marine or not.

Cancellation The cancellation clause states how the insurance company and the insured can go about cancelling the policy. The *first named insured* in the policy may cancel the policy by mailing or delivering to the insurance company advance written notice of the cancellation, stating the date on which coverage is to cease.

The *insurance company* may cancel by giving written notice to the first named insured. Ten days' notice is required when the insurer cancels for nonpayment of premium; otherwise, thirty days' notice is required. State laws may require longer advance notice and may restrict the reasons for which an insurance company may cancel a policy. State requirements may or may not be reflected in an endorsement to the policy. To effect cancellation, the insurance company must mail or deliver notice to the *last known mailing address* of the first named insured shown in the policy. The notice must state the effective date of the cancellation.

When the insurance company cancels, a pro rata refund of unearned premium must be sent to the first named insured. The pro rata refund is equal to the number of days left on the policy divided by 365, times the annual premium. When the insured cancels, a short rate refund is due. The short rate is generally 90 percent of the pro rata refund. An exception to the short rate rule applies when the insured cancels because he or she no longer has an insurable interest in the covered property. In such cases, manual rules state that the insurer should make a pro rata refund, but there is no provision in the policy itself addressing such situations.

Changes Modifications in the policy may be made by the named insured listed first in the declarations, if the insurance company consents. To effect a change, the insurer issues a written endorsement that is made a part of the policy.

Perhaps the most significant part of the changes provision is that it *limits* policy changes. The provision states that the written policy contains all agreements between insurance company and insured and that these agreements can be amended or waived *only* when the insurance company issues a written endorsement and makes it a part of the policy.

Examination of Books and Records The insurance company has the contractual right to examine the insured's books and records that related to the insurance policy during the policy period and for up to three years after the policy has expired. This condition is included so that the insurance company can verify that statements made by the insured are accurate and, in the case of auditable policies, to determine the correct premium.

Insurance premiums for commercial insurance policies are often based on such things as annual sales, dollar value of goods in stock, or similar things that are recorded in the insured's financial records. *Premium auditors,* employed by insurance companies, need to examine these financial records in order to determine the proper premium to charge. The examination of books and records provision makes it clear that the insured must permit the premium auditor to examine the books or records as necessary.

Inspections and Surveys Insurance companies employ *loss control representatives* to inspect the premises and operations of businesses that apply for insurance. While the policy is in force, loss control representatives may also make inspections and surveys, give reports to the insured, and recommend changes the insurance company would like to see made.

The inspections and surveys provision makes it clear that the insurance company has the right to make such inspections and surveys. The condition also states that these are not safety inspections, that the insurance company does not take on the responsibility of protecting workers or the public from injury, and that the insurance company does not warrant that the business it inspected is safe or healthful or complies with any applicable laws. This disclaimer is included because certain courts have held insurers liable for losses supposedly related to the inadequacy of such inspections.

This clause gives not only the insurer, but also various rating and advisory organizations, the right to inspect. An ISO subsidiary, Commercial Risk Services, Inc. (CRS) conducts property rating surveys on commercial properties to help insurers set accurate premiums for those buildings. This policy provision gives the CRS inspector the right to enter the property.

CRS and other organizations also provide loss control service to insurers for a fee. These organizations must also be permitted to make inspections and surveys, according to policy terms.

Transfer of Rights and Duties Under the Policy This provision deals with two situations in which it may be desirable to "assign" the policy to another party. The first situation occurs, for example, when the named insured sells insured property and desires to transfer the insurance to the new owner along with other assets. The provision states that the named insured's rights and duties cannot be transferred without the insurer's written consent. Insurance is a two-party contract, and the insurance company needs to be able to decide whether it wants to protect each individual insured; such underwriting approval would not be possible if coverage could be transferred at will from one person to another.

The second situation occurs when a named insured dies. The property or business usually continues to exist—and to be exposed to loss. In such a case the insured's rights and duties in connection with covered property are automatically transferred to anyone having proper temporary custody of property. Coverage also applies to the named insured's legal representative, once he or she is appointed. The legal representative is not protected for other ventures, but only while performing duties as a legal representative.

AAIS INLAND MARINE PROGRAM

In many respects, the ISO commercial inland marine provisions are representative of the provisions used in the commercial inland marine forms of the American Association of Insurance Services.

The AAIS inland marine program uses simplified language and a modular approach to policy construction like those of ISO's program. The AAIS inland marine forms may be used as the inland marine component of any commercial package policy whether or not the other modules consist of AAIS forms. An AAIS inland marine policy consists of the following parts:

- an advisory declarations page;
- a common policy conditions form like ISO's;
- an inland marine general terms form, containing definitions, perils excluded, duties in event of loss, loss settlement provisions, and other conditions that generally apply to all coverage forms;
- one or more coverage forms, performing the same function as the ISO coverage forms; and
- any endorsement as may be required to add optional coverages or make other modifications.

A significant difference in policy construction is that AAIS policies contain some exclusions (those that apply to all coverage forms) in the general terms form and others in the coverage forms, while all ISO exclusions are contained in the coverage forms. Moreover, the AAIS coverage forms contain schedules for the same information that is ordinarily shown in separate, advisory declarations pages for the ISO coverage forms. The AAIS forms specify that this information may be shown on a separate schedule or declarations.

In addition, some of the filed AAIS forms provide specified perils coverage, while others are of the "all-risks" type. This is due in part to the fact that AAIS has filed forms for some coverages not serviced by ISO, insuring classes of property that may not be suitable for "all-risks" coverage. Actually, neither "all" nor "risks" is used in the AAIS version of the "all-risks" insuring agreement, which states:

> We cover direct physical loss to covered property unless the loss is caused by a peril that is excluded. The loss must be due to an external cause.

Like ISO's dropping of "all" from "all-risks," AAIS's elimination of the entire term can be viewed as a precaution for avoiding court interpretations that tend to downplay the effect of exclusions in a contract that purports in any manner to cover all risks of loss.

NONFILED FORMS

Nonfiled forms are those that generally need not be filed with state insurance regulators. Insurers therefore have great freedom in writing the provisions for nonfiled forms. The extent to which insurers exercise that freedom varies, depending on the class of property being insured, the insurer's underwriting philosophy and policy-drafting expertise, and the relative bargaining power of the insured.

For some nonfiled classes, there is much uniformity among the contracts used by different insurers even though there is no standard filed form. For these classes, an insurer is likely to keep a supply of printed forms on hand to be used much like the filed forms. In drafting such forms, the insurer may begin with standard filed wording and make whatever modifications are necessary for the particular class. For some classes, which were formerly filed but no longer serviced by ISO or AAIS, an insurer may simply use the old filed form. AAIS publishes advisory information for the nonfiled classes, including nonfiled forms, in the AAIS *Inland Marine Guide.*

In other cases, the policy is a one-of-a-kind typed (or computer-printed) manuscript form. Often such manuscript forms are prepared by insurance brokers on behalf of their clients or by risk managers on behalf of their employers and submitted to the insurer with the application for insurance. Typically, the prospective insured is a large corporation that has special insurance needs or whose insurance involves such large premiums that the insurer is willing to negotiate over policy terms and rates. When such submissions are received, it is up to the insurer's underwriters and legal counsel to analyze the language and either approve it or insist on modifications. An insurer with a large book of inland marine business and many years' experience in inland marine underwriting is more likely to consider submissions of this sort than is an inexperienced insurer with a small book of inland marine business.

Apart from these generalizations, little more can be said without examining the provisions customarily used for insuring each class of property that can be insured on a nonfiled basis. That task is left to the chapters that follow.

SUMMARY

The forms described in this chapter are the industry standards found in the commercial inland marine forms filed by the Insurance

Services Office (ISO) and the American Association of Insurance Services (AAIS).

The ISO commerical inland marine program provides forms and endorsements that can be used as either a monoline inland marine policy or as the inland marine portion of a commercial package policy. Rules and rating procedures are contained in the ISO Commercial Lines Manual.

ISO commercial inland marine coverage forms follow a standard format, the major headings of which include:

- Coverage. The coverage section ordinarily contains at least four major provisions—covered property, property not covered, covered causes of loss, and additional coverage—collapse.
- Exclusions. The exclusions follow a three-tier format. Although exclusions may vary from one form to the next, a certain number are found in all or many of the ISO commercial inland marine coverage forms.
- Limits of Insurance. This section states that the most the insurer will pay for loss in any one occurrence is the applicable limit of insurance shown in the declarations.
- Deductible. Most coverage forms carry a mandatory minimum deductible.
- Additional Conditions. Each coverage form contains one or more additional conditions which supplement those of the commercial inland marine conditions and common policy conditions forms.
- Definitions. The definitions section usually defines only the word "loss."

The commercial inland marine conditions apply to all inland marine coverage forms except as amended by the additional conditions.

The common policy conditions form contains the general conditions concerning such matters as cancellation and changes in the policy, which can apply to any commercial lines policy, whether inland marine or not.

In many respects, the ISO commercial inland marine provisions are representative of the provisions used in the commercial inland marine forms of the American Association of Insurance Services. The AAIS program uses simplified language and a modular approach to policy construction similar to ISO's. A significant difference between the two programs is that some AAIS forms provide specified perils coverage, while ISO forms all apply on an "all-risks" basis.

Nonfiled forms are those that generally need not be filed with state insurance regulators. For some nonfiled classes, there is much uniformity among the contracts used by different insurers even though there is no standard filed form. In other cases, the policy is a one-of-a-kind manuscript form.

Chapter Notes

1. 692 Fed. (2nd) 551 (1982).
2. 140 Cal. App. (3rd) 720 (1983).
3. A reproduction of the Guiding Principles can be found in *The Fire, Casualty, and Surety Bulletins,* Personal Lines Volume (Cincinnati, OH: National Underwriter Co.), General Gp-1 through 42.
4. This discussion of the no benefit to bailee clause and loan receipts follows William H. Rodda. *Marine Insurance: Ocean and Inland* (Englewood Cliffs, NJ: Prentice-Hall, 1970), pp. 475-76.
5. The discussion of common policy conditions is adapted from the manuscript for Chapter 3 of William H. Rodda, James S. Trieschmann, Eric A. Wiening, and Bob A. Hedges, *Commercial Property Risk Management and Insurance,* 3rd. ed. (Malvern, PA: American Institute for Property and Liability Underwriters, 1988).

CHAPTER 3

Transportation Loss Exposures*

INTRODUCTION

Inland marine insurance originated as a way to cover property in the course of inland transportation. Today, property in transit, whether by highway, railroad, air, or inland waterway, continues to be a principal class of inland marine business. Because of the various modes of transportation and, more importantly, the various types of carriers that transport property, the loss exposures resulting from the shipment of property are complex and the corresponding insurance coverages are many. Consequently, two chapters of this book are devoted to the subject of transportation loss exposures and transportation insurance. This chapter examines transportation loss exposures and their treatment by risk management methods other than insurance. Chapter 4 surveys the various insurance policies used to cover transportation loss exposures.

TRANSPORTATION LOSS EXPOSURES

The loss exposures resulting from the transportation of property are analyzed here according to:

- the property subject to loss,

*Portions of this chapter are adapted from the manuscript for Chapters 9 and 10 of William H. Rodda, James S. Trieschmann, Eric A. Wiening, and Bob A. Hedges, *Commercial Property Risk Management and Insurance,* 3rd. ed. (Malvern, PA: American Institute for Property and Liability Underwriters, 1988).

- the perils that may cause loss,
- the potential financial consequences of the loss, and
- the parties affected by loss.

Property Subject to Loss

There is no perfect system for classifying commercial property. One widely used system, however, divides all property into real property and personal property. The major distinction between the two is "moveability." Real property can be (and often is) converted into personal property when it is moved. Therefore inland transportation exposures are concerned with personal property. This category, however, is very broad indeed. Generally only land, large buildings, and other large structures cannot be moved. Some of the property exposed to loss in transit includes money and securities, inventory, furniture, equipment, supplies, clothing, machinery, data processing equipment, valuable papers, fine arts, and many other types of property.

Perils Affecting Property in Transit

Property in transit is subject to virtually all the loss causes that are common to fixed-location property. In addition, it is exposed to perils related to transportation.

Fire may occur in warehouses or while property is en route in a truck, railcar, or aircraft. Conveyances may be overturned, upset, or demolished by a *windstorm* with resultant damage to goods being conveyed. Property in transit may be exposed to loss by *aircraft damage, vehicle damage, riot and civil commotion, explosion, smoke, vandalism,* and so forth.

Property in transit is particularly subject to *crime* loss. The greatest exposure is faced by property of high value and low bulk—cigarettes, for example. However, bulky items, such as a load of steel, may also be stolen. Hijackers can be interested in property of low unit cost and high marketability, as in one hijacking of a semitrailer of panty hose. Exposure to crime loss is relatively high for property in transit, because tight security is difficult when property is being moved about.

The chances of *flood* loss to property in the course of actual movement are perhaps somewhat less than the chances of loss to property at a fixed location in a flood zone. Many floods can be anticipated in advance, giving railroads and truck lines time to move their vehicles out of the flood area.

Earthquakes are not yet predictable, yet there have been relatively few serious earthquake losses to property actually in transit. There is still an exposure, however. A train wreck could be caused by the disruption of tracks in an earthquake. Cargo losses do occur when trucks are driven or parked in an area where an earthquake occurs.

Property in transit, because it is in transit, is exposed to loss resulting from the peril of *collision* or *upset* of the conveyance. Trucks or railroad cars may become involved in a collision with a fixed object or other vehicle. Airplanes may crash. Upset or overturn may occur whether a single vehicle or multiple vehicles are involved.

Misdelivery and *nondelivery* of property are further perils to which property in transit is exposed. If a parcel is not delivered, or if it is delivered to the wrong party, then the shipper, carrier, or consignee (buyer) faces a loss.

Property in transit is also subject to loss caused by *wear and tear, deterioration, loss of refrigeration, excessive heat,* and other miscellaneous perils. The potential for loss due to these perils depends in part on the nature of the property. Meat, for example, may be particularly subject to damage caused by loss of refrigeration. On the other hand, liquids or sensitive electronic components may be damaged by cold or freezing temperatures. The exposure to such miscellaneous perils may be increased or decreased depending on the type of packing and mode of transportation.

Potential Financial Consequences

As discussed in Chapter 1, loss of property or damage to it may reduce the value of the property, cause an increase in the owner's (or other party's) expenses, or reduce the owner's (or other party's) income. All three consequences of property loss can result from loss to property in transit.

By far, the most usual consequence is reduction in value of property. If, for example, a truckload of canned goods is destroyed in transit, the owner will have lost the value of the goods. (The carrier, depending on the circumstances, may also have incurred a liability to the owner equal to the value of the destroyed property.)

In many cases, loss to property in transit does not result in any significant increase in expenses or loss of income. Merchandise, tools, or other property essential to the owner's operations often can be replaced without increased expenses or loss of income. However, the loss of a custom-built or hard-to-replace item without which the owner cannot operate could result in both extra expense and loss of income. For example, if a custom-built boiler were damaged in transit, it might take several weeks for the manufacturer to build a replacement. The owner of the lost boiler might therefore suffer a loss of business income due to shutdown while a replacement was being built. Or, the owner might incur extra expense to rent substitute quarters or heating equipment.

Parties Affected by Loss

When property in transit is lost, damaged, or destroyed, the financial impact depends upon the parties involved and their legal situation. Usually there are at least two parties involved: (1) the shipper (consignor) or receiver (consignee), and (2) the carrier. The terms of the sale, as well as legal principles and practices, determine at what point ownership of the goods being transported passes from the shipper (seller) to the consignee (buyer). Regardless of ownership, the carriers having custody of the property bear some legal liability for loss, damage, or destruction of property in their custody.

When property is transported by a carrier that does not own the property, it is sometimes assumed that all loss exposures have been transferred to the carrier. Although many exposures can be transferred to a carrier, such transfers do not usually include all exposures of the shipper or consignee. Moreover, those transfers that can be made will be ineffective if the carrier is insolvent. Furthermore, it is often difficult to determine precisely the point at which exposures are transferred to or from a carrier. Throughout the following discussion the reader should therefore keep in mind the distinct exposures of:

- the shipper,
- the carrier,
- the consignee, and
- the owner, if different from the preceding.

TYPES OF CARRIERS

Carriers are persons or organizations having custody of property in transit from one place to another. In this country the five most important modes of freight movement are railroads, trucks, waterways, pipelines, and aircraft. The economic characteristics of these modes vary considerably.

Exhibit 3-1 shows how each of the major modes may be ranked. To interpret the numbers in this table, 1 is the highest ranking and 5 is the lowest. For example, air is the most expensive and has a ranking of 1. It ranks third in dependability and fifth in fuel efficiency (indicating it is the least fuel efficient of the modes). It is interesting to observe the rankings for "loss and damage." Pipelines are ranked highest on losses, while railroads are lowest.

Exhibit 3-1
Modes of Transportation*

Characteristic	Rail	Air	Highway	Pipeline	Water
Cost	2.9¢/ton-mile	$45/ton-mile	15.3¢/ton-mile	Under 1¢/ton-mile	0.45¢/ton-mile on rivers 0.52¢/ton-mile on Great Lakes
Cost Ranking	3	1	2	4	5
Speed	3	1	2	5	4
Dependability	4	3	2	1	5
Capability	2	4	3	5	1
Fuel efficiency	3	5	4	1	2
Loss or damage	5	3	4	1	2

* Reprinted with permission from *Introduction to Logistics Management* (Englewood Cliffs, NJ: Prentice-Hall, 1986), p. 46.

Basic Legal Types

Another way of classifying carriers is by their legal or regulatory status. On this basis, it is helpful to examine common carriers, contract carriers, exempt carriers, and private carriers.

As the railroads grew to major importance in American business, a number of problems developed. For example, rates were controlled in monopoly fashion, secret rebates were common, unscrupulous schemes were developed for investments in railroad "securities," and discrimination in prices and services was common. In response to these abuses, the federal government, under the authority of the Commerce Clause in the United States Constitution, passed the Interstate Commerce Act. The basic purpose of the Act was to provide a comprehensive program to regulate interstate commerce.

The Interstate Commerce Act has been amended a number of times. It is the basic statutory law that applies to interstate commerce—that is, shipments that cross state lines. (Shipments that do not cross state lines are described as *intrastate* commerce.)

Exempt Carriers and Commodities As noted above, the basic statutory law is designed to regulate interstate commerce. A problem is created, however, for carriers, shippers, and insurers involved in short-haul business in and around cities that border state lines. In other words, it may not be reasonable to impose the complexities of the Interstate Commerce Act on those who are involved in short distances that happen to cross state lines. Thus, the law provides for "exempt zones." These are territories that are excluded from statutory regulation. An "exempt zone" may be entirely within a state or cross state lines. For example, the "exempt zone" for the New York City area includes the city of New York and twenty miles in all directions surrounding the city. This encompasses parts of Westchester County and Long Island in New York State and parts of New Jersey and Connecticut.

Certain commodities have been designated by state and federal statutes to be "exempt commodities," and as such are free from statutory control. Carriers hauling these commodities are subject only to the common law. This exemption was originally established to allow farmers to haul their products over public roads. Therefore, "unprocessed" products of agriculture and fishing are largely exempt from statutory regulation. Over the years many specific products have been included in the exempt category.[1]

Common Carriers In the early English common law, certain activities were considered essential to community life and were affected with the "public interest." At one time these "common callings" included common carriers, common innkeepers, common merchants, common brokers, common schoolmasters, common surgeons, and others. Special authorization was required to perform in these occupations. Now all of the public employments mentioned above have lost their name and special status, except for common carriers (and possibly to some extent, common innkeepers).

A common carrier is one that undertakes to carry persons or goods of all persons who choose to employ it. At least this is the key characteristic of common carriage. Actually, a common carrier is not obligated to serve *everyone,* to carry *everything,* or to serve *everywhere.*

Common carriers usually hold themselves out to carry only certain types of goods. For example, a common carrier trucking company that hauls milk may refuse to carry furniture or chemicals. An air common carrier may refuse to carry heavy products. A common carrier may choose to restrict its activities to certain types of shipments and is obligated to serve only those users who fall within this category. In other words, generally there can be no discrimination within the category served by the common carrier. In some circumstances, however, a common carrier may refuse service even within its usual category of goods. A common carrier may refuse to carry shipments of extreme value, and shipments that are improperly packed, illegal, or dangerous. Sometimes riots or strikes may create an unreasonable hazard. Goods that may contaminate other goods may be refused. A common carrier also may decline a shipment when the proper vehicular equipment is not available or when there is no room on the carrier's facilities.[2]

As a general rule, railroads have few restrictions on what they will carry. Many trucking companies also carry a broad range of commodities. Some trucking carriers, however, restrict their services to furniture, frozen goods, or chemicals. Oil pipelines, by definition, are very restrictive.

A common carrier is not required to serve everywhere. The obligation to the public is limited to the points the carrier normally serves.

The above discussion is concerned only with the common law obligations of common carriers. In actual practice, some shippers may be discouraged from using common carriers for economic reasons.

A common carrier, in practically all cases in the United States, operates under authority granted by a federal or a state regulatory body. The federal regulator is the Interstate Commerce Commission (ICC); the states have comparable bodies (known as Public Utilities Commissions or by other names). The authority granted to a common carrier defines the geographical area in which the carrier is authorized to operate and the commodities it may haul.

- *Bus companies* have authority to carry passengers between points named in the authorization, and may also be authorized to carry cargo under certain conditions.
- *Railroads* often have authority to carry both passengers and cargo.
- *Airlines* generally have authority to carry both passengers and cargo.
- *Truck lines* usually are limited to the carrying of cargo between points named in the authorization.

As a result of the easing of ICC regulations during the 1980s (called "deregulation" without complete accuracy), it has become easier for truckers to expand into new areas. Previously, a trucker was required to show a need for its services before being authorized to serve a new territory. After deregulation, a carrier has only to show its ability to provide the service. The result has been to increase competition among carriers.

Contract Carriers A considerable volume of cargo shipment is handled by contract carriers. These carriers do not have authorized routes such as are granted to common carriers. Contract carriers are relatively free to carry cargo for anybody between any points, and operate under individually negotiated contracts of carriage.

The essential difference between a common carrier and a contract carrier is that the common carrier offers its service to the general public, whereas the contract carrier operates under special and individual contracts of agreement. This is a generalization that oversimplifies the scope of activities of common and contract carriers. In practice a differentiation between the two often is difficult to make.

Common and contract carriers engaged in interstate commerce, except those operating in exempt zones or carrying exempt commodities, must be licensed by the ICC. The license granted a common carrier is identified as a "certificate of public convenience or necessity." Contract carriers are issued a "permit."

Although it is not always easy to distinguish a common carrier from a contract carrier, a few practical observations may be helpful.

- Railroads generally operated as common carriers before passage of the Staggers Rail Act of 1980. It is now not unusual for a railroad to operate as a contract carrier.
- A large portion of motor truck operations is performed by contract. A trucking company may be authorized to operate as a contract carrier for some shipments, and as a common carrier for other shipments. To determine loss exposures, it is necessary to determine whether a particular shipment is being handled under a motor truck carrier's authorization as a common carrier or as a contract carrier.
- The scheduled airlines are common carriers operating under authority granted by an agency of the federal government or, in a few cases, under authority granted by state bodies. These same airlines also operate as contract carriers in many cases, carrying either passengers on charter trips or special loads of cargo under contract.

Private Carriers The Motor Carrier Act of 1935 set up the present three categories of carriers—common carriers, contract carriers, and private carriers. The Act defines a "private carrier" as one that carries its own goods or goods for which it is the lessee or bailee.

When cargo is carried by its owner on the owner's trucks, there is no chance of recovery for loss or damage from a carrier. The only chance of recovery from another party is when some third party causes an accident in which cargo becomes damaged or lost.

Another effect of the 1980s "deregulation" of motor carriers is that private carriers are permitted to act as contract carriers on back haul. Thus, a private carrier that transports its own goods on an outgoing trip can contract to carry property belonging to someone else on the return trip. This avoids the necessity of the private carrier's returning with an empty truck. The obligation of the carrier to the shipper or owner in such a case is that of a contract carrier.

Specialized Carriers

In addition to the basic legal types discussed above, some carriers are classified as "specialty" carriers.

Household Goods Carriers These carriers operate under rules and regulations tailored for the unique conditions of the class, the most recent being the Household Goods Transportation Act of 1980.

A household goods carrier is limited to the carriage of "household goods," as defined in the Household Goods Transportation Act. The definition encompasses a much broader scope of property than what would ordinarily be considered household goods. The definition is as follows:

1. personal effects and property used or to be used in a dwelling when part of the equipment or supply of such dwelling;
2. furniture, fixtures, equipment, and the property of stores, offices, museums, institutions, hospitals, or other establishments when a part of the stock, equipment, or supply of such stores, offices, museums, institutions, hospitals, or other establishments;
3. articles, including objects of art, displays, and exhibits, which because of their unusual nature or value require specialized handling and equipment usually employed in moving household goods.

Heavy Specialized Carriers Motor carriers who specialize in hauling heavy equipment, and who are members of the Heavy Specialized Carriers Conference, may require that the insurer guarantee their compliance with rules of the Heavy Specialized Carriers Conference in Washington, D.C.

Indirect Carriers

Indirect carriers serve as carriers to the public by purchasing transportation services from direct carriers. Their economic existence is based on the differences in rates between small and large shipments.

Freight Forwarders A freight forwarder is a person or organization that holds itself out to the general public (other than as an express, pipeline, rail, sleeping car, motor, or water carrier) to:

- assemble and consolidate shipments,
- assume responsibility for the transportation from the place of receipt to the place of destination, and
- use for any part of the transportation a carrier subject to the ICC.

Freight forwarders are used in most transportation modes. *Surface freight forwarders* are very active in rail and truck service. These companies solicit small shipments and combine them into carload,

Exhibit 3-2
Trailers on Flatcar ("Piggyback")*

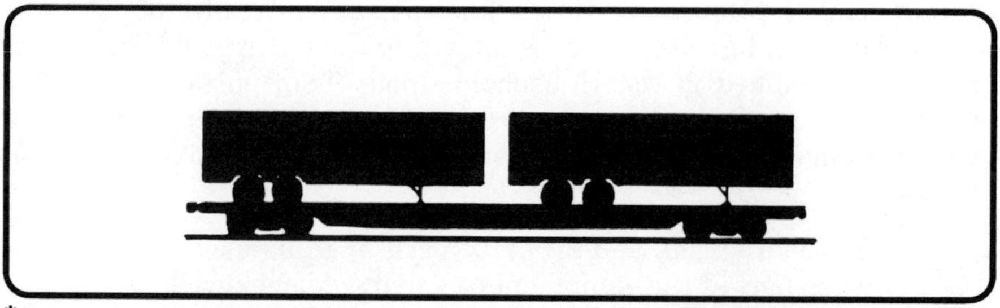

* Reprinted with permission from Association of American Railroads.

piggyback, or container loads (discussed below). *Air freight forwarders* offer similar services. Although a surface freight forwarder is classified by the ICC as a common carrier, it cannot operate its own trucks outside an exempt zone.

Consolidators A consolidator, as an agent of the shipper, consolidates shipments to take advantage of bulk rates. It may operate its *own vehicles* only within an exempt zone. Transportation outside the exempt zone may be arranged by the consolidator on behalf of the shipper, but it may not control the freight at destination. The consolidator is not responsible for losses outside the exempt area.

Shippers Associations These organizations are very similar to freight forwarders. The difference is that shippers associations operate as nonprofit organizations to reduce the costs of shipments to their members.

Intermodal Services

Different types of carriers often provide coordinated (combination) services. The best known of these approaches is rail-truck, commonly called "piggyback," but officially designated as "trailer on flatcar" (TOFC). An illustration of "piggyback" service is shown in Exhibit 3-2. This service is offered by railroads alone and in conjunction with forwarders and motor carriers.

Truck-air service is another combination service. Several air carriers have purchased motor carriers for this purpose. Other intermodal combinations include truck-water, rail-water, and air-water.

LIABILITY OF CARRIERS

A common carrier might be tempted to be careless in the handling of property if it did not have a responsibility for safe carriage and delivery. Therefore, a fairly early principle of common law is that a firm making a business of carrying persons or property for a consideration is responsible for their safe delivery.

This liability of the common carrier makes it probable that the shipper of goods can recover from a common carrier for the value of property that is lost or damaged while in the custody of the common carrier. However, the liability of a common carrier is subject to certain exceptions and limitations. Moreover, the common carrier's exposures may be affected by the terms of the bill of lading, and the common carrier's exposures exist only during the period within which property is legally in the carrier's custody.

The comments that follow are more applicable to *surface* transport, i.e., transport by highway, railroad, or pipeline, than to transport by other modes. The liabilities of domestic air and water carriers, as well as the liabilities of private carriers, freight forwarders, and consolidators, are discussed separately at the end of this section in terms of their variations from the general rules of common carrier liability that follow.

Exceptions to Common Carrier Liability

A common carrier can do little to control loss due to some calamities. Therefore, such a carrier is not held responsible for (1) acts of God, (2) acts of the public enemy, (3) exercise of public authority, (4) fault or neglect on the part of the shipper, or (5) inherent vice or the nature of the property. The following explanations of each of these limitations will show that they are generally unusual occurrences.

1. *Acts of God*—Acts of God are occurrences of nature, such as tornadoes, storms, earthquakes, and floods. Although generally not responsible for loss by an "act of God," the common carrier might be liable for damage by one of these occurrences if the event could have been foreseen and action by the carrier could have prevented the loss. A flood some years ago caused damage to cargo in railroad freight cars in the Kansas City, Missouri, yards. The railroad denied liability for the damage on the ground that the damage resulted from an act of God. The courts decided, however, that the railroad had had enough advance warning that the railroad yard would be flooded. It could have taken measures to protect the cargo. Since such measures were not taken, the railroad was responsible for the loss.

2. *Acts of the Public Enemy*—The "public enemy" referred to is a nation or government at war with the nation in which the carrier is domiciled. It does not refer to individual criminals or even groups of criminals not involved in warfare. Although absolved from liability for "acts of the public enemy," a common carrier is responsible for loss resulting from the acts of criminals, even if the criminal is recognized as "public enemy number one." The status of actions by some terrorist groups is uncertain.
3. *Exercise of Public Authority*—An exercise of public authority would be any act that is taken by a public official acting with his or her governmental authority. Confiscation of cargo under quarantine rules would be an example. The common carrier would not be legally liable for such a loss.
4. *Fault or Neglect on the Part of the Shipper*—A shipper may be negligent in packing or shipping some type of property that obviously would be damaged by ordinary handling in transit. The common carrier is not held liable for damage that results directly from such negligence on the part of the shipper.
5. *Inherent Vice or the Nature of the Property*—Inherent vice is a condition within a particular type of property that tends to make the property destroy itself. The deterioration of natural rubber over a period of time when it is not in use is often cited as an example of inherent vice. It was decided by a court in one case that injury to cattle when they were stampeded by the passage of a railroad train constituted an inherent vice. The court said that it is the nature of cattle to stampede under such circumstances.[3]

In summary, a common carrier is liable for most cases of loss or damage that occur to property in the custody of the common carrier. It is rare that the common carrier can escape liability because of loss or damage even from one of the five exemptions that have been described.

Limitations on Common Carrier Liability

There are some limitations on the extent of a common carrier's liability that may be invoked by the common carrier even when it has liability for the loss or damage. This holds when a specified value, or limitation of liability, is specified in the contract of carriage—particularly when the common carrier has in effect a different schedule of charges according to the values declared. One of the extreme examples of this principle was a case where a federal court upheld a $50 limitation on a $4,880 mink coat. The valuation was placed on the coat by a hotel employee who delivered the coat to an express company on behalf of the owner. The court decided that the hotel employee was the agent of the coat owner and that the $50 limitation in the express company's receipt was binding.[4]

It is standard practice in connection with many common carrier contracts to state a dollar limitation on the value of the property, or for the contract to specify a dollar limit of liability according to some units of measuring the property shipped. Liability for household goods usually is limited to a specified dollar amount per pound or per 100 pounds of property. The lower rates charged by the carrier when these dollar limitations are in effect are called *released rates.*

Another limitation in the liability of a common carrier occurs when the liability is reduced to that of a bailee. (The more limited liability of a bailee is discussed in Chapter 6.) The contract of carriage (bill of lading) may provide that the liability of the carrier will become that of a bailee after the property has been delivered to a terminal in the consignee's locality and the consignee has been notified that the property is there. It is considered reasonable for the extreme liability of the common carrier to be mitigated after a reasonable length of time if the consignee neglects to pick up the property after having been notified that it is available for pickup.

When the shipper has the facilities to load and seal a railroad car, the carrier has no opportunity to check the nature, quality, weight, or quantity of the load. Sometimes an organization with a railroad sidetrack loads and sends entire carloads without any checking of the contents by the rail carrier. The bill of lading in such cases is stamped with the words "shipper's weight, load, and count" or words with that intent. The common carrier is then not liable for any loss resulting from short load or count unless it can be proved that the car was entered and goods removed en route. Many well-managed carriers maintain careful records of the seals on cars and trucks. It is possible to enter a car or truck and to reseal it, but this does not often happen.

Bills of Lading

The bill of lading issued by a common carrier serves as a receipt from the carrier for the goods being transported. In addition, it serves as the contract of carriage between the shipper and carrier, setting forth the obligations and responsibilities of each party. There are several types of bills of lading; some of the more common types are described below.

- *Released Bill of Lading*—On a released bill of lading, the carrier is released from liability above a certain amount specified in the contract. As previously noted, this may be a specific number of dollars, or it may be an agreed or declared value according to some unit of measurement. The carrier may have filed tariffs that specify various charges according to the type of property to be carried and the values to be declared. (A "tariff" is a schedule of charges and conditions under which the carrier operates.)

- *Straight Bill of Lading*—The straight bill of lading does not include any limitation on the value to be paid by the carrier in case of loss. The charges for transporting the property may be paid by the shipper or by the consignee, depending on the conditions of the contract. The straight bill of lading will specify whether shipment is prepaid by the shipper or whether the charges are to be collected from the consignee.
- *Order Bill of Lading*—The order bill of lading serves as a contract of shipment (the same as a straight bill of lading) possibly with limitation on liability for values (as in a released bill of lading) and also as a method of shipping on a cash-on-delivery arrangement. The order bill of lading is extensively used in ocean commerce. When property is shipped under an order bill of lading, the consignee does not receive the goods from the carrier until they have been paid for, usually through an arrangement with a bank. Common carriers such as railroads and truck lines often do not want to take the responsibility for handling the money that would be required for a cash-on-delivery arrangement directly through the carrier. The money is handled through banking channels. The carrier delivers the property to the consignee upon receiving instructions from the financial institution that the agreed payment has been made.
- *Through Bill of Lading*—A through bill of lading covers shipments by more than one transportation company with a fixed charge for the entire service. (Such a shipment is known as an interline shipment.) A through bill of lading may be either a straight or order bill of lading marked "Through." "Section 20(11) of the Interstate Commerce Act (49 U.S.C. 11707) makes the origin or destination carrier on a through bill of lading jointly and severally liable for the 'full actual loss' suffered en route. Section 20(12) gives the carrier that pays such a claim the right to sue the responsible carrier in the event it does not reimburse the paying carrier, and it may recover attorney's fees as well."[5] The shipper can file a claim against either the carrier of origin or the carrier that made the delivery. This rule

of joint and several liability does not apply to intrastate shipments or unregulated shipments.

A mistake on the bill of lading in the description of the goods may bring about a situation similar to that which arises under a shipper's weight, load, and count situation. A carrier may be able to prove that it did not actually receive the goods described in the bill of lading, and it might be able to limit its liability to the shipper or the consignee to the value of the goods actually received. This situation can arise in the case of sealed packages whose contents are incorrectly described. However, the carrier may be liable to the consignee as an innocent third party even though it did not actually receive the goods described. Complicated situations often have to be resolved in court.

When Carrier's Loss Exposures Begin and End

A common carrier's exposure to loss begins when goods have been delivered to and accepted by the carrier. The carrier's exposures end when the carrier has delivered the property to the consignee. However, in any particular case, the point at which loss exposure actually is transferred may be difficult to define.

Delivery to the Carrier Delivery of goods to the carrier is usually clearly established in the case of package shipments. For example, the shipper may deliver the packages to the carrier at a freight depot. Actual receipt by the carrier of the property under these circumstances constitutes delivery to the carrier, and the property is in the custody of the carrier from that point on. Some carriers provide a pickup service at the shipper's premises. Here again, actual receipt of the property by the carrier constitutes delivery to the carrier with custody in the hands of the carrier from that point on.

But there can be a question as to when delivery is made to the carrier in the case of carload shipments from a railroad siding. The issuance of a bill of lading by the carrier upon notice that the car is ready ordinarily constitutes acknowledgment of delivery to the carrier. This may be true even though the railroad has not yet moved the car. The situation becomes a bit cloudy in cases where the bill of lading is issued before the car is fully loaded. Sometimes a shipper loading the car during the late afternoon may ask the freight agent to complete the bill of lading so that the car can be moved by the railroad during the night. It would become a question of fact to determine whether the railroad actually received the goods in such situations where the bill of lading was issued before the car had been fully loaded.

Delivery by the Carrier Questions also arise regarding whether delivery actually has been made by the carrier to the consignee. Delivery by the carrier to the consignee's premises usually is evidenced by a receipt that the carrier takes from the consignee upon delivery. A question can arise when the carrier's delivery person arrives before the consignee's place of business is open and leaves the goods outside the door. There would be no receipt to prove delivery in such a case, and the carrier probably would be held liable for nondelivery. There is also the possibility that an imposter at the consignee's premises might receive the shipment, sign the receipt, and abscond with the goods. Here again there would be a question of fact as to whether the delivery actually was made.

A different situation occurs where the consignee is obligated to pick up the shipment at the carrier's freight depot. Usually, the carrier's liability as a carrier continues for forty-eight hours after written notice of arrival has been sent or given to the consignee. The liability of the carrier becomes that of a warehouseman (or bailee) at the expiration of that time. The liability of the carrier as a warehouseman or bailee is limited compared to the extensive liability as a carrier. The consignee must make sure that the goods are picked up before the forty-eight hour limit expires. The burden of proof of negligence is on the consignee after the liability of the carrier changes to that of a warehouseman.

Railroad shipments may be made on what are called "public team tracks." (A public team track is a railroad sidetrack with a driveway alongside that enables consignees to park their trucks at the railroad freight car door and unload goods.) The consignee has the obligation to remove goods within the forty-eight hour period after notification has been given that the carload is on the team tracks ready for pickup by the consignee. It is, of course, an obligation of the carrier to provide security for property parked on public team tracks.

Sidetrack Agreements In the case of cars delivered to a private or semiprivate sidetrack, delivery by the carrier is made by placing the railroad car on the sidetrack at a reasonable hour for unloading. The sidetrack agreement between the railroad and the consignee may specify what is to be considered as delivery. There is no forty-eight hour requirement for notice of sidetrack deliveries. The delivery is really the equivalent of the delivery of a package to the premises of the consignee.

The sidetrack agreement may provide that the railroad may place carload freight on the siding at its convenience and that such placing constitutes delivery. The placing of a railroad car on the siding at a late-night hour might make the contents vulnerable to theft—an additional consideration in evaluating loss exposures.

Claims Against the Common Carrier

The claimant against a common carrier must meet certain conditions in order to recover the value of goods. Sometimes this is not easy to do. The paragraph regarding claims in a typical bill of lading reads:

> Section 2(b) As a condition precedent to recovery, claims must be filed in writing with the receiving or delivering carrier, or carrier issuing this bill of lading, or carrier on whose line the loss, damage, injury or delay occurred, within nine months after delivery of the property (or, in the case of export traffic, within nine months after delivery at port of export) or in case of failure to make delivery, then within nine months after a reasonable time for delivery has elapsed; and suits shall be instituted against any carrier only within two years and one day from the day when notice in writing is given by the carrier to the claimant that the carrier has disallowed the claim or any part or parts thereof specified in the notice. Where claims are not filed or suits are not instituted thereon in accordance with the foregoing provisions, no carrier hereunder shall be liable, and such claims will not be paid.

A shipper of goods must realize that common carriers generally enforce strictly the requirements of the bill of lading for making claim against the carrier.

The consignee must note any shortages or damages upon receipt of the goods. Claim must be filed promptly upon the discovery of a loss. The claim must clearly be a claim for damages and it must be for a dollar amount.

There are circumstances where the shipper or consignee can collect damages for unreasonable delay in delivery. But government regulations do not allow a common carrier to promise expedited service or a definite delivery date unless the carrier has filed a tariff providing the conditions under which such expedited service will be provided.

To collect from the carrier for loss or damage, a firm must pursue the claim promptly and in strict accordance with the provisions of the bill of lading. Suit must be filed within the time limit prescribed. Sometimes a claimant assumes negotiations by the carrier for settlement will act as a waiver of the time limit for filing suit, but this is not the case.

It is important to realize that the interest of the carrier and the interest of the claimant are adverse. The common carrier seeks, by strict compliance with the contract conditions, to reduce or eliminate its liability. The shipper or consignee who is claimant against the carrier must pursue the claim with equal vigor.

State statutes and regulations differ in some details from ICC regulations. These differences may affect the requirement for notice to the consignee, or they may affect the liability of the common carrier when an intrastate shipment arrives at the carrier's freight depot at the destination. These possible differences in the exact liability of a common carrier must be determined in any case where they might affect the exposure to loss of a shipper, a consignee, or (for liability) a common carrier.

There may be other details of difference in liability and possibilities of recovery where the shipment may proceed for a certain portion of its journey by water. For example, a barge or lighter used in connection with a rail journey is normally considered as part of the rail journey—loss or damage occurring during such lighterage should be settled according to the general rules of land transportation rather than the rules applying to ocean transportation. An ocean carrier in that case might occasionally assume liability by contract in order to provide comparable security with that provided by railroads or trucks.

Measure of Damages

When a common carrier becomes liable for loss or damage, it must pay the full amount of the loss, subject of course to any of the limitations discussed above. The amount of loss is usually determined as the market value of the lost or damaged property had it arrived in good condition at its destination. Often the invoice price of the property (less any trade discounts) is an accurate measure of market value. Freight charges on the lost or damaged property, if already paid, may also be claimed if not included in the invoice price. The expenses connected with filing a claim—such as telephone calls, tracing, and inspection—may not be claimed.[6]

Moreover, it is unusual for a consignee to be able to collect damages from a common carrier for *loss of use* of property following its damage or destruction, even though the carrier is liable for the value of the property itself. According to one authority, "special damages" (such as loss of use) "are not ordinarily recoverable from a carrier unless the carrier actually knew, or reasonably would be expected to know, that such special damages would naturally follow upon failure to safely and promptly transport the property."[7]

When partially damaged property is repairable, the consignee may accept the property, have it repaired, and make claim with the carrier for the actual loss. Or, the consignee may dispose of the property and make claim with the carrier for the full value of the actual loss.

When property is totally damaged, the consignee may refuse to accept delivery and then make claim for the full value of the property. In this case, the carrier may take possession of the property and dispose of it as the carrier sees fit. If the carrier fails to exercise that right, the consignee may dispose of the property in a way that will serve the best interests of the carrier. If the property is sold for salvage, the proceeds are deducted from the carrier's claim settlement.[8]

Differences Among Liabilities of Carriers

The preceding discussion of carrier liability is based on general characteristics of the liability of common carriers. In actual practice, the liability of a railroad differs in some respects from the liability of an air carrier, the liability of a trucker differs in some respects from the liability of a water carrier, and so on. Some of the unique aspects of carrier liability for the various types of common carriers, as well as contract carriers, are described below.

The mode of transportation and the liability of the carrier(s) involved are important facts in underwriting transportation insurance. The mode of transportation is a measure of the exposure, and the liability of the carrier is the foundation for a recovery through subrogation.

Rail Carriers and Motor Carriers Both rail and motor carriers have essentially the same liability under their respective bills of lading. They can limit their liability without prior approval from the ICC. Railroads and their customers may also negotiate separate contracts that define the carrier's liability for loss or damage to cargo. Railroads may also make provision for a deductible, which could be applied to an already released valuation.

The "piggyback" or TOFC (trailer on flatcar) service provided by rail carriers may involve more than one bill of lading. Under one plan, the motor carrier working in conjunction with the railroad issues the bill of lading. Under another plan, the railroad issues the bill of lading. Under a third plan, there can be three bills of lading in effect: one issued by the motor carrier making the delivery to the railroad, another issued by the railroad, and a third issued by the motor carrier making the delivery. Rail and truck service provided by railroads in connection with piggyback plans is exempt from ICC regulation, provided the motor carrier is a subsidiary of the railroad. Other motor carriers not so affiliated who participate in piggyback operations do not enjoy this exemption.

The dollar amount of a rail or motor carrier's liability depends on the terms of each individual bill of lading.

Domestic Water Carriers Domestic interstate water carriers have less liability for loss or damage than common carriers engaged in land transportation. In addition to the usual exemptions from common carrier liability, loss due to perils of the waters, errors in navigation, rescue efforts, and fire are additional exemptions from the liability of interstate water carriers. Consequently, the liability of domestic water carriers is relatively limited.

Domestic Air Carriers Prior to 1977 domestic air carriers limited their liability based on the precepts of the common law. In essence, carriers were relieved of liability unless they were proven negligent. The burden of proof of negligence was on the claimant. The limitation per shipment was $.50 per pound or $50, whichever was higher. The declaration of a higher value was not normally permitted. Carriers usually disclaimed liability for any special or consequential damages.

In 1977 the Civil Aeronautics Board changed the liability of domestic air carriers from that of negligence to one similar to that governing surface carriers. The $.50 per pound limitation was changed to the amount used on international air cargo shipments. Shippers were permitted to declare a higher valuation on individual articles provided an excess value charge was paid.

In late 1977 Congress passed a bill giving air carriers the freedom to revert to the old rules, maintain the latest rules, or use a combination of both. As a result there is no uniformity with respect to the liability accruing to domestic air carriers.

International Air Carriers The liability of carriers engaged in international air freight is established by the rules of the Warsaw Convention, a treaty signed by the representatives of various governments in Warsaw in 1929. Under these rules an air carrier is not liable for loss if it can show that it took all the necessary steps to avoid the loss, or that the loss was caused by pilot error. The burden of proof is on the carrier.

Household Goods Carriers Household goods carriers engaged in interstate commerce use a standard bill of lading entitled "Uniform Household Goods Bill of Lading and Freight Bill." Under the terms of the bill of lading the carrier is liable for physical loss or damage from any external cause, except for condition or flavor of perishable goods, and except for loss caused by or resulting from the following:

1. an act, omission, or order of the shipper;
2. insects, moth, vermin, and ordinary wear and tear;
3. defect or inherent vice, including atmospheric conditions such as temperature or humidity changes;
4. war; and

5. acts of God, when the shipment is released to $.60 per pound per article.

Household goods carriers may limit their liability to: (1) $.60 per pound per article; (2) $1.25 for each pound of weight in the shipment; or (3) the lump sum declared by the shipper. The shipper is obliged to choose one of the foregoing. If the choice is $.60 per pound or a lump sum, that choice must be recorded on the bill of lading in the shipper's handwriting, over the shipper's signature. If no choice is made, the shipment is released to $1.25 per pound.

Because of their specialized moving equipment, household goods carriers often carry property that has a substantial value and a high susceptibility to loss. Electronic data processing equipment is included in this category. When carrying such equipment the carrier can release its liability through released rates orders. Under released rates orders the carrier's liability may be limited to $5 per pound or raised beyond that in $1 increments, up to $10 per pound.

As the result of the liberalizing provisions of the Household Goods Transportation Act of 1980, new price and service options are being made available to shippers. Some carriers now have ICC approval for tariffs that enable them to offer replacement cost on articles lost or damaged while in their custody. Previous practice was to pay claims based on actual cash value, computed as replacement cost less depreciation. If an item could not be replaced the most recent consumer price index factor was applied to original cost, and the result adjusted for depreciation.

In the *Federal Register* on March 11, 1981, the ICC announced that a household goods carrier could "... sell, or offer to sell or procure for any shipper, any kind of insurance...." For this to be effective the shipment must be released to $.60 per pound. It was further stipulated that the certificate of insurance be in plain English, although no definition of plain English was offered. Prior to this ruling the issuance of certificates of insurance on interstate shipments was prohibited.

Freight Forwarders Freight forwarders are included in the provisions of the Interstate Commerce Act, and as such are subject to the jurisdiction of the ICC. A freight forwarder is a common carrier who consolidates shipments and arranges for their transportation using carriers subject to ICC jurisdiction. Freight forwarders file their own tariffs with the ICC, covering shipments from point of origin to destination. The Motor Carrier Act of 1980 permits freight forwarders to file released value rates without getting prior approval from the ICC. The ICC may, however, require that they also publish full value rates. Freight forwarders have the same liability as motor carriers.

Consolidators Consolidators (also called packinghouses) generally do not assume liability for loss to goods in transit although they may arrange for the transportation. Consolidators are liable as bailees and, in the absence of any other agreement made with their customers, are liable only for loss caused by their negligence.

Contract Carriers The basic liability of a contract carrier is for negligence in the handling of the cargo. It is generally considered to be against public policy for anyone selling a service to contract away his or her entire liability for negligence. Therefore, the contract carrier in general would be liable for any loss or damage that resulted from its negligence in its handling of the cargo. However, the liability can be affected by the provisions of the contract. The contract carrier may assume complete liability for loss or damage; on the other hand, the contract can contain some restrictions or limitations that reduce the carrier's liability.

WHEN TITLE PASSES

Many shipments are made to transport property from a seller to a buyer. When that is the case, an essential aspect of the loss exposure during transit is the question of when title to the property being sold passes from the seller to the buyer. As a general rule, the party that has title bears the risk of loss in transit.

Sales of personal property are governed largely by the Uniform Commercial Code. The *Uniform Commercial Code* was written by a large number of experts on American law under the auspices of the National Commission on Uniform State Laws. It organizes, clarifies, and in some ways changes the law regarding commercial transactions. The Uniform Commercial Code is only one of several codes on various phases of American law which, at the urging of the National Commission, have been adopted by many states.

The Code permits the buyer and seller to stipulate by agreement when title will pass between them. If they make no stipulation, the Code provides that title passes to the buyer at the time and place at which the seller completes physical delivery of the goods as required by the terms of the contract, even though the seller may retain a security interest in the goods. Precisely where and when the physical delivery required by the contract becomes complete depends on the wording of the contract.

In most commercial sales of personal property, the buyer and the seller agree on when title passes, as well as other terms of the sale, according to customary shipping terms. There are several types of shipping terms.

1. *F.O.B. Point of Shipment* (Origin). F.O.B. is an abbreviation of "Free on Board." These terms obligate the *seller* to assume the responsibility for loss or damage until the property is in the possession of the carrier and a clean bill of lading has been issued. Thereafter, the *buyer* assumes the responsibility for any loss or damage.
2. *F.O.B. Destination.* These terms obligate the seller to transport the goods to the destination stated, and tender proper delivery upon arrival. The *seller* assumes the responsibility for loss or damage until proper delivery has been made. There are many variations on F.O.B. terms. Eight variations on F.O.B. terms are depicted in Exhibit 3-3.
3. *F.A.S. Vessel* (Named Port). F.A.S. means "Free Along Side." These terms obligate the *seller* to transport the property to the named port and place it alongside the vessel. The *seller* is responsible for loss or damage until such placement is made.
4. *C.I.F.* This is an abbreviation of Cost, Insurance, and Freight. It is a term used in overseas shipments. The *seller* agrees to arrange for transportation and pay the freight (shipping charges), arrange and pay for insurance, and mail the necessary shipping documents to the buyer. The risk of loss passes to the buyer when the goods have been loaded aboard the vessel or when they have been delivered into the custody of the ocean carrier.
5. *C. & F.* This is an abbreviation for Cost and Freight. The terms are the same as C.I.F. terms, with the exception of the requirement to obtain and pay for insurance.

Insurable Interests of Buyer and Seller[9] In theory, the party holding title to property involved in a sale bears the risk of loss or damage to the property. In practice, however, a seller may be exposed to loss after title has passed to a buyer; and a buyer may be exposed to loss before title has passed from the seller to the buyer.

For example, a seller may have a security interest in sold property. If that property is destroyed in transit, after title has passed to the buyer, and the buyer is unable to continue making payments on the property, there will be no property of any value for the seller to repossess.

On the other hand, a buyer may have ordered custom-made machine parts that take two months to manufacture. If these parts are destroyed in transit before title passes to the buyer, the buyer could nevertheless suffer loss of business income while the parts are being remade.

Consequently, a seller's insurable interest in property does not

Exhibit 3-3
The Effect of Selling Terms: When Does Title Pass*

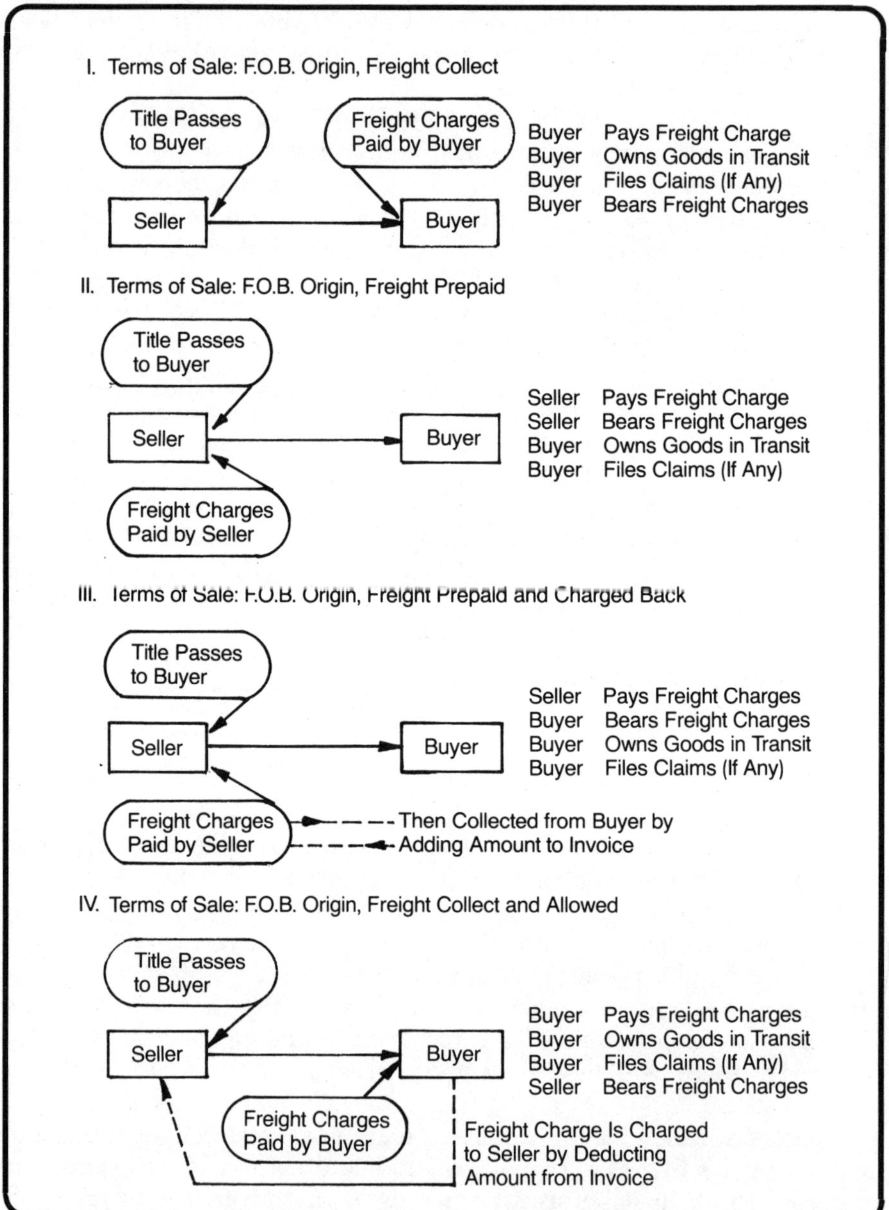

continued on next page

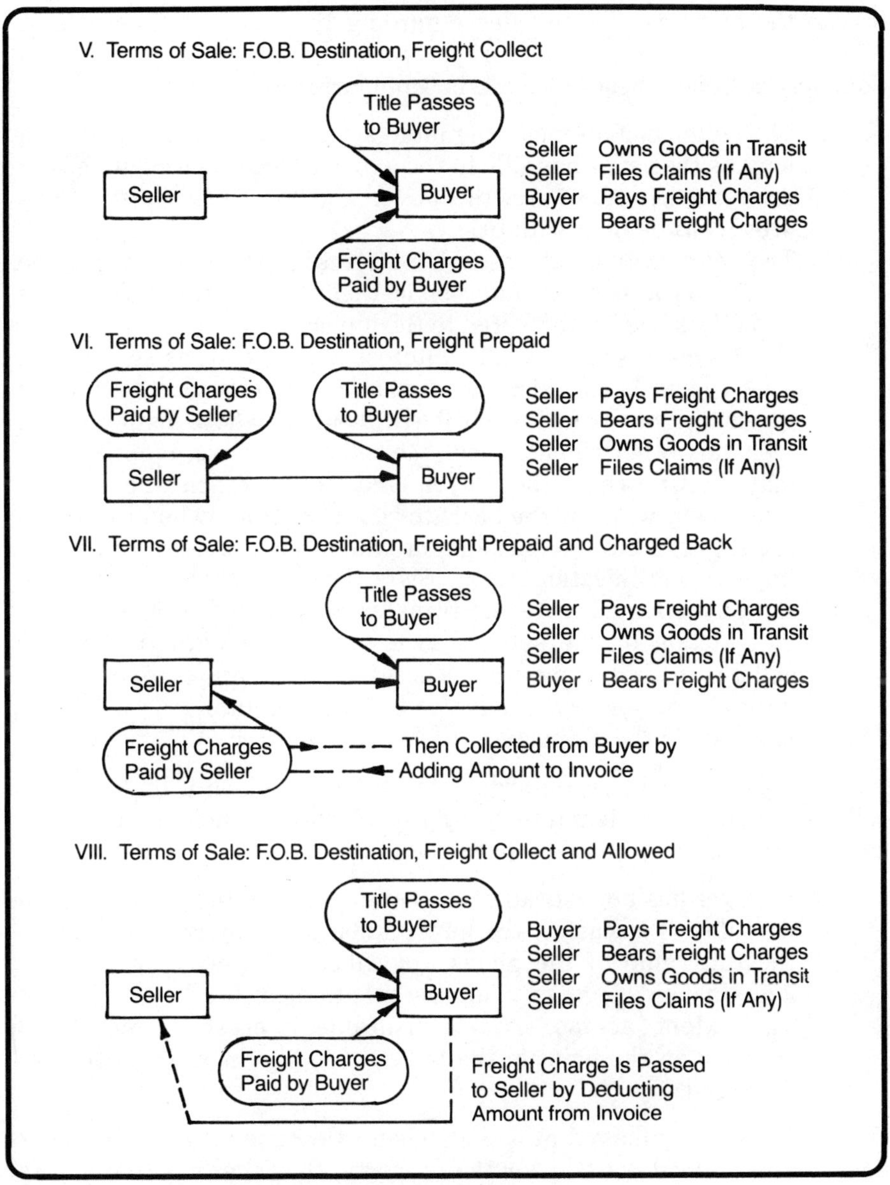

* Reprinted with permission from Robert Milsop.

necessarily end when title in the property passes to the buyer. And a buyer has an insurable interest in property before actually acquiring title to the property. Three rules regarding the insurable interests of sellers and buyers of personal property are spelled out in the Uniform Commercial Code. These rules can be summarized as follows:

1. The *seller* has an insurable interest in damage to the goods as long as the seller has title to the goods in accordance with either an agreement between the buyer and the seller or the Code provisions dealing with title.
2. The *seller* retains an insurable interest in the goods while the seller has a security interest in them, even after title to the goods has been transferred to the buyer.
3. The *buyer* has an insurable interest in the goods as soon as the goods have been "identified," that is, as soon as the specific goods the buyer is to take have been somehow distinguished from any other similar goods the seller may have. Identification may occur when the buyer and seller reach the mutual agreement which is the basis for their contract, when the goods are segregated in a package, or when they are delivered to the buyer. Identification can create an insurable interest for the buyer long before the transfer of title to the buyer or the satisfaction of the seller's security interest extinguishes the seller's insurable interest. Therefore, it is quite common for *both the buyer and the seller* to have simultaneous insurable interests in the property.

The foregoing rules regarding the times at which a buyer and a seller have an insurable interest in goods also affect the extent of each entity's insurable interest in those goods:

- A *buyer* has no insurable interest in goods until they have been identified; thereafter, the buyer's insurable interest is equal to the full value of the goods, regardless of whether the buyer actually holds legal or equitable title to them.
- The extent of the *seller's* insurable interest in the goods depends on the point in the transaction at which the goods are damaged.

If the goods are damaged at a time when title remains with the seller and the buyer need not pay for the property, the seller's potential loss and insurable interest both equal the full value of the property. If the property is destroyed after title has passed to the buyer and the buyer has paid for them, the seller faces no potential loss from damage to the goods and has no insurable interest in them. If the goods are destroyed at any time when the seller has a valid security interest, the seller's potential loss (and insurable interest) is limited to the unpaid balance of the debt.

Because a buyer and a seller may both have simultaneous insurable interests in the same goods, and because the buyer's insurable interest is never less than their full value, the sum of a buyer's and a seller's insurable interests in the same goods may exceed their full value.

MEASURING AND TREATING TRANSIT LOSS EXPOSURES

Measuring Transit Loss Exposures

The severity exposure of property in transit varies materially with the kind of property being shipped. The mobile television equipment sent by motor truck to cover a presidential convention may be worth as much as $5 million. In such a case, the exposure in a single loss is quite severe, but the equipment may be transported infrequently.

A different situation is presented by an organization that regularly ships small quantities of goods. The exposure to loss here is continuous, but any single loss may be relatively small. For example, a retail mail order operation selling men's slacks may ship huge quantities of merchandise directly to retail consumers, but the average value of any single shipment may be less than $100. In other cases, the continuous exposure may be substantial. A diamond merchant, for example, will frequently carry several hundred thousand dollars worth of diamonds from city to city.

In evaluating the frequency and severity potential of the loss exposure, a number of factors should be considered, including the type and value of merchandise, the radius of operations, the condition of the equipment carrying the cargo, the caliber of drivers handling the vehicles or merchandise, the terrain and climatic variations where the load will be carried, the past record of the carrier, and the crime rate in areas through which the merchandise will pass.

When measuring transit loss exposures, both frequency and severity statistics should be further analyzed to determine predictability. For firms handling large numbers of shipments stable in value, losses may be predicted with a high degree of confidence. When volume is lower or value is variable, it is much more difficult to plan for probable loss costs.

Controlling Transit Loss Exposures

Various control measures may be used to lower loss frequency or severity potential and to improve predictability.

As with all loss exposures, *avoidance* should be considered. If it is not necessary to move something, it is not necessary to incur transit exposures.

One set of *noninsurance transfers* has already been discussed. Shippers (and consignees) can often lessen their exposures by transferring custody of the property to a carrier or by transferring title before (or after) property is moved. Conversely, carriers can minimize their exposures by the terms of bills of lading and by arranging pickup and delivery schedules to minimize the time period during which property is in the carrier's custody.

The points of attack for transit *loss control* are (1) the susceptibility of the property itself to damage or loss, (2) the effectiveness of its packaging as a means of protection, (3) the selection of means, routes, and times for shipments, and (4) the system used to control carelessness and dishonesty of employees of shippers and consignees.

Susceptibility of Property to Loss and Damage Types of property vary in fragility, in susceptibility to damage by dampness, extremes of temperatures, vermin, and so on, and in attractiveness to thieves. In many cases, the risk manager can do little about these. The nature of the property is what it is; it usually cannot be significantly altered without undesirable results. For example, raw silk is inherently subject to discoloration by water, and silk cannot be changed. Jewelry is inherently attractive to thieves, and that cannot be changed. While steel is less brittle than cast iron, substitution is usually unacceptable because of cost. However, there are cases where undue vulnerability to loss can be remedied. A particular part may not have adequate reason for being weak and unsupportive, and the extra cost of a stronger material may be paid for by the savings in breakage. Shipment may be made with goods roughly finished, rather than in a finely finished state. In general, any feature that increases probable loss frequency or severity should be questioned to determine whether it really is necessary.

Packaging Packaging may be able substantially to overcome susceptibility to loss. Most brittle objects *can* be shipped with little probability of breakage when the packaging is adequate. The theft rate on jewelry and negotiable securities is much lower when their packages do not suggest what kind of property is inside (for example, the package does not specify the shipper as "Stone and Sons, Diamond Merchants"). Parts may be sent separately to reduce attractiveness of individual packages to thieves. Use of very large shipment units—containerization—has proved successful in reducing damage and theft. This has worked for land cargoes, as well as for ocean cargoes.

Selection of Means, Routes, and Times of Shipments Land transit avoids or reduces some exposures associated with water transit (e.g., exposure to dampness), but adds or increases others (for example, the peril of collision). Air transit likewise avoids some surface perils, and reduces time of transit exposure but creates some other perils of its own. Some cargoes are more safely transmitted by rail, others by truck. Mail or express handling is warranted to protect cargoes of special value. The means of transport can be selected with an eye to the perils to which particular property is especially susceptible.

Different carriers—different truck lines, different rail lines, different ship lines—have different records as to rates of loss and damage. Sometimes carriage on a shipper's own equipment or by contract carrier produces fewer losses than use of common carriers. (However, if the shipper is not prepared to invest adequately in equipment and in management and maintenance, carriage by its own equipment can produce increased rates of loss.)

Routing and timing, too, affect loss rates. As noted before, some locales have worse theft rates than others. Seasonal congestion at truck, rail, and ship docks increases loss and damage. There is more loss during trips (land, sea, or air) in bad weather than in good.

Some organizations employ freight transportation specialists who carefully manage selection of carriers and routes. Other organizations do not have such experts; then someone needs to see that, in getting advice and making decisions on shipping, the effects on loss and damage are considered.

Systems to Control Carelessness and Dishonesty A large portion of transit loss can arise from deliberate or accidental miscounts, erroneous or illegible shipping labels, spurious or hypercritical rejections of shipments by consignees, and other human tendencies and weaknesses. Accounting and supervisory systems that apply to shipments in and out, and arrangements and relations with the parties at the other end (sending or receiving), are the major methods of controlling such losses. Also important are the arrangements for handling shipments received in damaged or incomplete condition. These should be efficiently returned or disposed of, and payments should be adjusted accordingly.

Retaining Transit Loss Exposures

Transit loss exposures often lend themselves to retention. The considerations involved in deciding whether to retain losses to property in transit depend on whether the organization considering retention is a shipper or a carrier.

Retention for Shippers Retention of losses to property in transit is often feasible for a shipper. Values exposed to individual loss events are often small relative to the total shipped, with the number of exposure units large enough to make losses fairly predictable. However, any decision to retain or insure transit losses should also consider not only pure loss costs but also the value of the insurer services in:

- providing immediate claims payments,
- collecting from carriers that may ultimately be held responsible for loss payments,
- servicing claims in remote locations,
- providing loss control recommendations to lower loss frequency and severity, and
- filling a need for other risk management advice and services.

Retention for Carriers Not all carriers purchase insurance. Whether losses are insured or retained depends largely on the type of carrier and the scope of its operation.

- The operations of a large railroad are so extensive that the railroad can afford to handle its own claims for loss or damage to cargo. A small railroad might carry cargo liability insurance.
- Airlines may or may not carry cargo liability insurance; the choice depends on the size of the airline and the extent of its cargo handling activities.
- Very large truck lines may retain their cargo liability exposure, possibly supplementing retention with some kind of deductible or excess insurance coverage. (Even if it has a substantial ability to absorb losses, a truck line might find it desirable to carry a catastrophe policy to protect itself against loss by the total destruction of a cargo terminal.)
- Many truckers do carry motor truck cargo insurance, which is described in Chapter 4.

Insuring Transit Loss Exposures

Owing to the complexity of transit loss exposures, particularly the different parties that can have an interest in property being transported, there are several forms of transportation insurance used to cover these interests. The various types of transportation insurance are examined in Chapter 4.

SUMMARY

Loss exposures resulting from the shipment of property are complex and the corresponding insurance coverages are many. In this chapter, the loss exposures resulting from the transportation of property are analyzed according to the property subject to loss, the perils that may cause loss, the potential financial consequences of the loss, and the parties affected by loss.

Carriers are persons or organizations having custody of property in transit from one place to another. In this country, the five important modes of freight movement are railroads, trucks, waterways, pipelines, and aircraft, the economic characteristics of which vary considerably. Another way to classify carriers is by their legal or regulatory status—as common carriers, contract carriers, exempt carriers, or private carriers. In addition to these basic legal types of carriers, some carriers are classified as "specialty" carriers, such as household goods carriers and heavy specialized carriers.

Indirect carriers serve as carriers to the public by purchasing transportation services from direct carriers. These include freight forwarders, consolidators, and shippers associations.

Different types of carriers often provide coordinated (combination) services, the best known of which is the rail-truck combination, commonly called "piggyback" but officially designated as "trailer on flatcar" (TOFC).

A firm making a business of carrying persons or property for a consideration is responsible for their safe delivery. This liability of the common carrier makes it probable that the shipper of goods can recover from a common carrier for the value of property that is lost or damaged while in the custody of the common carrier, with certain exceptions and limitations.

The bill of lading issued by a common carrier serves as a receipt from the carrier for the goods being transported. There are several types of bills of lading: released bill of lading, straight bill of lading, order bill of lading, and through bill of lading, among others.

A common carrier's exposure to loss begins when goods have been delivered to and accepted by the carrier. The carrier's exposures end when the carrier has delivered the property to the consignee. However, in any particular case, the point at which loss exposure actually is transferred may be difficult to define. When a carrier becomes liable for loss or damage, it must pay the full amount of the loss, subject to any limitations. The amount of loss is usually determined as the market value of the lost or damaged property had it arrived in good condition at its destination.

Differences exist among the liabilities of the various types of carriers. The mode of transportation and the liability of the carriers involved are important factors in underwriting transportation insurance. The mode of transportation is a measure of the exposure, and the liability of the carrier is the foundation for a recovery through subrogation.

Many shipments are made to transport property from a seller to a buyer. When that is the case, an essential aspect of the loss exposure during transit is the question of when title to the property being sold passes from the seller to the buyer. As a general rule, the party that has title bears the risk of loss in transit. However, there are cases in which a seller may be exposed to loss after title has passed to a buyer and a buyer may be exposed to loss before title has passed from the seller to the buyer.

In evaluating the frequency and severity potential of the loss exposure to property in transit, factors that should be considered include the type and value of the merchandise, the radius of operations, the condition of the equipment carrying the cargo, the caliber of drivers handling the vehicles or merchandise, the terrain and climatic variations where the load will be carried, the past record of the carrier, and the crime rate in areas through which the merchandise will pass.

Transit loss exposures often lend themselves to retention. The considerations involved in deciding whether to retain losses to property in transit depend on whether the organization considering retention is a shipper or a carrier.

Chapter Notes

1. A comprehensive list of exempt commodities can be found in "Interstate Commerce Commission Administrative Ruling No. 119."
2. Donald V. Harper, *Transportation in America: Users, Carriers, Government,* 2nd. ed. (Englewood Cliffs, NJ: Prentice-Hall, 1982), p. 124-25.
3. Texas & P. Rwy. Co. v. Prunty, 233 S.W. 625 (Tex. Civ. App. 1921).
4. Feinberg v. Railway Express Agency, 163 F.2d 998 (1947); cert. den., 322 U.S. 847 92 L.Ed. 230 (1948).
5. William J. Augello, *Freight Claims in Plain English* (Huntington, NY: Shippers National Freight Claim Council, 1982).
6. *Transportation in America,* pp. 129, 130.
7. John McKnight Miller, *The Law of Freight Loss and Damage Claims,* 2nd ed., additional revisions by Fritz R. Kahn (Dubuque, IA: W.C. Brown, Co., 1961), p. 788, sec. 524.1.
8. *Transportation in America,* p. 130.
9. Portions of this section are adapted from C. Arthur Williams, Jr., George L. Head, Ronald C. Horn, and G. William Glendenning, *Principles of Risk Management and Insurance,* Vol. II, 2nd. ed. (Malvern, PA: American Institute for Property and Liability Underwriters, 1981), pp. 33-34.

CHAPTER 4

Transportation Insurance

INTRODUCTION

This chapter describes the types of insurance used to insure the transportation exposures analyzed in Chapter 3. Transportation insurance can be divided into two kinds: that which insures the shipper's interest in property being transported and that which insures the carrier's liability for loss to property being transported.

The first form of insurance discussed in this chapter is annual transit insurance, which insures the interest of the shipper in property being transported by a carrier. In some cases, incidental transportation by the owner of the property is covered as well. *Annual* transit policies are so named because they cover all shipments made during the policy period, which is usually for one year. By contrast, *trip* transit policies are used to insure property for a specified trip only.

Motor truck cargo insurance is discussed next. This coverage can be arranged to cover a carrier's liability for damage to cargo being transported by the carrier, to cover damage to property being transported on the owner's trucks, or to cover both exposures. Although the motor truck cargo policy covers cargo only while transported by truck, other policies can be written to cover cargo transported by air, rail, and water carriers.

Another type of transportation insurance described in this chapter covers money and securities being transported by armored car or messenger. This coverage may be written to cover the interest of a property owner (typically a financial institution making local shipments of money and securities) or the interest of an armored car company transporting property of others.

Property sent by mail, instead of by common or contract carrier, is ordinarily insured under specialized forms. One such form, for insuring first class, certified, registered, and express mail sent through the United States Postal Service, is the mail coverage form of Insurance Services Office. Other types of mail coverage are parcel post insurance and transit cash letter coverage. All three forms of mail coverage are described in this chapter.

ANNUAL TRANSIT INSURANCE

Annual transit policies indemnify the owner of property for loss that may occur to property while being carried from one point to another. These policies cover property while it is in the custody of others and not under the control of the owner, although the coverage may be written to cover incidental shipments being carried on vehicles belonging to the owner of the property.

The Need for Coverage

As seen in Chapter 3, common carriers generally are legally liable for loss or damage to goods in their custody. Because of this, many owners of cargo assume all loss exposures have been transferred to the carrier and that no further treatment is necessary.

There are several reasons why transfer of the exposure to the carrier is not always fully effective:

- time and effort are required to collect from carriers;
- limitations may exist on the dollar amount of liability of carriers (recall that the liability of the carrier may be limited to a certain amount in total, or a certain amount per pound);
- carriers are not liable for all causes of loss—acts of God and acts of the public enemy, for example; and
- a carrier may not be financially capable of paying claims.

Consequently, a shipper may choose to transfer the exposure to an insurer by buying annual transit insurance.

Almost any type of business or institution that has incoming or outgoing shipments may have a need for transit insurance—manufacturers, processors, wholesalers, retailers, department and discount stores, dealers, museums, libraries, and warehousemen, to name a few.

Insurance Coverage

Annual transit insurance is a nonfiled class of business. As such, policies are tailored to fit the circumstances of individual insureds. Standardization has not been feasible because of the variety of merchandise shipped and the differing modes of transportation. No two merchants receive their goods from the same set of shippers or over the same routes. Therefore rates and policy conditions are those agreed upon by the insured and the underwriter.

Covered Perils. Annual transit policies may be written on an "all-risks" basis or for named perils. If a policy is written on an "all-risks" basis, several exclusions (of the type usually associated with "all-risks" coverage) will be used. Loss caused by the following perils might be excluded in an "all-risks" transit policy:

- insects, vermin, inherent vice, or contamination;
- war or nuclear damage;
- rough handling, breakage, marring, scratching, chipping, denting, bending, or chafing;
- leakage of liquids
- shrinkage, evaporation, or loss of weight

If the "all-risks" approach provides a broader scope of coverage than is desired by the underwriter or the insured, a named perils policy may be used instead. A named perils transit policy might insure:

- while the property is on land, against fire, lightning, cyclone, tornado, flood, strike, riot, vandalism or malicious mischief, and collision, derailment, or overturn of the transporting vehicle;
- while the property is waterborne, against fire and perils of the seas, including the insured's liability for general average and salvage charges[1]; and
- theft of an entire shipping package, excluding pilferage.

Collision is frequently restricted in such a way that the coming together of railroad cars during coupling operations is not deemed to be a collision. This is an important limitation, because switching operations on railroads may result in violent bumps as the cars are coupled.

Property Not Covered Most of the property exclusions in transit policies are used to eliminate coverage on property that is more appropriately insured in other types of policies. Property commonly excluded consists of:

- accounts, bills, currency, deeds, evidences of debt, money, notes, securities, stamps, precious stones, fine arts, jewelry, or other similar valuables;
- property shipped by mail or parcel post;
- import shipments, until ocean marine insurance has ceased to cover;
- export shipments, after laden on board export coveyance, or under the protection of ocean marine insurance, whichever first occurs; and
- property shipped under an "on deck" bill of lading.

An "on deck" bill of lading stipulates that the cargo will be shipped on the deck of the vessel. Because of the higher likelihood of damage to "on deck" shipments during ocean transit, the underwriter may be unwilling to assume any risk for such shipments, even after they are unloaded from the vessel.

Covered Locations Coverage applies wherever the property may be while it is in transit within the territorial limits specified in the policy. This would include domestic waterborne shipments, although there may be some limitations specified for these. Transit policies may exclude coverage for property on the Mississippi River, the Ohio River, or the Great Lakes, or on any other waters where the underwriter feels there is a hazard not contemplated by the rates acceptable to the prospective policyholder.

Waterborne coverage included in transit policies does not apply to exports or imports. However, land coverage does ordinarily apply to imports after ocean marine coverage on the property ceases; and to exports until ocean marine coverage begins.

Many transit policies cover only while the covered property is in the custody of a specified class or classes of carrier—air, truck, rail, and so on. (As mentioned earlier, it is possible to write an annual transit policy to cover the property while it is on the insured's own vehicles, but this coverage must be spelled out specifically in the policy.) The questions of when property actually comes within the custody of the carrier and when it is removed from custody are important in determining whether coverage applies under a transit policy. The property is not in the custody of a carrier until it is actually at the carrier's location or accepted by the carrier to be placed on the carrier's vehicle. In one case, a cargo owner put cargo into the hands of an imposter under the mistaken belief that this trucker was a representative of the carrier. A court ruled that delivery to the imposter did not constitute delivery to a carrier, and the insurance policy did not cover the loss. The goods were never in the custody of a carrier and consequently were never covered by the policy.[2] In some cases, underwriters will agree to insure this exposure.

A common clause in a transit policy extends the coverage to property while it is on wharves, piers, and bulkheads, in depots and stations, or on platforms if it is in the custody of a common carrier incidental to transportation. This is a clarification of coverage, as property at these locations would be covered so long as it is in transit.

Another clause that seeks to make the coverage continuous has been adopted from the ocean marine "warehouse to warehouse" clause. It reads:

> This insurance attaches from the time the goods leave the factory, store or warehouse at initial point of shipment, and covers thereafter continuously, in due course of transportation, until same are delivered at store or warehouse at destination.

The purpose of this clause is to prevent lapse of coverage if the goods are placed temporarily in a storage location while in the course of transit. It is not intended to extend coverage to an actual storage situation when the goods are no longer in a state of transit.

However, there are cases in which coverage may be needed while the goods are temporarily not in transit. One such case is where property is sent to be processed. A similar situation arises when property is delivered on consignment for sale or distribution. In both of these cases, a transportation policy may be extended to provide coverage at the fixed locations. Separate limits generally are required at these locations. The underwriter also may want to amend the coverage provided at a location.

Valuation Transit policies may or may not include a clause that indicates how valuation of property is determined in the event of loss or damage. If there is no such valuation clause, the insurance company would be liable for the actual amount of loss at the time and place of occurrence. It would be the duty of the insured to present a proof of loss setting out the value and supporting data.

A policy may specify that the value is the invoice cost at the time and place of shipment. This type of valuation could result in a difference between the liability of the insurance company to the insured and the liability of the common carrier, because the common carrier is liable for the actual loss (subject, perhaps, to the limitations discussed in Chapter 3) and cannot specify a method of valuation.

The most common type of valuation clause states that the goods are to be valued at the amount of invoice, including prepaid or advanced freight, together with any costs or charges that have occurred since the shipment began. In the absence of an invoice the property is to be valued at its actual cash market value at destination on the day of loss.

Limits of Insurance Annual transit policies generally specify separate limits of insurance for each type of transit used. The types of transit include railroads, motor trucks, scheduled air transportation carriers, and messengers. A separate limit may be included for property on the insured's own vehicles, if property on such vehicles is covered.

Another limit of insurance applies to any one disaster. A conflagration or forest fire might involve several locations within a community. A hurricane or flood might involve several communities and could destroy a number of shipments spread over a large area. The insurance company must know the maximum amount it could pay as a result of such an occurrence. The determination of this limit depends upon the total amount of goods in transit within the same geographical area over a period of several days or perhaps several weeks. The limit usually includes both the loss or damage itself and any salvage charges or other expenses. A commonly used clause reads:

> This company shall not be liable for more than _____ dollars in any one casualty, either in case of partial or total loss, or salvage charges or other expenses or charges, or all combined.

Recoveries from Common Carriers In order to protect their interests and be able to recover from carriers, insurance companies have inserted in transit policies a provision to the effect that the insurance "shall in no wise inure directly or indirectly to the benefit of any carrier or other bailee." As discussed in Chapter 2, this type of clause preserves the insurer's right to subrogate against the carrier or bailee. As described below, subrogation plays an important part in the rating and underwriting of transportation policies.

Many policies have an additional clause strengthening the position of the insurance company. Usually called "impairment of recovery rights," this clause provides that any act of the insured, whether prior or subsequent to the loss, that impairs the right of the insured to collect the full value of any loss or damage from a carrier or bailee shall invalidate the policy. Impairment of the insured's right to collect would in turn impair the insurance company's right to collect under a subrogation agreement. However, the clause sometimes goes on to state that the insured is permitted to accept the ordinary bills of lading issued by carriers for hire. These ordinary bills of lading could include released valuation conditions, and their acceptance would, in absence of the exception just described, be a violation of the "impairment of recovery rights" provision. Some "impairment of recovery rights" clauses make provision only for acts of the insured subsequent to the loss. Such clauses make unnecessary any reference to bills of lading accepted by the insured.

Recoveries against a carrier are important in transit insurance. In fact, some policyholders wish to make their own collections from the carriers but still want insurance protection. These policyholders often have their own traffic departments and are in frequent contact with their carriers.

Contingent transit coverage provides indemnification for a loss only after the insured has exhausted every effort to collect from the carrier. The rates are low because the insurance company does not have to bother with numerous claims and does not have the trouble of collecting them under subrogation. This form of coverage is desirable only for the policyholder who is capable of making collections, and who needs coverage only for those catastrophes for which the common carrier is not liable. The coverage under these policies is the same as that under other transit forms, but loss payment is contingent upon the insured's making the primary effort to collect.

Passage of Title to Goods in Transit The sales contract between shipper and consignee usually specifies that the goods are shipped F.O.B. a designated point, either the point of shipment or the destination. As noted in Chapter 3, the abbreviation "F.O.B." means "free on board" and originated in the shipping of goods by water carrier. The usual arrangement is for goods to be shipped F.O.B. the point where the carrier's liability begins. That is, the shipper delivers the goods to the railroad company or puts them in the custody of the motor or air carrier.

The terms of the sales contract in this respect are important, because the title to the goods ordinarily passes from shipper to consignee at the point where they are F.O.B. If they are sent F.O.B. point of shipment, they usually belong to the consignee from then on, and any claim to be made against a carrier for loss or damage must be made by the consignee. If they are shipped F.O.B. the consignee's location, the title remains with the shipper until they are delivered, and the shipper would make claim against the carrier for any loss.

There may be circumstances in which a shipper is responsible for delivery of goods to the consignee even though technically the shipper has made delivery when the goods are placed in the hands of the carrier under an F.O.B. point of shipment arrangement. The shipper may wish to assume this responsibility for business reasons. In such cases the shipper's transit policy should include coverage on shipments until they are delivered to the consignee, regardless of the terms of the F.O.B. provisions in the sales contract. This extension may be granted by a simple clause reading substantially as follows:

> This policy is hereby extended to cover shipments sold F.O.B. point of shipment or otherwise, and the interest of the insured in such shipments is admitted.

Annual transit policies covering incoming goods ordinarily cover the property from the time it is placed in the hands of the carrier at point of shipment. In writing such a policy, inquiry should be made regarding the customs of a particular business, in order to avoid overlapping insurance coverage between shipper and consignee.

Premium Payments The premium for an annual transit policy is based upon the total value of all goods covered during the term of the policy. The premium is computed by applying the rate to the value of the goods insured (that is, the value of all the goods shipped that come within the definition of coverage in the policy).

It is usually impossible for a merchant to determine accurately in advance what his or her annual sales and merchandise receipts and shipments will be. Consequently, it is customary for annual transit policies to be written on a reporting basis. Annual adjustment of premium is common. The insured estimates receipts or shipments as closely as possible and pays an estimated annual premium. At the expiration of the policy, the insured makes a report to the insurance company of the actual values covered by the policy. An adjustment is then made in the premium, and the insured pays any extra premium due or receives a refund of any overpayment.

Some transit policies produce sufficient premium to justify a monthly reporting of values and monthly premium payment. Insurance company practices differ in regard to what constitutes a premium large enough for monthly reporting. The factor to be considered is the expense to both insured and insurance company of handling the reports and payments.

It is customary for the insurer to require a deposit premium that may be a quarter or a third of the estimated annual premium. In many cases, the monthly premiums for the first few months are charged against the deposit premium, and the insured starts making actual payments only when the deposit is exhausted. Sometimes the policy provides that the premium payments start immediately, and the insurer holds the deposit until expiration, upon which a final adjustment is made. The latter arrangement may be used if the insurer has doubts as to the insured's ability or willingness to pay all the premium.

The policy contains a clause governing the reporting of values. This clause constitutes an agreement that the insured will report to the insurer the actual values shipped that are covered by the policy. The same clause usually contains the rate and the provisions for payment of premium. Premiums may be due either when the report is made or within an agreed upon number of days after reporting.

The policy usually requires that the insured keep a record of all values shipped that are covered by the policy. That is, the insured must not only report them to the insurance company but also keep an accurate record that the company may check at a later date. Many insurance companies make it a practice to have an auditor check the books of the insured before final settlement is made at the expiration of the policy. The knowledge that such a check will be made is a deterrent to the insured who might be tempted to omit part of the values. An audit will also reveal mistakes, which may be in favor of either the insured or the insurer.

It is possible to write transit policies on a continuous reporting basis. These differ from the policies just described only in that the policy has no expiration date and continues in effect until canceled by either party. Monthly reporting is required just as in a policy that expires annually, and the company makes its audits periodically to see that values are being reported accurately.

Occasionally policies are written for a flat annual premium with no provision for adjustment. This can be done in the case of a small, steady business, which is not likely to fluctuate from year to year. Insurers require prospects to submit reports of previous shipments and insurance experience. Many underwriters consider at least three years' reports to be necessary for a satisfactory estimate. At expiration and before the next year's policy is issued, a careful underwriter will again examine the record to see whether any change in rate or premium is justified.

Underwriting

The major underwriting considerations for transit insurance include:

1. The commodity and its susceptibility to loss or damage. Clothing and textiles are leading targets for cargo theft, along with jewelry, food, electronic equipment, and furs. Susceptibility to breakage, spoilage, and other causes of loss must also be considered.
2. The modes of transportation used and the type of carrier. For example, many underwriters believe there is a greater hazard to property in the custody of truckers than in the hands of railroads.

3. The type of bill of lading used, the extent of released value, and the terms of sale. The terms of sale, such as F.O.B. destination, will indicate the portion of the trip that will be at the shipper's risk.
4. Loss experience of the shipper.
5. Distance property will be shipped.
6. The type of packing and container used. Containerization reduces many handling and pilferage losses.
7. The limits of insurance desired and the type of valuation clause employed.

When including coverage for owner's goods on an owner's truck, there is no possibility of subrogation from a carrier. This would tend to justify a higher rate. However, the absence of subrogation recoveries could be balanced out by superior handling on the part of the insured, who has direct supervision of the property while it is in transit.

MOTOR TRUCK CARGO INSURANCE

Annual transit insurance applies to the property of *shippers.* The insurance is written to protect the *owners* of such property from loss in transit. The *carrier* that is transporting the property from one place to another also has an insurable interest in the property because of the carrier's legal liability to the property owner. A loss of cargo may require that the carrier pay the owner for the value of the property, and this gives the carrier an insurable interest. This insurable interest is generally covered by a *motor truck cargo policy* purchased by the carrier.

Motor truck cargo insurance also may protect the owner of goods. When the insured is the owner, the policy provides direct property damage coverage (not legal liability coverage as above).

In volume of premiums written, motor truck cargo insurance accounts for a substantial share of the inland marine market. It is a nonfiled class, which permits the underwriter and producer great latitude in the coverage provided and the rate charged. Trucking companies differ widely in their methods of operation, in the commodities hauled, in the territories served, and in the length of hauls. While there are no filed forms or rates for motor truck cargo insurance, most insurers maintain a stock of printed forms for issuing motor truck cargo policies. These forms can be modified by endorsement to fit the needs of a particular insured.

Carriers Forms

A *carriers* form of motor truck cargo insurance policy indemnifies the insured (the trucker) for loss or damage resulting from legal liability as a carrier. The policy does not insure against loss of the property unless the insured is legally liable for the loss.

For example, suppose a trucker had an insurance policy that insured (among other things) legal liability for loss of property by flood, but it is determined that the circumstances under which the flood caused the loss constituted an act of God. If it is determined that the trucker is not liable for such a loss resulting from an act of God, the insurance company would have no duty under its policy to pay the loss.

The motor truck cargo carrier's policy is issued to cover the single interest of the trucker. It does not cover the interest of the shipper, owner, or consignee of the cargo. Such policies are not written to cover more than one trucker under a single policy and seldom cover the interest of a railroad or other carrier in connection with the operations of the motor carrier.

Covered Perils In addition to paying only those losses for which the insured is legally liable, carriers forms also require that loss must result from a covered cause in order for the insurance to respond. A form may restrict the coverage to liability for loss resulting from specified perils or insure virtually any loss for which the carrier may be liable under the bill of lading, shipping receipt, or other contract of carriage issued by the carrier.

Bill of Lading Form. The latter type of policy, the so-called *bill of lading form,* is ordinarily subject to certain exclusions and so in that respect functions like an "all-risks" policy. Usually the exclusions are few. The following exclusions, for example, might be found in a bill of lading form:

- governmental action, nuclear hazard, war and military action (see Chapter 2);
- delay, loss of use, loss of market, or any other consequential loss;
- trick or device and unauthorized instructions (see Chapter 2);
- dishonest acts of the insured, the insured's employees, or anyone else entrusted with the property;
- any quality in the property that causes it to damage or destroy itself ("inherent vice");
- insects, vermin, or rodents;
- breakage; breakdown or failure of any refrigeration system; contamination; corrosion, rust, dampness or dryness, cold or heat; any change in appearance, smell, texture, or taste; however, in some policies, the foregoing types of loss may be covered if caused by fire, lightning, windstorm, hail, smoke, explosion, rioters, strikers, civil commotion, vandalism, earth-

quake, flood, theft or attempted theft, or accident to the vehicle carrying the property.

Also, carriers forms often contain an exclusion of any costs or penalties the insured incurs for violating any law or regulation that applies to denial of claims or delay in paying customers' claims for loss to covered property.

Named Perils Form. When a carriers form is written on a named perils basis, the covered causes of loss generally include some or all of the perils listed below. Naturally, as these policies are nonfiled, there can be some variation among different insurers' forms.

a. Fire, lightning or explosion;
b. Windstorm;
c. Collision of the conveyance with any other vehicle or object;
d. Overturn of the conveyance;
e. Collapse of bridge, wharf, dock, platform or culvert;
f. Stranding, sinking, burning, or collision of any regular ferry, including General Average and Salvage Charges;
g. Flood, meaning the rising of any natural body of water;
h. Theft, but excluding pilferage.

Another peril that can be added is damage resulting from dropping the insured property while it is being loaded or unloaded. Loading and unloading may be restricted to operations immediately adjacent to the vehicle, or extended to provide coverage for property being carried into or from, or hoisted into or lowered from, a building.

Peril c., collision of the conveyance with any other vehicle or object, does not provide coverage for a loss resulting from the *cargo* striking a vehicle or object. Collision of the load can be included as another peril insured against.

A restrictive collision clause that sometimes appears excludes loss resulting from the transporting vehicle coming into contact with the roadbed or curbing, or with a stationary object or trailer while backing up for the purpose of loading or unloading, or while coupling or uncoupling.

Named perils forms are usually subject to many of the same exclusions contained in bill of lading forms, as listed earlier.

Covered Property It is customary to insert in the policy a description of the goods hauled. In the case of a common carrier hauling all kinds of goods, the description could be "general merchandise." The coverage applies to goods for which the carrier is legally liable as carrier, bailee, or warehouseman under tariff, or bill of lading or shipping receipt issued by the insured. The broad phraseology is used in order to include circumstances in which the trucker would be in the position of a bailee or warehouseman in regard to some particular shipment.

The policy is written to cover only "lawful goods and merchandise," because it is against public policy to insure unlawful goods, and it also is considered poor underwriting practice to insure illegal operations. Illegal operations would be subject to loss by racketeering or to confiscation by legal authority.

Certain types of property are typically listed as not being covered:

- accounts, bills, deeds, evidences of debt, money, notes, securities, jewelry, precious stones, or other similar valuables;
- paintings, statuary, and other works of art or virtu, unless there is a total loss in specie;
- property carried gratuitously or as an accommodation.

Limitations Some forms limit the amount of insurance on loss resulting from the theft of certain commodities such as alcohol, wine, liquor, cigars, cigarettes, tobacco, or furs to 10 percent (or some other percentage) of the amount of insurance that would otherwise apply. Loss by breakage of eggs is sometimes limited to a nominal dollar amount.

Live animals, fish, or birds are usually covered only against loss by death resulting directly from specified perils or destruction made necessary by injuries resulting from a specified peril. Death from natural causes is not covered.

Losses to paintings and other works of art usually are paid only in cases of total loss from a peril insured against. Some policies contain a dollar or percentage limitation on the amount that will be paid for fine arts losses.

Time Period Covered As motor truck cargo policies provide coverage for property in transit, it is necessary to know when transit begins and ends. This is not always easy to determine. Whether or not property was in transit when a loss occurred has been the subject of a good deal of litigation.

In general, the courts have held that transit does not begin at the same time for an owner carrying its own goods as for a carrier hauling the goods of others. For an owner carrying its own goods, transit begins when the goods leave the starting point on the way to their destination. With a carrier for hire, transit begins when the goods have been placed in the carrier's custody, ready for delivery. The issuing of a bill of lading by the carrier does not necessarily mean it has taken custody of the property. In one case, goods left on a shipper's platform were held not to be in transit while on the platform, despite the fact that the carrier had signed a bill of lading.[3]

Transit does not necessarily end when movement ceases. With respect to property in the custody of a carrier, temporary storage for the convenience of the carrier, shipper, or consignee is not an interruption of transit. Other detainments for the purpose of facilitating transportation, such as reloading or sorting, are not interruptions of transit. However, to quote one authority, "when goods in transit reach some intermediate point where the movement is stopped for the purpose of having something done to the goods not related to the transportation, then the transportation has ceased, and a period of storage has begun."[4]

With respect to property being transported by the owner of the property, transit is not interrupted by any stops that are normal to the route, including overnight stops. Any other stops, or any storage en route, would be an interruption of transit.

Transit ceases when the property has been delivered at its destination. Many disputes have arisen over what constitutes an effective delivery. Generally speaking, delivery has not been completed if anything remains to be done to effectuate delivery. The carrier must tender delivery at a reasonable time, within working hours. If a carrier tenders delivery fifteen minutes before a consignee's closing time, and the consignee refuses delivery as it would not have sufficient time to unload the cargo, it may well be argued that the property is still in transit, even though the carrier stores the property in its warehouse overnight. If a carrier tenders delivery to a consignee in ample time to unload, and the consignee requests that the property be held by the carrier and delivered again the next day, there is a good presumption that transit had ceased when the initial delivery was refused.

Goods delivered to an imposter have been held to be still in transit. It has been determined that delivery made under these circumstances is not a true delivery, and that transit did not end.

The foregoing are broad generalities on a very complex issue. Each case is unique. All the individual facts of each case must be considered separately when making a judgment as to when transit began or ended.

Locations Covered Motor truck cargo policies often show a *radius of operations*. Experience has shown that the hazard of a motor truck operation increases with the distance traveled by the trucks. Rates are determined upon the basis of the radius of operations from the insured's headquarters as stated in the policy; losses occurring beyond that radius are not intended to be covered.

A local hauler is one that operates within a radius of approximately fifty miles. The risk presented by this class of trucker usually is considered to be less than that presented by a long-haul trucker.

An intermediate hauler may operate over a radius of 200 miles; its operations are characterized by the fact that the drivers are out and back the same day. It is not necessary for them to drive on night runs or to be away from home overnight. On the longer hauls of several hundred miles, the drivers may operate at night, and driver fatigue seems to be an important cause of loss. Long-distance operations must carry high value loads to be profitable, and the losses that do occur on these runs are likely to involve large amounts.

Scheduling of Vehicles A policy may or may not list the trucks covered. On smaller policies it is customary to list the trucks, with a complete identification by motor and serial number. Cargo is covered only while in transit on a described truck. In policies covering larger operations, the trucks are not listed, and all operations of the insured are covered, including any with hired trucks used temporarily.

Most scheduled vehicle forms contain a substitution clause allowing the insured to substitute another vehicle when a scheduled vehicle is disabled. In some instances, provision is made to insure property on a newly acquired vehicle, if all of the insured's other vehicles are scheduled. Most scheduled vehicle forms do not cover property while on a vehicle of another carrier who has accepted property from the insured on an interline basis.

Limits of Insurance Policies include a limit of insurance per truck and a catastrophe limit of insurance when more than one truck is involved or when terminal coverage (see below) is included. If the trucks are listed specifically in the policy, a limit of insurance for each truck is shown.

Extensions of Coverage An extension of coverage may be built into a motor truck cargo form or added by endorsement. Following are some of the extensions of coverage commonly found in carriers forms.

Terminal Coverage. The insuring clause of a motor truck cargo policy usually covers the legal liability of the insured for loss or damage to goods "when loaded for shipment on and in transit in or on the vehicles owned, operated or hired for or by the named insured. . . ." In the early days of motor truck operations, this was a satisfactory coverage because the trucker picked up the goods at the shipper's door and delivered them to the consignee's place of business without any transfer from one truck to another.

The trucking industry became more and more complicated, and truckers established terminals at which goods are sorted by routes and transshipped. A motor common carrier ordinarily is responsible for the safety of goods while they are in a terminal in course of transit to the same extent as when they are in the trucks. Most policies now contain an extension of coverage to terminals while the goods are in the custody of the insured and while they are in due course of transit. These extensions of insurance coverage to terminals sometimes limit the coverage to twenty-four, forty-eight, or seventy-two hours, depending on the needs of the insured and the length of time the goods are likely to be in a terminal during transfer.

Earned Freight and Debris Removal. Motor truck cargo policies often provide nominal amounts of coverage for two additional exposures. The earned freight extension provides coverage for freight charges that have been earned but are uncollectible due to a loss insured against.

The debris removal extension covers the expense necessary to remove cargo debris following an insured loss.

Other Provisions Several other provisions are common to carriers' forms, as described below.

Indemnity Agreement. The indemnity agreement states that the insured must reimburse the insurer for any sums the insurer is required to pay because of the attachment to the policy of any federal, state, or provincial endorsement. (These types of endorsement are discussed below.)

Fines and Assessments. The fines and assessments provision excludes coverage for any penalties the insured is required to pay as the result of the violation of any law or regulation relating to the delay in the payment, denial, or settlement of any claim.

Coinsurance. Very few carriers forms contain a coinsurance clause, because the carrier rarely knows the full value of shipments. When effective, coinsurance applies separately to the limits on vehicles and the limits on terminals.

Valuation. Valuation clauses in carriers forms vary. One approach is to value the property at the lesser of actual cash value or the amount for which the insured is liable under the shipping document. Another approach is to value the property at the least of the following:

1. the amount of invoice, including prepaid or advanced freight (or in the absence of an invoice, the actual cash market value at the destination on the day of loss);
2. the value shown on the shipping list or bill of lading; or
3. the cost to repair or replace the property with other of like kind and quality.

Settlement of Loss with Owners of Property. The insurer reserves the right to adjust a claim with the owner of the property.

Deductible. Deductibles play an important role in the underwriting of motor truck cargo policies. The size of the deductible varies with the rate and the exposure.

Gross Receipts Reporting Clause. As discussed later in this chapter, gross receipts of a trucker are often the basis for rating motor truck cargo insurance. Thus, policies rated on this basis include a provision requiring the insured to report its gross receipts. The wording of this clause varies considerably. A typical clause defines gross receipts as the total amount to which the insured is entitled (both collected and uncollected) for the transportation of property, whether the shipment originates with the insured or another carrier. Some forms more specifically outline what should be, and what should not be, included as gross receipts. Many forms require that the report of gross receipts be received no later than thirty days after the end of each reporting period.

Federal and State Filings

Motor truck carriers of cargo operating within federal jurisdiction are required to provide evidence that suitable cargo insurance is in force. This requirement is met by having their insurance policy amended by the attachment of a standard form numbered BMC 32, entitled "Endorsement for Motor Common Carrier Policies of Insurance for Cargo Liability Under Section 215, Interstate Commerce Act." To evidence that this endorsement has been attached, the insurance company is required to file another form, BMC 34, with the Interstate Commerce Commission.

The endorsement states that the insurance company agrees to pay the shipper or consignee for all loss or damage, up to $5,000 on any one motor vehicle, and $10,000 in any one loss, for which the motor carrier may be held legally liable. This agreement is binding on the insurance company "regardless of whether the motor vehicles, terminals, warehouses and other facilities used in connection with the transportation of the property hereby insured are specifically described in the policy or not." In the same vein, the company is liable for a loss which is less than the deductible amount shown in the policy.

In actual practice, the carrier pays the shipper for any valid claims not covered under its insurance policy. If the carrier does not honor a claim, however, the shipper has the right to approach the insurance company directly for redress. The insurance company, upon paying the claim, assumes the right to recover from the carrier any payments it makes under the filing. In most cases, however, the carrier has not honored the shipper's claim because it was financially unable to do so. The insurer, then, has little hope of any recovery from the carrier.

Filings are made on an "until cancelled" basis and require a thirty day notice of cancellation (form BMC 35) to the ICC. If coverage is cancelled and rewritten by another insurer, the new insurer may assume liability during the thirty day period by a letter of agreement with the previous company.

Most states have passed legislation requiring motor carriers operating within the state to make a filing similar to that required by the ICC. The filing is made with the state regulatory body, in most states called the Public Service Commission or the Public Utilities Commission. The state filing has the same effect as the federal filing, although the limits for which the insurance company is held liable vary from state to state. Some states require only intrastate carriers to file. Other states require both intrastate and interstate carriers to file.[5]

The great majority of states requiring state filings have adopted uniform documents for filing the required evidence of insurance. The Inland Marine Underwriters Association was particularly active in the pursuit of this uniformity, and made a significant contribution toward bringing it about. The certificate of insurance filed with the state is NARUC form H. The endorsement attached to the policy is NARUC form I. The notice of cancellation is NARUC form K. NARUC is an acronym for the National Association of Regulatory Utility Commissioners, the organization that promulgated the forms.

Owners Forms

Owners forms are similar to carriers forms in their format and in the coverage they provide. There are, however, some basic differences. Some of them are as follows:

1. The owners policy covers only the owner's interest in its own goods. It does not cover the insured's liability for damage to property of others.
2. The owners form does not have a provision for a schedule of terminals.
3. Owners forms generally exclude coverage for tarpaulins and other similar coverings.
4. Owners forms invariably include a coinsurance clause, usually 100 percent.
5. Valuation clauses in owners forms usually value property at the amount of invoice, including prepaid or advanced freight. In the absence of an invoice, the valuation is actual cash market value at the destination on the day of loss.
6. An owners form is sometimes extended to provide coverage for property while it is located on the owner's premises prior to transit, or at a stopover while transit is interrupted. Coverage is generally limited to a specified number of days or hours.

Owners carrying their own goods are private carriers. The insurance policy on property being carried by a private carrier covers direct damage and not the insured's legal liability. If the property is damaged or lost as a result of one of the perils insured against, the loss must be paid by the insurance company. There is no possibility of avoiding loss payment on the ground that the trucker is not liable for the loss. There is not even the remote possibility of a loss being considered not payable because it is the result of an act of God. The policy must be underwritten on the basis of the commodity hauled and the hazards covered by the policy.

It might be expected that experience with private carriers would be worse because of the insurance company's more extensive liability. This is not the case. The average experience with private carriers is better than that with common and contract carriers. There appear to be several reasons for this. Many private carriers operate over shorter routes than common or contract carriers; their operations are more likely to be short and medium hauls. It is also probable that an owner tends to take better care of its own property than it would of property belonging to others.

Another favorable aspect is the absence of the terminal hazard that results when the goods of many shippers are mixed together and sorted for distribution over various routes. The owner's truck goes from point of shipment directly to its destination. The cargo is not reshuffled at terminals en route, where it may be lost and mis-shipped. Owners policies do not cover the terminal hazard, because inland marine policies ordinarily do not cover owners' goods on their own premises. Therefore, there are no large terminal fires to be charged against the loss record of the private carrier.

Many owners can afford to maintain their trucks in optimal condition. They may not be under pressure to make runs to keep customers, since trucking is a minor part of their operations.

Specialized Motor Truck Cargo Policies

In addition to the carriers and owners forms, there are special forms of motor truck cargo insurance for household goods carriers and carloading companies and freight consolidators. The operations and exposures of these types of carriers or bailees are described in Chapter 3. The following sections describe the corresponding insurance treatments.

Household Goods Carriers Small household goods carriers not involved with warehousing can be insured on the customary motor truck cargo carriers form. Larger carriers usually are insured on a specialized form designed to insure all their operations. While these forms vary from one insurer to another, the coverage described below is typical.

Section 1. Carrier's Liability. This section insures the carrier's liability for loss to property in transit, including temporary "storage in transit." Household goods carriers' tariffs include a specific number of days for "storage in transit." Premium for this section is collected on a gross receipts reporting basis.

Section 2. Warehouse Legal Liability. After the "storage in transit" period has expired, the carrier becomes liable as a warehouseman, and is responsible only for loss caused by its negligence. This section insures loss arising out of that responsibility. Storage locations are scheduled, with an amount of insurance shown for each. A flat annual premium is generally charged for this section.

Section 3. Customers' Household Goods. This section provides for the issuance of a policy of insurance (certificate) at the shipper's request. The certificate may provide insurance for property in transit, or property in transit and in storage. The policy provides rates for each of these exposures. A copy of each certificate, including the premium for property in transit, is sent to the insurance company. Premium for the storage exposure is generally collected on a monthly reporting basis. Cancellation of the master policy does not cancel the certificates. An individual notice of cancellation must be sent to each certificate holder.

Section 4. Accrued Charges. This section insures accrued charges rendered uncollectible under the customers' household goods section of the policy.

Section 5. Additional Charges and Expenses. This section insures additional charges such as those for packing, recrating, etc., incurred under the customers' household goods section of the policy.

Section 6. Moving Equipment. This section insures property of the insured such as dollies, burlap, skids, etc.

Section 7. Government Agency Contracts. This section covers the insured's liability for property accepted under contracts made with a government agency.

Section 8. Military Traffic Management Agency Endorsement. This endorsement states the policy is amended to comply with the requirements of the Department of Defense as respects transportation of household goods for both military and civilian employees.

Coverage for Carloading Companies or Freight Consolidators Freight brokers and consolidators perform much the same service in the motor truck field that the carloading company performs in the railroad freight field. Some of these concerns qualify as common carriers, and their legal liability may be covered in the same way as that of a trucker. Each insured is rated individually. The policy is arranged to fit (1) the terminal hazards of the insured's operation, (2) the insured's trucking operations, if any, and (3) the contracts with other truckers. Many consolidating operations are actually local truckers and can be insured in the same way as other local trucking concerns.

Underwriting

To better understand the operation of a motor truck cargo account, the underwriter should be familiar with the type of equipment used to haul covered property. Some of the common types are shown in Exhibit 4-1.

Some of the factors to be considered when underwriting motor truck cargo insurance are:

1. type of carrier (common, contract, etc.);
2. number of vehicles;
3. routes over which the insured operates;
4. commodities carried;
5. average value per truckload;
6. amounts of insurance required;
7. terminal locations and security arrangements;
8. protective devices on trucks;
9. filing requirements (ICC or state); and
10. annual gross receipts.

Past loss history is also important. The insured's financial condition is critical, particularly if federal or state filings are required. The Central Analysis Bureau (CAB), located in New York City, functions as a clearinghouse for financial information on motor carriers. The CAB analyzes the financial statements of motor carriers and makes their analysis known to their client companies through quarterly and annual reports, or by telephone if the need for immediate information arises. When a carrier is found to be in weak financial condition the underwriter might well consider some type of financial guarantee to satisfy claims for which the insurer would be held liable under a filing. Escrow deposits and irrevocable letters of credit are two types of guarantees commonly in use.

Target Commodities An important consideration in evaluating the theft exposure is the type of commodities hauled. Underwriters often insert a limitation in the policy providing that limited amounts of coverage apply to "target" commodities that are especially susceptible to theft. This limitation may be by percentage. For example, a policy may provide that not more than 20 percent of the limit of insurance shall apply on the special commodities. The limitation may also be expressed in dollars. The commodities listed in many policies include meat, fish, furs, liquors, silks, rayons, woolens, tires, tubes, tobacco products, radios, televisions, clothing, and textiles.

When insuring target commodities, underwriters often require an extra measure of protection against loss by theft. This is particularly true when the carrier is operating in areas with a high incidence of theft. Some of these extra precautions include the following:

1. The requirement that an alarm system be maintained on the vehicles. Standard endorsements have been developed for use with the equipment furnished by the major alarm manufacturers.
2. An attendance agreement. This provision requires that a permanent employee of the insured, or a person whose sole duty it is to attend the vehicle, be in or on the vehicle at the time the loss occurs.
3. A locked car agreement. This states the requirement that, at the time of loss, the body of the vehicle from which the theft occurred be fully enclosed, and that the theft be the result of forcible entry, evidenced by visible marks.
4. A convoy. In some instances the requirement that the transporting conveyance be part of a convoy might be the most practical form of protection. An alternative is the requirement that the transporting conveyance be followed by another vehicle.

Refrigerated Shipments Many carrier forms exclude loss or damage caused by or resulting from breakdown of refrigeration equipment. Underwriters are sometimes asked to delete this exclusion. When that is done, a requirement mandating periodic inspections of the equipment is often incorporated in the form. When underwriting refrigerated shipments, the availability of other refrigerating facilities along the route is a factor to consider. Prompt removal of the goods from a disabled vehicle into another refrigerating facility may lessen or preclude a loss.

Terminals From the insurance company's standpoint, the extension of coverage to terminals poses a serious additional hazard. The largest insured motor truck cargo losses have been in terminal fires. The highest value regularly carried in a single motor truck may be only a fraction of the value concentrated in a terminal. The fire hazard of

Exhibit 4-1
Common Types of Trucks*

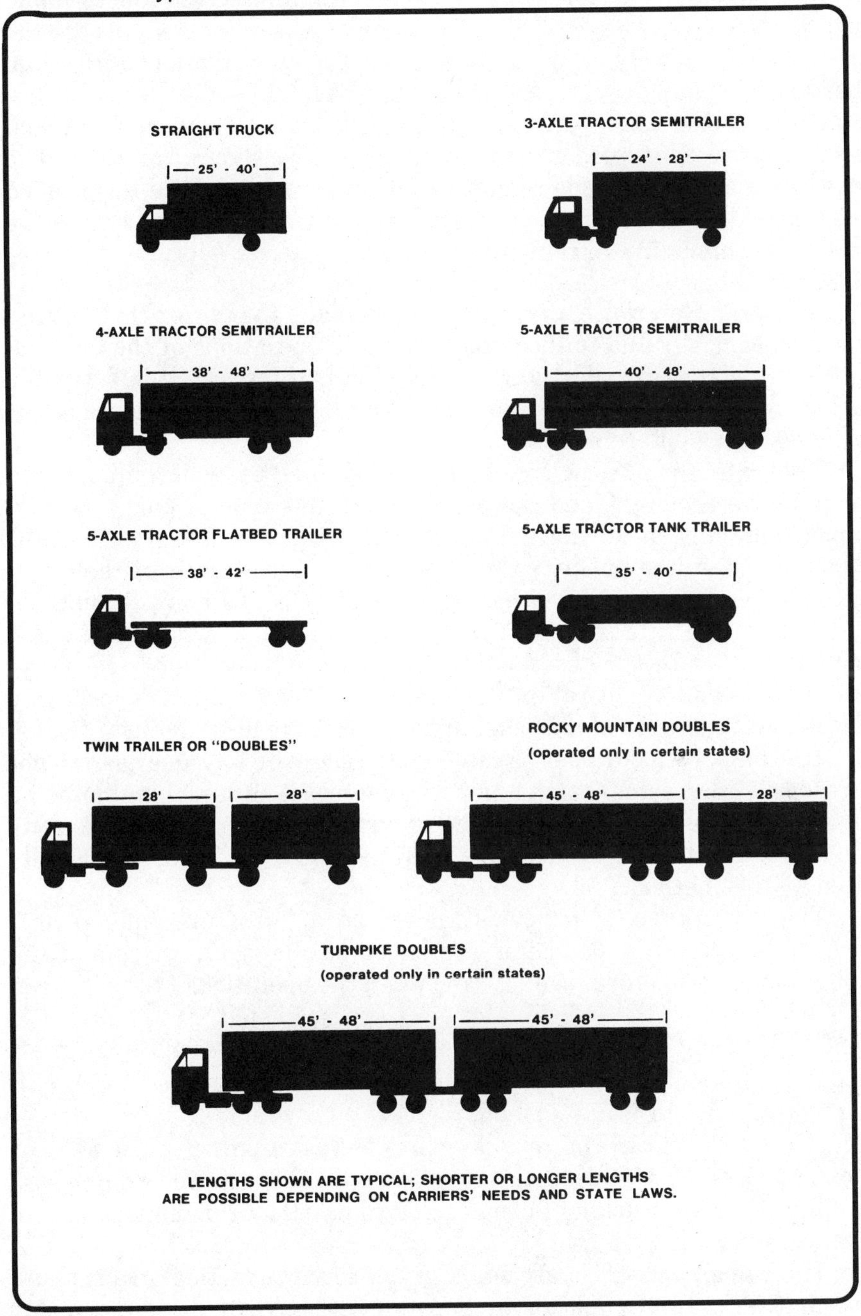

* Reprinted with permission of the American Trucking Associations.

each terminal is underwritten with caution, and the insurance company is entitled to a considerable additional premium when the terminal hazard is covered. The published fire insurance rate for contents for the terminal customarily is used as a basis for the additional premium charge.

Most forms make provision for a schedule of terminals. When terminals are scheduled a limit of insurance is shown for each. The schedule may also include a limit of insurance for any one unspecified terminal. All forms contain a catastrophe limit, which puts a cap on the various sublimits for vehicles and terminals.

Rating Reference already has been made to policies that list the trucks specifically and to those that cover all operations of the insured. In the first type of policy, a specific amount of insurance is listed for each truck. The amount of the policy is the total of all the amounts applying to the different trucks.

The rate for the policy is multiplied by the policy amount to compute the premium, and the premium for this type of policy usually is paid annually in advance. For example, suppose there were eight trucks listed on the policy, with $10,000 coverage on four of them and $20,000 coverage on the other four. The policy amount would be $120,000. If the rate were $3 per $100, the premium would be $3,600. Factors that affect rates include the limit of insurance, coverage provided, radius of operation, terminals, deductible amount, property carried, and presence of alarms. Larger risks have fleet credits.

The limit of insurance payable as a result of any one loss is not necessarily the same as the policy amount. A lesser limit may be specified. In the example used in the previous paragraph, a limit for any one loss might be set, for example at $75,000. Owner forms are usually rated by this method.

The other type of policy is known as a "gross receipts form," because the premium payments are based on the gross receipts of the motor carrier. This form usually covers all the operations of the insured as a trucker, and the individual trucks are not listed. Frequently it is used in insuring the larger truck operations. There would be a great deal of additional work involved in endorsing the insurance policy if it were necessary to issue an endorsement every time a large trucker secured a new truck. The rate is expressed as an amount per $100 of gross receipts. The insured agrees to keep an accurate record of gross receipts from the trucking business and to pay the premium at the rate given in the policy.

The calculation of a rate for a gross receipts method of premium payment is largely a matter of knowing the exposures of the motor carrier. The underwriter considers the previous loss experience, the limits of insurance requested, the commodities hauled, terminal exposures (if any), radius of operations, degree of cooperation by the insured, and other relevant factors. A premium is then calculated to cover expected and catastrophic losses. That premium is then divided by the expected gross receipts to determine the rate.

There is no uniformity in method or in the rates that result, because each underwriter has his or her own experience and judgment to use as a basis for quotations.

Use of Owner Operators Many carriers today are making increasing use of owner operators to haul products for their customers. The owner operator works under the operating authority of the carrier who issued the bill of lading and who hired the owner operator. The carrier issuing the bill of lading is liable to the shipper for any loss while the goods are in the custody of the owner operator. However, the carrier may be reimbursed by the owner operator if the terms of the contract make the owner operator liable, as is usually the case. Owner operators may or may not have insurance to effect payment to the carrier. A responsible carrier will deal only with owner operators it knows and can trust.

When policies are issued on a scheduled vehicle basis, the owner operator's vehicle will probably not be scheduled. This may present a problem in the event of a loss while the property is in the custody of the owner operator. When vehicles are not scheduled and premium is collected on a gross receipts basis, the carrier should report the full amount collected for the shipment, not just the amount that it retains for its own account. Seventy-five percent of the shipping charge may have gone to the owner operator who made the delivery, leaving the carrier with 25 percent. The carrier, however, had the ultimate liability for the entire trip.

A trip lease is an agreement made by one carrier with another, similar in arrangement to the agreements made with owner operators. The difference is in the parties who are signatory to the agreement. The owner operator is generally an individual who owns a tractor and trailer and offers trucking services to any carrier. A trip lease is thought of as an agreement by two carriers with established routes. One carrier may not have the particular equipment needed for the delivery of a certain property and will enter into a trip lease agreement to use the other carrier's equipment and driver.

TRIP TRANSIT INSURANCE

Annual transit policies are written on a *full term basis,* i.e., for a year or continuously (until cancelled). By contrast, the trip transit policy is written to cover a single trip. It fills the needs of an insured who does not have annual transit insurance and wishes to cover a particular transit exposure.

A trip transit policy can be written to cover the interest of an owner transporting its own property on its own (or rented) trucks, a shipper having property shipped by a carrier, or the carrier itself.

Insurance Coverage

Insurance companies generally have printed forms to cover trip transit exposures. As trip transit is a nonfiled class, printed conditions vary from one insurance company to another.

A typical policy might cover "shipments made on or about (date) of merchandise consisting of (description of property) while in transit from (origin) to (destination) while in the custody of (carrier) and while contained in or on the (conveyance)." The property is generally valued at the amount of invoice or, in the absence of invoice, actual cash market value at time and place of loss. This valuation clause may be changed to another basis when necessary. The policy is usually subject to a 100 percent coinsurance clause.

Both named perils and "all-risks" forms are available. Named perils usually include fire; flood; cyclone, tornado, or windstorm; collapse of bridge or culvert; collision of the transporting conveyance with any other vehicle or object; derailment or overturn of the transporting conveyance; stranding, sinking, burning, or collision of the transporting vessel, including general average and salvage charges. Some forms include coverage for theft. Others require addition of theft coverage by endorsement.

The usual exclusions eliminate coverage for loss caused by or resulting from delay, loss of market, or loss of use; inherent vice or gradual deterioration; strikes or riots; employee dishonesty; war; and nuclear occurrences.

Coverage for an exhibition can be written under a trip transit policy by endorsing the policy to cover at the location of the exhibit. Transit coverage may be provided both to and from the exhibit. Special precautions might be required at the exhibit location to minimize the exposure to loss by theft.

Underwriting

An infinite variety of exposures can be insured under trip transit policies, from the commonplace household furniture shipment to the movement of a building containing operating telephone equipment. The underwriter has the opportunity for close scrutiny of a trip transit risk, as the property to be insured, the route, and the carrier are all known.

The susceptibility of the property to the perils of transportation must be determined. Commodities subject to breakage should be packaged properly and suitable precautions taken to prevent loss during loading, unloading, or rigging. Property with an inordinate theft exposure should be given the protection needed. If the insured is a shipper, the extent of the carrier's liability should be determined to assess subrogation possibilities. If the insured is a carrier, the extent of its liability will determine the amount the insurance company has at risk.

When insurance is to be provided for the movement of goods from one building into another building, the policy should clearly specify when coverage begins and coverage ends. This will preclude any question as to whether or not the property was "in transit" when the loss occurred. The same clarity is needed when insuring goods in transit and "until installed." An installation may be a simple process of setting the object in place, or may involve a more complicated procedure, including testing. If testing is to be covered, full details of the process should be obtained and evaluated by the underwriter.

Coverage for consequential loss requires careful investigation. A request may be made to insure loss of income in the event that a piece of equipment is damaged in transit and is inoperable upon arrival. A small property damage loss can trigger a substantial claim for loss of income. The availability of replacement parts should be established, as well as the time needed for replacement.

Rates are a matter of judgment and vary considerably depending on the exposure. Deductibles are an important consideration, especially in such exposures as loading, unloading, and rigging. Smaller deductibles are used for the movement of household furnishings and other property on which small breakage claims can be expected.

ARMORED CAR AND MESSENGER INSURANCE

Armored cars are used extensively for the delivery of money and securities. There are also occasions when banks and investment houses transfer valuable property by messenger, either armed or unarmed, depending on the value of the property. These are similar to the situations covered under mail policies, but armored car and messenger service may be more convenient for short hauls. Such service is used for the transfer of funds within a city and for the delivery of payrolls to large industrial concerns.

Armored car and messenger insurance can be written for the account of the shipper or to cover the liability of the carrier. When the shipper is a financial institution, the coverage can be written as a separate policy or added by endorsement to a mail policy. Frequently a financial institution has a bankers blanket bond that gives protection on shipments by armored car or messenger. However, the institution may need protection for armored car and messenger shipments in excess of the limits provided by the blanket bond. Armored car and messenger is not a filed class of business, even when written in conjunction with registered mail.

Insurance Coverage

Typically, armored car and messenger coverage is provided on an "all-risks" basis, with few exclusions. The employee dishonesty exclusion is absent from some policies, but present in others.

Armored car and messenger policies cover stocks, bonds, coupons, notes, bills of lading, other commercial papers, and documents of value. Insured also are gold, silver, and platinum, coins, paper money, and bullion.

Separate limits of insurance generally apply to property being transported by the armored car, property in the custody of messengers under armed guard, and property in the custody of messengers not under armed guard. Separate limits may also apply to coins and paper money, and property other than coins and paper money, while this property is being transported by the various modes mentioned above. The policy usually excludes any loss on a shipment if the value of the shipment exceeds the limit in the policy, unless the insurer is notified in advance. This provision is considered necessary because the larger the shipment, the greater the temptation to a thief. The insured must be careful to keep shipments within the policy limits or notify the insurer of any excess before the shipment is made.

When written for the account of the shipper, the policy may be designated as excess over an applicable brokers or bankers blanket bond. When written for the account of an armored car and messenger company that requires a high limit of insurance, the policy is often written on a participation basis by more than one insurer.

An armored car and messenger policy may be written with a deductible, the deductible being the amount of the blanket bond. The deductible is ordinarily in excess of $100,000. The same approach may be used if the insured has primary crime insurance covering messenger robbery. (Coverage forms C, D, and H of the ISO commercial crime program all provide coverage for robbery of messengers and armored cars carrying covered property outside the insured premises.)

The premium for an armored car and messenger policy usually is on a flat basis and depends upon the hazards of the operation, the amount of the primary coverage, and the amount of property shipped during the year.

Rating and Underwriting

Rates are based on the hazards of the insured's operations and apply to each $100 of value shipped. When paper money is shipped by aircraft in the custody of a messenger, it is customary to charge an extra rate. Shipments must be reported to the insurance company and premium paid thereon.

It is possible to issue a trip policy either to cover an unusual shipment or for a person or firm that infrequently ships valuables by armored car or messenger. This sort of policy is used at times to cover securities and money when a financial institution is moving to a new location.

Armored car and messenger insurance is a specialty class written by a relatively small number of insurers. Because armored car and messenger policies are tailored to meet insureds' individual needs, the underwriter must know each prospect's methods of doing business in order to prepare a policy giving complete protection. For example, when a bank has a contract to deliver payrolls to its clients, it needs protection to the premises of the consignee. In other cases, the armored car company may take the responsibility for delivery and carry insurance on the shipments, and the bank's policy may cover only to the point at which the armored car company's responsibility begins. Banks with branches need protection for funds being transferred between the branches and the main bank. Securities houses use messengers to deliver securities to their clients. The variations are endless.

MAIL COVERAGE

Property in custody of the United States Postal Service (USPS) can be insured through the purchase of insurance from the USPS. The limits of insurance offered by the USPS, as well as the rates for such insurance, depend on the type of mail service being used. However, mail insurance is also available through commercial insurance companies. Many who are aware of its availability favor the use of commercial insurance because:

- it eliminates the need to stand in line at the post office;
- the cost is frequently lower than that of government insurance;
- the amount of insurance available from the USPS is limited; and
- commercial insurance may provide for faster claim settlements.

Traditionally, commercial insurers have offered several different forms of mail insurance corresponding to different types of mail handled by the USPS: parcel post, first class, registered, certified, and express. Currently, Insurance Services Office offers a single mail coverage form that can be used to insure all of the above types except parcel post. Similarly, registered, certified, and express mail can be insured through forms filed by the American Association of Insurance Services. The ISO mail coverage form is discussed below.

Mail that does not meet eligibility requirements for the filed form is insured on a nonfiled basis. Two common types of nonfiled mail coverage are parcel post insurance and transit cash letter insurance. Both are discussed here as well.

ISO Mail Coverage Form

The filed rules for the ISO mail coverage form apply to first class mail, certified mail, USPS express mail, or registered mail sent by:

- banks, bankers, trust companies, insurance companies, security brokers, and investment corporations;
- other persons, firms, or corporations whose business is mainly of a fiduciary character; and
- corporations acting as security transfer agents or registrars for their own security issues.

Mail coverage for any other person or organization is a nonfiled class of business.

Covered Property The mail coverage form only covers "valuables" of the kind likely to be mailed by those eligible for coverage. When sent by first class mail, certified mail, USPS express mail, or registered mail, the following are covered property:

a. Bonds, stock certificates, certificates of deposit and other securities;
b. Coupons if detached from bonds; and
c. Postage and revenue stamps; postal, express and other money orders; checks, drafts, notes, bills of lading, warehouse receipts and other commercial papers; other documents and papers of value except unsold travelers checks and currency.

The following are also included as covered property when sent by registered mail:

d. Bullion, platinum and other precious metals; and
e. Currency, unsold travelers checks, food stamps, jewelry, watches, precious and semi-precious stones and similar valuable property.

Property of the types specified in (a) through (e) above is covered only if (1) recorded for insurance purposes prior to loss and (2) sent by the type of mail for which a limit of insurance is shown in the policy declarations. To illustrate the second requirement, property sent by registered mail is not covered unless the declarations show a limit of insurance for registered mail. The requirement regarding records is explained in more detail later in this discussion.

When Coverage Applies Property is covered while in the care, custody, or control of a government postal service, and also while in transit to or from the government post office by common carrier or messenger. The form refers to "government postal service" instead of only the United States Postal Service because the policy territory (see below) includes Canada and, in the case of registered mail, the entire world.

Property is covered until it has been:

a. Delivered to the addressee at the address stated on the shipping package;
b. Delivered at the proper address in the event of non-delivery by reason of error in address or removal of addressee; or
c. Returned to the premises of the sender in the event of non-delivery.

Property is not covered while at the premises of any mail-receiving agency.

Covered Perils The mail form insures covered property on the "risks of loss" basis described in Chapter 2. The only exclusions in the form are the governmental action exclusion and the war and military action exclusion (both as discussed in Chapter 2), and an exclusion of any weapon employing atomic fission or fusion or any mine or torpedo. Consequently, the mail form covers an extremely broad scope of perils.

Limits of Insurance There are many different limits that may be shown in the mail declarations, depending on the types of mail used by the insured. Within each of three separate categories (first class and certified mail, USPS express mail, and registered mail) there are separate limits for:

- property in any one shipping package,
- property to any one addressee on any one day,
- property sent between the insured's offices or to its transfer agents, and
- property sent to others than those described above.

In addition, for USPS express mail, separate limits may be shown for non-negotiable securities, detached coupons, and all other covered property. (The coverage form defines non-negotiable securities as "securities that cannot be negotiated or converted to cash by unauthorized persons without resort to forgery." The rate for non-negotiable securities is considerably lower than the rates for negotiable securities and detached coupons.)

For registered mail, there are separate limits for (1) currency, unsold travelers checks, jewelry, watches, precious and semiprecious stones, and similar valuable property, and (2) all other covered property.

Conditions The mail form, like all other ISO commercial inland marine coverage forms, is subject to the provisions of the commercial inland marine conditions form, as discussed in Chapter 2. In addition, there are several conditions included in the mail form itself. These conditions relate to records, valuation, reports and premium, coverage territory, cancellation, duties in the event of loss, loss payment, and other insurance.

Records. One of the most important duties of the insured is to keep accurate records of all mailings of covered property. Each mailing must be recorded prior to loss, and the record must include:

- a description of the property,
- the destination of the property,
- the type of mail used, and
- the value of the property contained in each shipping package covered.

These records are important because they are used to report values at risk to the insurance company and the insurance company uses these reported values as the basis for determining policy premium. The recorded values for covered property are also used in valuing lost or damaged property.

The mail form contains an *errors and oversight extension* that allows for coverage even though the insured may have incorrectly recorded the value of property due to an error or oversight. In such a case, the extension states that the insurer will pay the actual value of the property (subject to the applicable limit of insurance) in the event of its loss. The insured must promptly notify the insurer after discovering any error or oversight and record the proper value.

Sometimes, an error or oversight can result in the value of covered property in one shipping package exceeding the applicable limit of insurance. In that case, the insurer will pay only the proportion of any loss that the applicable limit of insurance bears to the actual value of the property on the date of mailing. If, for example, the limit of insurance applicable to any one shipping package is $20,000, and the insured, because of an oversight, sends $30,000 of jewelry in a single package, the insured will be able to recover only $20,000/$30,000, or two-thirds, of the amount of loss. On a partial loss of $9,000 due to breakage, then, the insured could recover only $6,000.

Valuation. Covered property is valued at its *actual value,* but not less than its market value, *on the date of mailing.* In other words, property is valued at its actual value or its market value, whichever is *greater.*

The insurer agrees to furnish the bond or indemnity necessary to reissue or duplicate covered property after receiving the insured's statement of loss. If the lost property is recovered by its owner after its replacement and is not returned to the insured for cancellation, the insured's rights of recovery against the owner are transferred to the insurance company.

If the insured is required to deliver covered property before the property can be reissued or duplicated, the insurer will pay the cost of equivalent property purchased by the insured on an available market and will also pay loss of actual interest earnings and shipping and insurance charges. If it is impossible for the insured to reissue or duplicate the property or to purchase equivalent property, the insurer will pay the value of the property as of the *date of loss,* along with postage, insurance, and loss of actual interest.

The insurer will pay no more than 125 percent of the value the insured has recorded for bonds, stock certificates, certificates of deposit, and other securities. For all other covered property, the insurer will pay no more than the value the insured has recorded for the property.

For example, suppose that the insured mails securities with a market value of $1,000 and an actual value of $1,100 at the time of mailing, and records a value of $1,000. If the securities are lost in the mail, the insured will be able to recover the full $1,100, since that is the actual value of the securities and it does not exceed 125 percent of the value recorded by the insured.

Reports and Premium. Whatever reporting period is in effect—annual, monthly, or other—is shown in the reporting declarations form. Within thirty days after the end of each reporting period, the insured is required to report to the insurer the total values of all covered property sent during the preceding reporting period. The report must list values separately for each type of property and each type of mail for which a rate is shown in the declarations.

At the beginning of the policy period, the insurer charges a deposit premium. If the policy is written for an annual reporting period, the actual premium (computed using reported values) and the deposit premium are reconciled, and the insured either receives a refund or is charged an additional premium. If the policy is written for any other reporting period, computed premiums are applied to the deposit premium until it is used up. Thereafter, the insured is obligated to pay additional premiums computed during the policy period.

The mail coverage form carries a minimum annual premium that must be paid even if computed premiums are less than the minimum premium.

If mail coverage is cancelled, the insured must report promptly to the insurer the total values of all covered property sent up to the date and time of cancellation. The premium for that period is computed as described above, subject to a requirement that the insured must pay a minimum premium of at least one-twelfth of the minimum annual premium shown in the declarations for each month or part of a month that the coverage was in effect.

Cancellation. In addition to the above provisions regarding cancellation, the mail form contains a cancellation condition that supplements the regular cancellation condition of the commercial inland marine conditions form. This additional condition states that the coverage applies to all mailings of covered property made up to the date and time of cancellation. Thus, as long as property is mailed before the coverage is cancelled, a loss that occurs while such property is in the mail will be covered even if the loss occurs after the policy is cancelled.

Coverage Territory. Property sent by first class mail, certified mail, and USPS express mail is covered "within and between places in the United States, Puerto Rico, Canada, the United States Virgin Islands, and other territories and possessions of the United States." Registered mail is covered "between places anywhere in the world."

Duties in the Event of Loss. In addition to the requirements specified in the commercial inland marine conditions, the insured's statement of loss must also include proof of interest in the property; affidavit of mailing; affidavit of non-receipt by the addressee and, if the insurer requests, by the property owner; and, if applicable, receipts of mailing from any government postal service.

Loss Payment. The insurer promises to make good any covered loss within seven days after reaching agreement with the insured, the entry of final judgment, or the filing of an appraisal award.

Other Insurance. The mail form participates with other applicable insurance or indemnity on a pro rata basis, except in two situations.

- If the loss is a theft committed by employees of the sender or the addressee, the mail form is excess insurance over the amount covered by the other insurance or indemnity, whether it is collectible or not.

- If the loss results from any cause other than theft committed by employees of senders or addressees, and is covered by any blanket bond, the insurer issuing the mail form is "directly and primarily liable for that loss" and will have no recourse against any blanket bond.

Rating The inland marine division of the ISO Commercial Lines Manual shows rates only for shipments (1) within and between places in the United States except to or from Alaska or Hawaii; and (2) within the states of Alaska or Hawaii. The published rates are for limits of insurance up to $250,000 for each shipping package and up to $1,100,000 for any one addressee on any one day. Thus, rates for shipments between other points or for higher limits of insurance are nonfiled, and so are determined by the individual insurance company. The published mail rates apply per $1,000 of value.

Endorsements The ISO mail filing includes four coverage options that can be added to the mail coverage form by endorsements.

Transfer Agents Mail. The mail form can be endorsed to cover first class mail, certified mail, or registered mail sent by the insured while acting as a transfer agent, as a registrar, as a trustee under indentures governing debt securities (except for securities issued by the insured), or in any other agency capacity for the issuer of covered property.

Property covered under the transfer agents mail endorsement includes non-negotiable securities (as defined and limited in the endorsement) and fractional share or script certificates, subscription warrants, rights, and similar certificates in negotiable form, as long as the actual value in any one shipping package does not exceed $150 on the date of mailing. Covered property is insured only against nondelivery, subject to the exclusions of the regular mail form.

Negotiable Securities Sent Under Air Bill. By endorsement, the mail form can be extended to cover loss to negotiable securities sent under air bill of any carrier named in the declarations. Coverage under the endorsement applies only to property sent between places in the United States of America; however, property sent to or from Alaska or Hawaii is not covered. The insured must declare to the carrier the actual value of the property, but not less than its market value on the date the property is sent.

Securities Sent by the United States Treasury. Another coverage extension provides coverage on incoming shipments of securities sent by the United States Treasury Department or any other agency or corporation of the United States government. The endorsement covers shipments to the insured and shipments made to the insured's customers at the insured's direction. The coverage applies only to shipments made by registered mail.

Flat Premium per Shipping Package. The mail coverage form can be endorsed to allow the premium for first class or certified mail to be determined according to the number of packages sent by the insured.

Parcel Post Insurance

Parcel post is used commercially by many firms. In addition to the nationally known mail order houses, many other concerns sell entirely or largely by mail. Some of them handle specialty items not generally available in stores, and others cater to the people who like to purchase from catalogs rather than from store counters. Parcel post is used also by city stores for delivery to their suburban customers. The cost may be less than that of a parcel delivery service, and next-day service by parcel post is available in many areas.

Parcel post is a nonfiled class of business. Although the forms in use are not standardized, they generally track with the conditions of a form that at one time was filed. The following remarks describe that form.

Covered Perils The policy insures a package and its contents against loss or damage from any external cause, including nondelivery, subject to exclusions of war and nuclear reaction. Additional exclusions, expressed as limitations on the scope of property covered, are noted below.

Covered Property The types of property covered must be described specifically in the policy, and the property must be usual to the insured's business. The following types of property are specifically not covered:

1. accounts, bills, currency, deeds, evidences of debt, money, notes, or securities;
2. merchandise shipped on consignment unless shipped in fulfillment of an order or consigned to parties to whom the insured had previously sold merchandise;
3. perishable items, except against loss by fire, theft, pilferage, or nonarrival;
4. packages incorrectly addressed, inadequately packaged, or on which the postage is not fully prepaid;
5. shipment sent to transients at hotels, except sales personnel of the insured, unless sent by registered mail or government insured parcel post;

6. packages bearing descriptive labels, unless such labels are in compliance with the laws of regulatory authorities; and
7. packages not bearing the notation "Return Postage Guaranteed."

The policy covers only while the property is "actually in the custody of" the United States Postal Service (USPS). Frequently parcels are placed in collection boxes, and sometimes they are placed alongside or on top of them. Postal regulations do not require postal employees to pick up mail deposited outside a mail box, although it is a federal offense to steal mail so deposited. An insured that deposits packages outside collection boxes is taking a chance that its parcel post insurance will not cover such packages. Ordinarily, the policy covers only outgoing mail sent by the insured. However, coverage on returned shipments or incoming shipments can be arranged.

Locations Covered Domestic policies limit the coverage to the continental United States and Canada, but coverage on overseas and foreign shipments can be arranged. The policy does not cover while the property is in the hands of the insured's employee or other messenger on its way to the post office.

Occasionally there are requests for a trip parcel post policy to cover the shipment of a single package or group of packages. The premiums on domestic shipments are so small that this is seldom justified, but there are occasions when a trip policy is justified on a foreign shipment. The conditions would be the same for any other parcel post policy except that the individual shipment would be described in the policy in much the same manner as a shipment would be described under a trip transit policy.

Limits of Insurance Policy limits are nominal, perhaps $100 per package shipped by ordinary parcel post or unregistered mail, and $500 per package shipped by USPS-insured parcel post or registered mail. The underwriter has the option to increase these limits. The policy may contain a warranty to the effect that each package shipped by USPS-insured parcel post valued at $100 or less will be insured through the USPS for at least 50 percent of its actual value, and that each package in excess of $100 will be insured with the USPS for not less than $50.

C.O.D. Shipments When property is shipped C.O.D., the charge made by the USPS includes insurance for the full amount to be collected from the addressee, up to a maximum of $500. There is therefore, no need to insure C.O.D. shipments under a parcel post policy unless the C.O.D. amount is less than the value of the package, or the C.O.D. amount (and the policy limit) exceeds $500.

USPS and Commercial Insurance When property insured under a parcel post policy is also insured by the USPS, the USPS and the commercial insurer will apportion the loss in accordance with the following USPS formula:

$$\frac{\text{USPS Insurance or Actual Value (whichever is less)}}{\text{USPS Insurance or Actual Value (whichever is less)} + \text{Total Commercial Insurance or Actual Value (whichever is less)}} \times \begin{array}{c}\text{Actual Value or}\\ \text{Cost of Repairs}\end{array} = \begin{array}{c}\text{USPS}\\ \text{Liability}\end{array}$$

If the private parcel post policy has a deductible, the USPS will pay the full amount of the deductible (if less than the USPS limit of insurance) and then apply the formula to the balance of the remaining loss.

Premium Payment The policy is generally written on a reporting basis, with monthly, quarterly, or annual adjustment. The insured is required to keep a record of each shipment made and report the values shipped at the time interval agreed upon. Monthly and quarterly reporting policies have deposit premiums against which computed premiums are applied. When the deposit premium is used up, additional premiums are charged as the reports are rendered.

The premium on an annual adjustment policy is an estimated premium based on the estimate of annual shipments. It is adjusted when the report of actual shipments is received. Many parcel post policies are written on an "open" or "until cancelled" basis. On rare occasions a flat premium policy is issued.

Underwriting Fragile articles, such as china and glassware, and articles subject to theft, such as tobacco products, clothing, and perfume, pose special risks. No matter what the product, proper packaging is essential. Property insured by the USPS receives preferential treatment during transit and may be considered by underwriters in a more favorable light than property not insured by the USPS.

Rates are applied per $100 of value of shipments and vary considerably according to exposure and the loss experience of the insured. The rates for overseas shipments are sometimes three or four times the rate for domestic shipments. When overseas shipments are insured, a rate schedule showing separate rates for each country is made part of the policy. Underwriters should confirm that the Postal Service maintains parcel post service in each country on the schedule. Shipments to foreign countries should be registered or partially insured by the Postal Service when that service is available.

Transit Cash Letter

A *transit cash letter* is a letter sent by an insured bank to another bank, itemizing by separate amounts all checks, promissory notes, drafts, and similar items which the insured had accepted for deposit, payment, or collection, and which were enclosed with the letter. Insurance coverage provides for these items while they are in transit between the insured bank and the bank on which they had been drawn.

As this is a nonfiled class, there are considerable variations in insuring conditions. Transit may be by any means agreed upon by the insured and the insurance company, and may include coverage until delivery is made at the correct address if there was an error in the original address. Shipments returned to the insured by the addressee may also be covered.

In addition to coverage for property in transit, insurance can be included for loss of a cancelled check after it has been charged to the customer's account, and after a statement purporting to enclose the check has been sent to the customer. Extra expense incurred by the insured in identifying the depositors of lost items, and in assisting depositors to obtain duplicates of lost items, may also be insured.

The insuring agreement may cover loss resulting from nondelivery or be more limited in scope. In addition to an employee dishonesty exclusion, the policy generally excludes any loss sustained directly or indirectly by means of forgery.

Premiums may be collected on any basis selected—prepaid or reporting. One method of annual adjustment is based on "average sendings." An "average sending" is the total of the full face value of all items enclosed with all transit cash letters sent during the prior policy year, divided by the number of banking days during that period.

The limit of insurance in the policy may or may not have a direct relationship to the face amount of the checks and drafts included with the cash letter. Normally, the expense to the insurer will be that of duplicating or replacing the lost item. This procedure is greatly simplified if the insured maintains a photographic record of the item, or a manual record of the amount of each item, the bank on which it was drawn, and the name of the person presenting it.

SUMMARY

This chapter describes the types of insurance used to insure the transportation exposures analyzed in Chapter 3. Transportation insurance can be divided into two kinds: that which insures the shipper's interest in property being transported and that which insures the carrier's liability for loss to property being transported.

Annual transit insurance policies indemnify the owner of property for loss that may occur to property while being carried from one point to another. These policies usually cover property while it is in the custody of others and not under the control of the owner. For several reasons, transfer of liability for loss from the owner to the carrier is not always effective. Transit insurance may be purchased to cover this exposure.

Transit insurance is a nonfiled class of business that may be written on an "all-risks" or a named perils basis. Transit policies generally specify separate limits of insurance for each type of transit used. Major underwriting considerations for transit insurance include the commodity and its susceptibility to loss or damage, modes of transportation and type of carrier, type of bill of lading used and the terms of sale, loss experience of the shipper, distance property will be shipped, type of packing and container used, and the limits of insurance desired.

Motor truck cargo insurance covers the carrier's insurable interest in property being transported by the carrier. Carriers forms of motor truck cargo insurance indemnify the insured (the trucker) for loss or damage resulting from legal liability as a carrier. Owners forms cover only the owner's interest in its own goods. There are some special forms of motor truck cargo insurance for household goods carriers and carloading companies and freight consolidators. The rating and underwriting of motor truck cargo insurance depend largely on the type and quantity of merchandise hauled.

In contrast to annual transit policies, written on a full-term basis, trip transit policies are written to cover a single trip. Trip transit is a nonfiled class. A wide variety of exposures can be insured under trip transit policies.

Armored car and messenger insurance can be written for the account of the shipper or to cover the liability of the carrier. This is not a filed class of business, even when written in conjunction with registered mail. These policies cover stocks, bonds, coupons, notes, bills of lading, other commercial papers, and documents of value. Rates are based on the hazards of the insured's operations.

Although property in the custody of the United States Postal Service can be insured through the purchase of insurance from the USPS, commercial insurers traditionally have offered several different forms of mail insurance. Currently, Insurance Services Office offers a single mail coverage form that can be used to insure first class, registered, certified, and USPS express mail. The mail coverage form only covers valuables of the kind likely to be mailed by those eligible for coverage. Property is covered while in the care, custody, or control of a government postal service and also while in transit to or from the government post office by common carrier or messenger.

Parcel post insurance, a nonfiled class, insures a package and its contents against loss or damage from any external cause, including nondelivery, subject to certain exclusions. Insurance on a transit cash letter provides for checks, drafts, and similar items while in transit between the insured bank and the bank on which they had been drawn.

Chapter Notes

1. Under maritime law, liability for *general average* arises when a cargo owner who has not experienced loss during shipment is required to share in reimbursing the cargo owners who have experienced loss; liability for *salvage charges* arises when cargo owners are required to share expenses incurred in saving the vessel and cargo from impending loss.
2. Starlight Fabrics, Inc. v. Glens Falls Ins. Co., 297 N.Y. 426, 79 N.E. (2d) 812 (1948).
3. Armory Mgf. Co. v. Gulf Cen. & S.F. Ry. Co., 89 Texas 419, 37 S.W. 856 (1896).
4. Harold S. Daynard, *Handbook on Transportation Claims,* rev. ed. (New York: Roberts Publishing Corp., 1972), p. 123.
5. The Inland Marine Underwriters Association from time to time compiles these filing requirements and distributes them to IMUA member companies.

CHAPTER 5

Contractors Equipment Insurance*

INTRODUCTION

In terms of premium volume, contractors equipment is the largest class of commercial inland marine insurance. It far outstrips any other class of inland marine insurance.

Contractors equipment presents a greater diversity of exposures than any other inland marine class. Contracting operations are conducted in a variety of environments—above ground, underground, on water, in quarries, on hillsides, in forests—anywhere that people have seen fit to labor in the pursuit of their particular objectives.

This diversity of environments gives rise to a wide variety of insureds who are eligible for contractors equipment coverage. Road builders, building contractors, excavators, steel erectors, demolition contractors, bridge and tunnel contractors, and dam builders are all prospects. State, county, and municipal agencies having equipment for maintenance, road construction, and snow and trash removal, as well as landscape services, cemetery maintenance services, carpenters, and masons are also eligible. Shipyard contractors and mining and quarrying operations do not exhaust the list. The farmer with a bulldozer who builds ponds or clears land for others might also be included.

Some of the equipment commonly insured under contractors equipment policies includes tractors, cranes, graders, power shovels, forklifts, drills, front-end loaders, backhoes, bulldozers, draglines,

---

* Portions of this chapter are adapted from the American Association of Insurance Services *Inland Marine Guide*, with the permission of AAIS.

concrete mixers, derricks, pile drivers, and similar equipment. Each contracting specialty requires a type of equipment unique to its own operation. The equipment used in road building is quite unlike that used in strip mining, for example. The policy may also cover smaller items of equipment such as air compressors, portable electric generators, hoists, block and tackle, pneumatic tools, cables, chains, and ropes. Wheelbarrows, shovels, picks, and other hand tools may also be covered.

ELIGIBILITY

To be a subject of inland marine insurance, the equipment must, according to the Nation-Wide Marine Definition, be "of a mobile or floating nature." This requirement has been interpreted quite liberally. Seemingly fixed properties such as asphalt mixing plants and stone crushers have been judged eligible for contractors equipment insurance so long as they can be moved to a new location when the need arises.

The distinction between mobile equipment and vehicles designed for highway use is often blurred. Vehicles designed for highway use cannot be covered by an inland marine form under the Nation-Wide Marine Definition. However, the fact that a piece of equipment is mounted on rubber tires and can travel over a highway under its own power does not mean that the item is ineligible for inland marine coverage. The distinction should be based on the item's principal use. If the equipment is principally used to perform the work for which it was designed, at the site to which it is moved, then it is eligible for inland marine coverage regardless of its ability to travel over highways.

The distinction between highway and nonhighway use has resulted in some interesting coverage dichotomies. A truck-mounted cement mixer cannot be covered under an inland marine form unless it can be detached and operated independently from the truck. If the mixer cannot be detached then the mixer and the truck chassis must be considered as a means to transport the cement from one point to another rather than as a tool for use on the job site. Consequently the mixer and the truck to which it is attached must be covered under an automobile policy.

A truck-mounted cherry picker, on the other hand, is eligible for inland marine coverage. The primary purpose of its use is at a job site, even if the job site is actually in or along a roadbed. The truck chassis, however, must be covered under an automobile policy since its primary purpose is to transport the cherry picker.

Truck-mounted portable drilling rigs present a different picture. In this case the truck chassis often becomes a part of the drilling rig or the platform from which the rig operates once the job site is reached.

Consequently, both the truck chassis and the equipment it carries are eligible for inland marine coverage. In this case the truck chassis is designed more for rough terrain rather than highway transit. If the drilling rig is detached from the truck, then the truck chassis should be covered under an automobile form.

POLICY PROVISIONS

Contractors equipment insurance is a nonfiled class, which permits the underwriter to use the rate and policy provisions that best fit the risk. However, most insurance companies have printed forms and endorsements that they use when issuing contractors equipment policies. If these forms and endorsements do not provide the coverage needed to fit the requirements of a particular insured, they can be amended to do so. The discussion that follows describes the provisions typically found in contractors equipment policies. Many variations are possible.

Covered Property

A contractors equipment policy covers the insured against loss or damage to the mobile machinery, tools, and equipment used in the insured's business.

The property may be that of the insured or property of others for which the insured is liable. Many contractors rent or lease equipment from others and are obligated under the terms of the rental or leasing agreement to return the equipment in as good a condition as it was (normal wear and tear excepted) when they took possession of it.

The equipment to be insured can be individually itemized in the policy (scheduled), or written for a single total amount of insurance (blanketed). When property is individually itemized, it is customary to schedule only the higher valued items. If small tools or other lesser valued equipment are to be insured, a blanket amount for these items can be included with the schedule. A limit of insurance on any one item may be made to apply to the blanketed property.

When property is scheduled, each item should be fully described so that there is no question of its identification. Information such as the year, make, model, and serial or motor number should be included with the amount of insurance.

Blanket insurance eliminates the need for a schedule of equipment and is convenient for an insured who has a rapid turnover of equipment. Underwriters will want to see a list of the equipment in existence when the policy is written and may include an annual adjustment provision to adjust for fluctuations in values during the policy term. When written for a blanket amount, the policy usually contains a limitation on the maximum amount applicable to any one item.

When the insured rents or leases equipment from others and is not able to provide a schedule of this equipment, insurance might be provided in a blanket amount, not to exceed a specified limit per item. Under such an arrangement, the insured is ordinarily required to report to the insurer either (1) the cost of hire of the equipment, or (2) the values at risk, at an agreed upon interval—monthly, quarterly, semiannually, or annually.

Scheduled policies usually include an *acquisition clause* which automatically covers newly acquired property up to a specified amount, provided the acquisition is reported to the insurer within the required number of days.

The acquisition clause in scheduled policies generally covers the lesser of a specified dollar amount or a stipulated percentage of the total amount of insurance. For example, newly acquired property might be covered for no more than 25 percent of the total amount of the policy or $50,000, whichever is less.

Acquisition clauses that use the word "acquire" (as in "newly acquired property") cover property purchased by or leased or rented to the insured. If the policy has a separate arrangement for insuring rented or leased property, the acquisition clause could be restricted to newly acquired property that the insured actually *owns.*

Property Not Covered

Following is a list of property exclusions commonly found in contractors equipment policies. A given form may include several, but not necessarily all, of these exclusions. The wording is not standard, and may vary from one form to another.

- *Automobiles, motorcycles, motor trucks, trailers, and semitrailers.* Another version simply excludes "vehicles designed and principally used for highway transportation."
- *Aircraft and watercraft.*
- *Property loaned, leased, or rented to others.* This exclusion expresses the insurer's concern for the safekeeping of insured equipment in the hands of a third party. The underwriter might consider deleting this exclusion upon receipt of satisfactory information concerning the frequency that the property is leased, the reputation of the lessee, and the lessee's responsibility under the lease for loss or damage.

- *Property while waterborne, except while in transit by carriers for hire.* This exclusion recognizes the fact that waterborne exposures require special assessments. The underwriter might consider deleting this exclusion with respect to the entire policy or only for individual pieces of equipment.
- *Property while located underground.* If the underwriter is made aware of any underground exposures and feels they can be insured, the exclusion can be deleted. Policies insuring equipment in underground mines may use a form designed especially for that purpose.
- *Tires or tubes, unless loss is caused by fire, windstorm, or theft or is coincident with other loss or damage insured by the policy.* The exclusion allows limited coverage for property that is prone to vandalism loss. For example, the exclusion would eliminate coverage for an incident of tire slashing that was not "coincident with other loss or damage insured by the policy." If, however, vandals set fire to an entire piece of equipment, the tires would not be excluded.
- *Plans, blueprints, designs, specifications, or similar property.* These types of property are more properly insured under valuable papers and records insurance (Chapter 10).
- *Property intended for, or which has become a part of, any structure.* This exclusion eliminates coverage for property that should be insured under a builders risk policy or an installation floater (Chapter 7).
- *Consumable property such as fuel, grease, oil, asphalt, aggregate, paving materials, building materials, and supplies.*

Covered Perils

Contractors equipment policies are written on either an "all-risks" or a named perils basis. The "all-risks" version generally insures against "all risks of direct physical loss or damage from any external cause" except as excluded. Simplified language policies may omit the word "all." When coverage is on a named perils basis, the following perils are typically insured against. The wording is not standardized, so there are variations among forms.

- fire and lightning;
- windstorm and hail;
- explosion;
- flood (meaning rising of navigable waters);
- earthquake;

- collapse of bridge or culvert;
- theft;
- collision, upset, or overturn;
- perils of the sea as respects covered property on ferries; and
- vandalism or malicious mischief.

Policies designed to insure underground mining equipment often add the following perils:

- slate fall, roof fall, cave-in, landslide, or "squeeze"; and
- strikes, riot, and civil commotion.

"Squeeze" is the pressure of surrounding rock or coal on augers or drill bits used in mining operations, which can break the equipment.

Policies insuring exploratory oil or gas well drilling rigs usually add the peril "blowout or cratering." Blowout is the uncontrolled flow from inside the well of drilling fluid, oil, gas, or water. Cratering is the formation of a basin-like opening around the rig by the erosive action of air, oil, gas, or water. The perils and hazards peculiar to mining and well drilling are discussed in more detail later in this chapter.

Excluded Perils

A contractors equipment policy may contain some, but not necessarily all, of the exclusions listed below. Phraseology and the terms of the exclusions vary from one policy to another.

- *Weight of the load exceeding the manufacturer's rated capacity of the equipment.* The exclusion is enforceable only when the manufacturer's rated capacity for the equipment under the conditions in existence at the time of loss is known. That is not always easy to ascertain.
- *Crane or derrick booms while being operated, unless such loss is directly caused by fire, lightning, hail, windstorm, explosion, riot, riot attending a strike, aircraft, other vehicles, landslide, or overturning of the unit of which it is a part.* The exclusion is worded so as to prevent payment of claims resulting from such causes as metal fatigue, improper operation of the crane, and (if the "weight of the load" exclusion is not a part of the contract) a load too heavy for the equipment. Some versions of the boom damage exclusion apply to booms in excess of a certain number of feet. Other versions preclude payment of a loss unless outriggers or stabilizers are extended to their operating position at the time of loss. There are also variations in specified perils forms in which boom collapse is covered.

- *Mechanical or electrical breakdown or failure.* Sometimes this exclusion is worded to state that breakdown or failure caused by fire, lightning, or explosion is not excluded. Other forms may state that they cover loss by a covered peril that results from the breakdown or failure.
- *Wear and tear, gradual deterioration, rust, dampness of atmosphere, extremes of temperature, inherent vice, or latent defect.* Most inland marine policies exclude these types of loss. The exclusion is sometimes worded so that ensuing loss from specific listed perils is covered.
- *Dishonesty of the insured's employees or others to whom the property is entrusted, other than carriers for hire.* Although most inland marine policies contain an employee dishonesty exclusion, the wording is subject to considerable variation.
- *Unexplained loss, mysterious disappearance, and loss disclosed upon taking inventory.* This type of exclusion, which is described in Chapter 2, is commonly found in "all-risks" policies and named perils policies that cover theft.
- *Any repairing, adjusting, servicing, or maintenance operation unless fire or explosion ensues, and then only for loss by such ensuing fire or explosion.* This exclusion precludes coverage for the type of "business risk" that traditionally has been borne by the insured.
- *War and nuclear hazards.*

Special Exclusions For certain types of operations or locations, special exclusions in addition to the above may need to be added to the policy. Two examples are the brush burning exclusion and the muskeg exclusion.

Brush Burning Exclusion. A contractors equipment policy can be used to cover equipment at land-clearing and land-filling operations, as well as at trash dumps. These risks are often involved with large and ongoing fires to burn up tree stumps and other refuse. The equipment used is often old and subject to breakdown, especially if the equipment is used to move objects onto the fire. For this reason, when the exposure does or might exist, some underwriters will attach a *brush burning exclusion,* which eliminates coverage for loss that results while covered property is used to move brush, trash, or other subjects onto an existing fire.

Muskeg Exclusion. In Alaska and parts of Northern Canada, equipment is often used in remote areas, where it is subject to sinking into the permafrost or muskeg. Consequently, many underwriters exclude loss resulting from:

- breaking through ice;
- subsidence of ice; or
- sinking in permafrost or muskeg.

The exclusion may be added to the policy by endorsement. In that manner it can be made to apply only to those insureds for whom the exposure exists.

Locations Covered

The equipment usually is covered wherever it is located, subject only to the territorial limits of the policy. Territorial limits generally include the continental United States and Canada (sometimes excluding Alaska). Property located outside the United States can, at the option of the underwriter, be covered by endorsement.

Deductibles

Deductibles play an important part in the underwriting of contractors equipment. To the underwriter the proper deductible might make the difference between a profitable and an unprofitable account. As deductibles directly affect the rate, the insured is likewise desirous of striking a satisfactory balance between the premium it pays and the amount of loss retained for its own account.

Deductibles are administered in many ways. A policy may have one deductible that applies to any covered loss, or there may be separate deductibles applying to certain perils or properties. A separate deductible may apply to theft, or to boom damage, or to waterborne equipment, or to augers. The choice of deductible depends on the past experience of the risk; the size, type, and frequency of claims; and the exposures the insurer is assuming.

Deductibles may be a flat amount, such as $100, $1,000, or $2,500, or may be a percentage of the amount of insurance on the item involved in the loss. For example, a deductible might be expressed as: "1 percent of the sum insured, but not less than $1,000 nor more than $5,000."

Deductibles may be made to apply to the adjusted loss before applying the limit of insurance, or to the adjusted loss or limit of insurance, whichever is less. Individual company guidelines will dictate which practice is adopted.

Valuation

It is customary to insure contractors equipment on an actual cash value basis, which takes into account such factors as depreciation and obsolescence. Replacement cost is another option. Before considering replacement cost, or new for old, the underwriter must be sure that the items are actually replaceable. Obsolete equipment is not replaceable per se. The age of the equipment is another factor to consider, as well as the possible moral hazard. Replacement cost provisions are worded so that they are inoperative unless the lost or damaged property is actually repaired or replaced.

Some insurance companies extend policies written on an actual cash value basis to provide replacement cost on partial losses that do not exceed a stipulated percentage of the actual cash value (or insured amount) of the item.

Limit of Insurance

Scheduled policies have a limit of insurance that applies to each item, and sometimes a catastrophe limit that applies to two or more items involved in the same loss. The catastrophe limit might be considerably less than the total of all the scheduled items. For example, a policy with a schedule totaling $10 million might have a catastrophe limit of $5 million. The catastrophe limit protects the insurer in the unlikely event that all the scheduled items are destroyed in a single loss. By avoiding this catastrophe exposure, the insurer is able to offer a rate and policy terms that meet the insured's needs.

Blanket policies might have a catastrophe limit and a separate limit on any one item. For example, a policy written in a blanket amount of $5 million might have a per item limitation of $100,000.

Coinsurance

Policies written for blanket amounts are generally subject to 90 percent or 100 percent coinsurance. Scheduled policies are generally subject to at least 80 percent coinsurance, with the coinsurance provision applying separately to each item scheduled.

Coverage Extensions

Some of the coverage extensions found in contractors equipment policies are as follows:

- *Employees' tools and clothing.* Coverage is generally restricted to a loss occurring to employees' property at the job site, or in transit to the job site in vehicles of the insured. Two limits apply: an aggregate limit per occurrence and a limit per employee. There is usually a separate deductible for this coverage.

- *Debris removal.* This extension provides an additional amount of insurance to pay for removal of debris of covered property that has resulted from an insured loss.
- *Rental reimbursement.* This extension reimburses the insured for the expense of renting substitute equipment to replace covered equipment that has been damaged by a covered peril. The rental must be necessary to continue the normal operation of the insured's business. If idle substitute equipment is available, rental reimbursement coverage will not respond. There is generally a forty-eight or seventy-two hour waiting period before the insurance commences. Some forms have a limit per day as well as an overall limit for the coverage. Other forms limit payment to a specified percentage (e.g., 80 percent) of the actual rental cost. Coverage ends when the damaged property has been repaired or replaced, or the need for it no longer exists, whichever first occurs.
- *Business interruption and extra expense.* When a piece of equipment is damaged or destroyed, time element losses may result. Business interruption insurance indemnifies the insured for lost profits and continuing expenses while the business is shut down or curtailed by a covered cause of loss. Extra expense insurance reimburses the insured for the extra expenses incurred to continue operations after a loss from an insured peril. (See comments on business interruption in the section that follows.)

UNDERWRITING

As said at the outset of this chapter, contractors equipment involves a greater diversity of exposures than any other inland marine class. This diversity results largely from the wide range of operations that use mobile equipment. For example, the physical hazards to which a building contractor's equipment is exposed are vastly different from the physical hazards to which mining equipment is exposed. The underwriting of contractors equipment therefore requires knowledge of the different types of operations that use mobile equipment and the principal perils that threaten the equipment used in each operation.

Other considerations in underwriting contractors equipment include:

- size and value of individual items of equipment;

- type, age, maintenance, supervision, operating characteristics, and protection of equipment;
- experience and accident record of the equipment operators;
- financial status of the insured;
- concentration of equipment;
- past loss history; and
- labor relations.

Types of Operations

Some of the more common types of operations that use mobile equipment are described below, in terms of what equipment is used and what perils are likely to cause loss. Several types of equipment mentioned in the following sections are illustrated in Exhibit 5-1.

Road Building Equipment includes excavators, graders, asphalt and concrete finishers, ditchers, loaders, rollers, scrapers, earth movers, batching and mix plants. Work is generally on a level grade. Principal hazards are fire, theft, vandalism, and upset. If work is performed in mountainous terrain there may be a landslide or overturn exposure. If the insured engages in blasting, equipment may be subject to loss by flying debris or accidental detonation of explosives. Probable maximum loss (PML) is generally low as equipment is usually spread out. There may, however, be a concentration in a storage or repair area. Modern asphalt mixing plants have a large concentration of value in their control systems.

Ground-Level Open-Cut Quarry Operations These are stone or limestone quarries cut into mountains at ground level. Equipment includes crushers, conveyor systems, air compressors, screens, shovels, drills, Euclids, haulers, loaders, and bulk material handling equipment. Principal hazards are landslides, collapse of walls, and explosion. These exposures can be minimized with good supervision.

Strip Mining This is surface mining for copper, coal, or other ore where the overburden (earth and rock covering the ore) is not too thick. Equipment includes draglines, drills, shovels and loaders. Principal hazards are overturn of the equipment and those associated with blasting.

Sub-Level Quarry and Open-Pit Mining Operations Such operations are ordinarily of long duration as the pit evolves slowly through the gradual extraction of the resource being mined. The pit can be quite deep, requiring access roads cut into its sides to reach the bottom. Equipment working at ground level includes screens, crushers, conveyors, loaders, and materials handling equipment. Principal haz-

Exhibit 5-1
Examples of Construction Equipment*

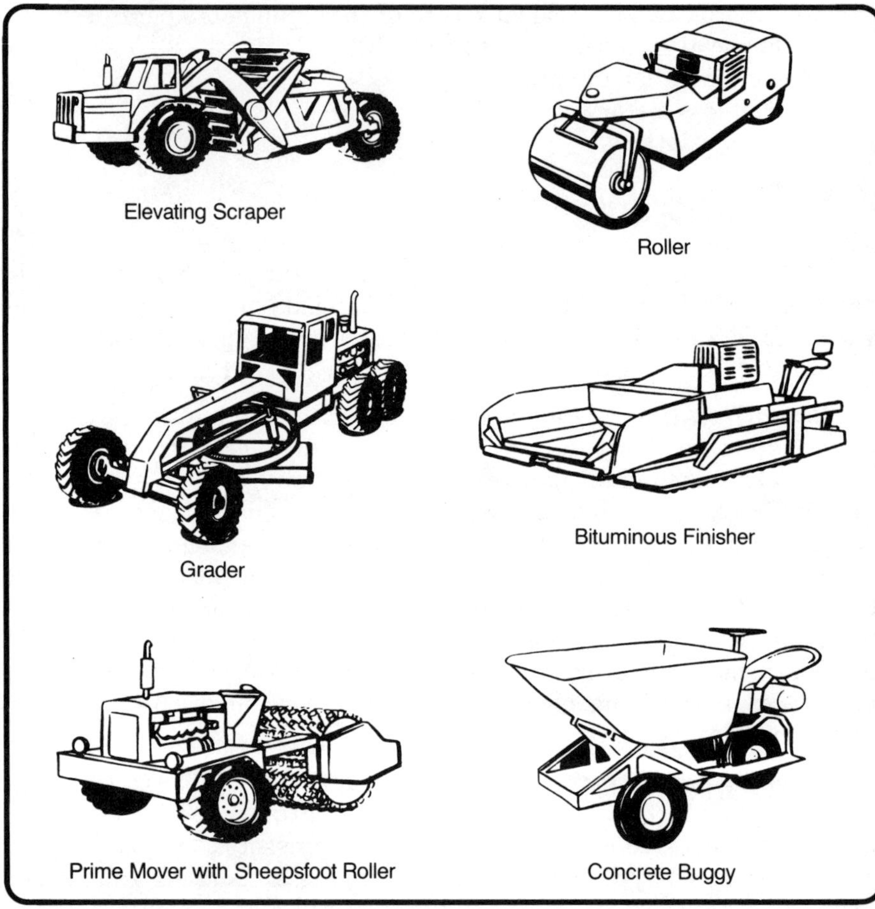

* Reprinted with permission from Associated Equipment Dealers

ards are overturn, falling rock, flooding, and explosion. Equipment on an access road can fall over the side.

Stevedoring Equipment includes forklifts, cherry pickers, gantry cranes, mechanical and hydraulic lifts, and materials-handling equipment. Equipment is generally well maintained. Many operations have a nearby maintenance shop and storage area. Principal hazards are fire and the possibility of the equipment's falling overboard.

Shipyard Operations Equipment includes forklifts, gantry cranes, cherry pickers, mobile cranes, burning and welding units, and locomotive cranes. Principal hazards are fire and windstorm. Shipyards

Exhibit 5-1, Continued

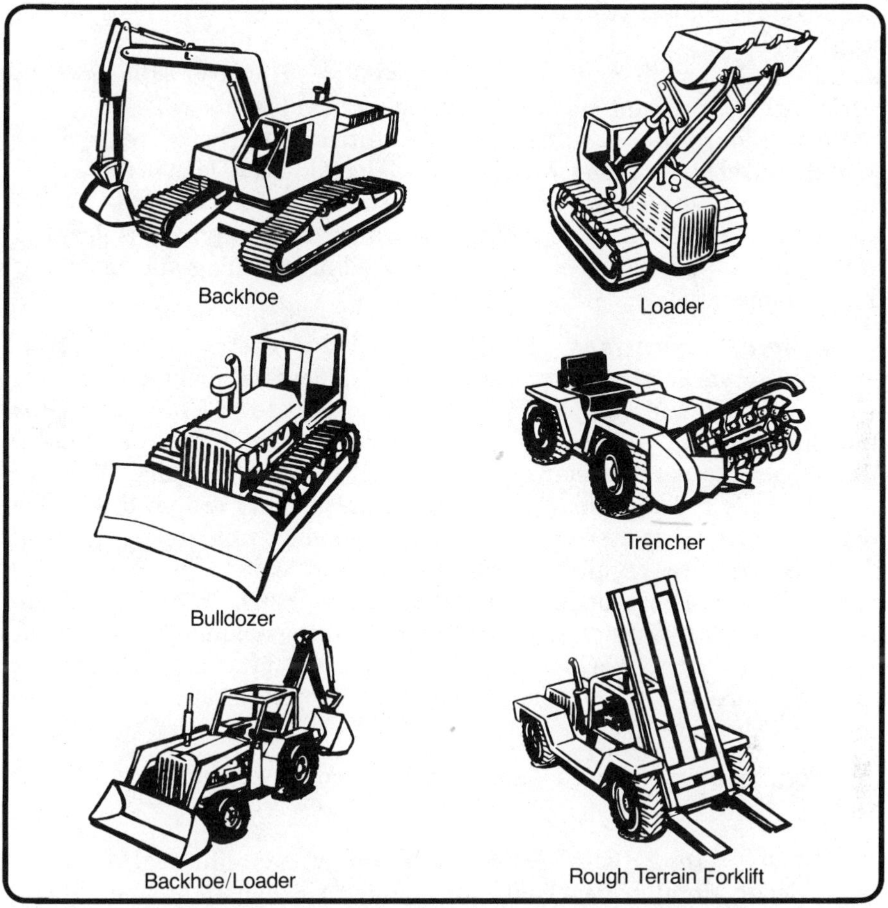

generally have the capacity to make their own repairs. Maintenance of equipment is usually good, as shipyards depend on their equipment to keep operating.

Building Contractors Equipment includes pile drivers, tower cranes, mobile cranes, derricks, and excavators. Hazards are fire, vandalism, windstorm, collision of crane booms with nearby structures, collapse of crane booms from overloading or improper operation of the crane, upset of excavating equipment, and upset of climbing cranes if footing is not secure. Cranes, which are used in many different types of operations, are described in more detail in a later section of this chapter.

Marine Contractors Waterborne equipment, consisting of cranes, compressors, pile drivers, and other pieces of equipment carried on barges, is subject to total loss. A piece of equipment that slips off the barge and sinks to the bottom of a river or other body of water may sustain little or no actual physical damage. However, the cost to retrieve the equipment may exceed its insured value.

An underwriter evaluating substantial waterborne exposures should consider obtaining a survey to determine the seaworthiness of the vessel to which the equipment is attached. Moreover, the underwriter should ascertain the manner in which the equipment is secured to the vessel, and the procedures to be used in installing and removing the equipment.

Logging Operations Equipment includes tractors, graders, tower/yarders, yarders, loaders, and skidders. Towers, or spars, are set with guy lines, and equipped with running lines to "reel in" logs. For downhill yarding, a tower of sixty to ninety feet in length is used. Mobile yarders with shorter spars are used for uphill yarding. Yarders are generally used in mountainous terrain. Skidders are used to move logs in relatively flat terrain. Tractors can skid logs on steeper grades. Hazards are fire resulting from overheated equipment or leaking hydraulic fluid, brush or forest fires, upset, overturn, theft, vandalism, and collapse of towers or spars. PML is often the amount of equipment in one "show" (one working site) that could not be removed from the path of a forest fire. The condition and availability of access roads are key considerations in estimating the PML.

Coal Mining There are three generally recognized grades of coal:

1. *Bituminous* (soft) coal may be either metallurgical or steam coal. Metallurgical coal is used in the production of steel. Steam (high sulphur) coal is used by electric utility plants. Deposits of bituminous coal are found throughout the country.
2. *Lignite* is indigenous to the western states. Strip mining is the method used to mine lignite.
3. *Anthracite* (hard) coal is found principally in eastern Pennsylvania. It has a low volatile content, which reduces the hazard from dust explosions. However, methane gas is present in most anthracite mines. Anthracite is chiefly mined by the room and pillar method (underground mining).

Underground Mining. There are basically three types of underground mines: shaft mines, slope mines, and drift mines. These types are illustrated in Exhibit 5-2.

A mine may have a number of working faces (working areas). The

PML is generally the value of the equipment working at one face. A working unit might consist of a cutter or continuous miner, roof drill, roof bolter, loader, and conveyor. The coal is removed by the cutter or continuous miner, and loaded onto a conveyor belt or placed in shuttle cars.

In some operations, a longwall miner is used. Unlike the continuous miner, which "chews" ever deeper into a coal seam, the longwall miner moves horizontally along the seam, making a long cut along the wall.

Hazards of underground mining are collapse of roof, fire, explosion, and flooding. Bituminous coal dust has a high hydrocarbon content and is very explosive. Hydrocarbon in its gaseous form, methane gas, is odorless, colorless, and highly flammable.

On occasion it is necessary to seal a mine to cut off the supply of oxygen and thereby extinguish a fire. Extinguishing a fire by that method may take six months to accomplish. The cost of sealing a mine can be insured as a coverage extension.

Strip Mining. Strip mining is used for mining coal (or other minerals) located relatively close to the surface of the earth. The method depends on the thickness of the overburden, the contour of the land, and the thickness of the coal seam. In flat terrain, draglines may remove the overburden. If necessary the exposed coal can be loosened by blasting. It is then picked up by shovels and loaded onto trucks. Draglines are not needed for stripping in hilly areas as a side of the hill is generally cut away to expose the coal seam. Bulldozers push blasted rock and earth down the side of the hill. Hazards are fire, overturn, collapse of dragline boom, and blasting. A typical strip mining operation is depicted in Exhibit 5-3.

Auger and Punch-Hole Mining. An auger is a drill that operates from a "bench," or notch cut into a hillside. It removes coal by drilling into a seam and propelling the coal backwards, much like a brace and bit. Augers may have single, twin, or quadruple bores, and can penetrate over 200 feet into a coal seam. The principal hazards are pressure on the bit (squeeze), which may cause it to break; and collapse of the face, called the "highwall," into which the auger is boring. Augers should be removed a sufficient distance from the highwall when they are not in use. This may not always be possible if the bench is too narrow. Narrow benches and narrow, unstable access roads present additional hazards for augers. See Exhibit 5-4.

Punch-hole mining employs a continuous miner that can operate from the same type of bench as an auger. The machine digs into the seam and a conveyor brings out the coal. Continuous miners can penetrate much farther into a coal seam than augers. Continuous miners operated by remote control can penetrate as far as 1,000 feet.

Exhibit 5-2
Three Types of Deep Mines

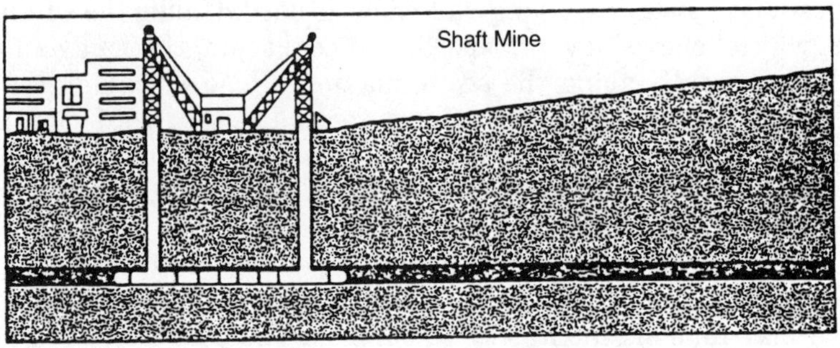

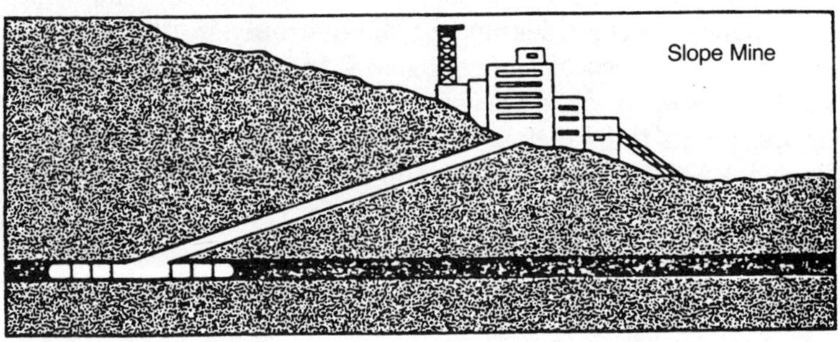

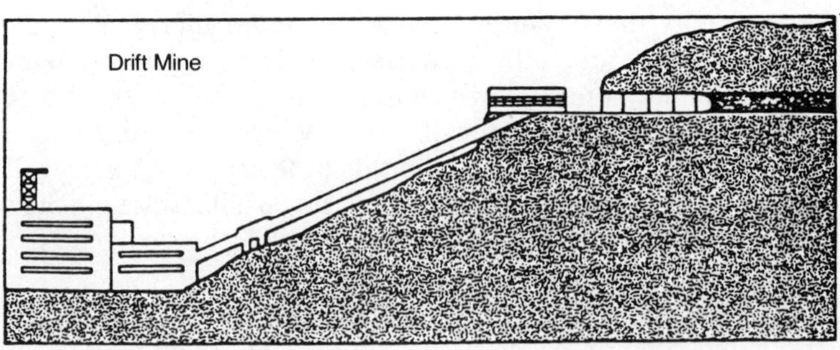

Exhibit 5-3
Typical Strip Mine

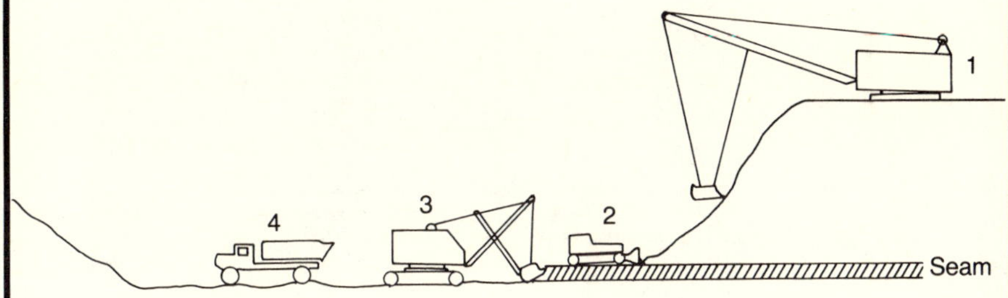

1. Drag line removes overburden which may be a few feet to over 100 feet.
2. Bulldozers remove loose slate and material.
3. Power shovels remove coal. Seam may be 2 feet to 10 feet thick.
4. Dump trucks carry coal to wash plants, crushers, etc.

Oil and Gas Well Exploratory Rigs and Well Servicing Equipment The big exploratory rigs drill the well either to or through the "pay-zone," or producing formation. Two of the major hazards to which this high valued equipment is subject are blowout and cratering. Blowout is the uncontrolled flow from inside the well of drilling fluid, oil, gas or water. Cratering is a basin-like opening formed around the rig by the erosive action of air, oil, gas, or water.

Well servicing, or "workover," units perform several functions. Exploratory rigs generally drill through the pay-zone. This operation, however, may be assigned to a servicing unit, which will "drill-in" and bring in the well. After the exploratory rig has drilled through the pay-zone, a servicing unit may be assigned the task of starting the flow of oil. This might be done by "shooting" the well, by lowering a charge to the pay-zone and setting it off to fracture the formation. Another method is "sand-fracturing." This entails fracturing the formation using a high pressure mixture of oil and sand or water and sand.

Servicing units, however, are mostly used on old existing wells to increase production. The old pipes are pulled and replaced and flow lines

Exhibit 5-4
Correct and Incorrect Uses of Augers

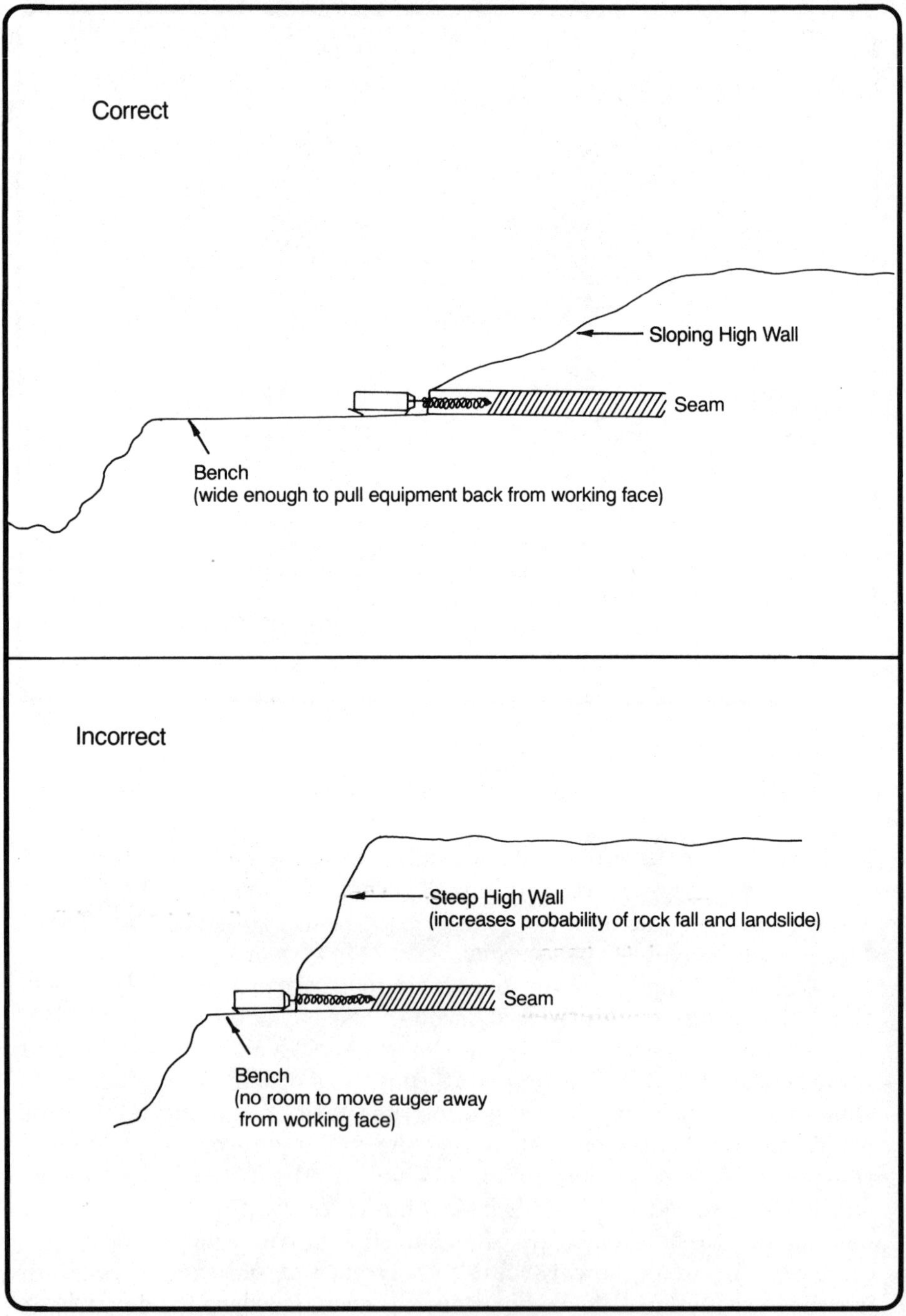

cleaned out. Hot oil units pump oil into the old lines to melt the paraffin and tar that have built up. Sand fracturing is also used on old wells.

A serious hazard facing a hot oil unit is fire. Sand fracturing units may be hooked up in series and may be subject to fire loss by breakage of hoses, especially when oil is in use. The main hazards for other servicing units are windstorm and fire.

Operations Involving Cranes Cranes are used in many different types of operations, including construction, quarrying, strip mining, stevedoring, and shipyard operations. Because of their substantial value and potential for serious loss, cranes are of special interest to the underwriter.

There are many different types of cranes. Some of them are illustrated in Exhibits 5-5, 5-6, and 5-7, and described below.

Overhead Cranes. Overhead cranes travel along fixed overhead rails and are generally used in manufacturing or assembly operations. The chief peril is fire.

Super or Mast Cranes. These cranes have long booms with great potential for collapse. They can be mounted on trucks, crawler treads, or rails. Truck and crawler mast cranes are commonplace at building construction sites.

Gantry Cranes. Gantry cranes are cranes mounted on traveling bridges or spans. The bridge or span is an inverted U-shaped structure that moves on rails. Gantry cranes are usually found at docks or shipyards. Their mobility and height combine to expose them to loss by windstorm. Sudden gusts of sufficient force can topple these cranes where they stand or move them along the rails at such speed that they hit the stops and upset. Proper tie-down procedures in the event of impending windstorm are essential.

Hammerhead or Tower Cranes. These cranes are more in the nature of a derrick than a crane. A derrick has a fixed base, while a crane has a mobile base. The boom of a hammerhead crane is perpendicular to the base structure (parallel to the ground). One end of the boom has a counterweight, so the boom is always under stress.

These cranes are used in building construction, and can either be "climbing" or free standing. Climbing cranes may have a telescoping base that enables them to move up with the building, or have as their base a beam that spans a stairwell or elevator shaft. The beam may rest on newly poured concrete, which could give way under the weight of the crane. Even light winds can affect hammerhead cranes.

Hydraulic Cranes. Hydraulic cranes have telescoping booms to which extensions can be added. They can be mounted on wheels or crawler treads, and have a variety of uses, from dockside work to

Exhibit 5-5
Lampson Transi-Lift® Mobile Crane*

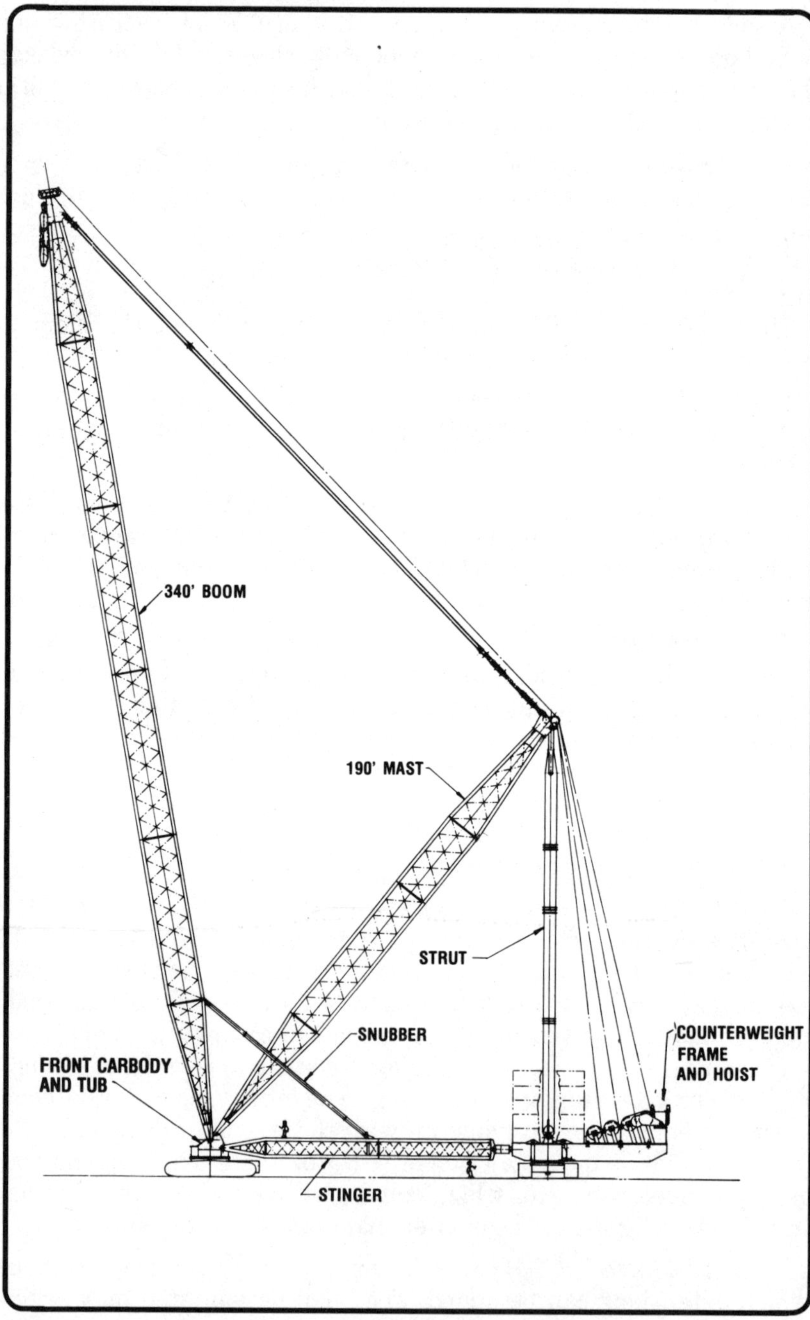

*Reprinted with permission from Neil F. Lampson, Inc., Kennewick, WA.

Exhibit 5-6
Liebherr Hammerhead Tower Crane*

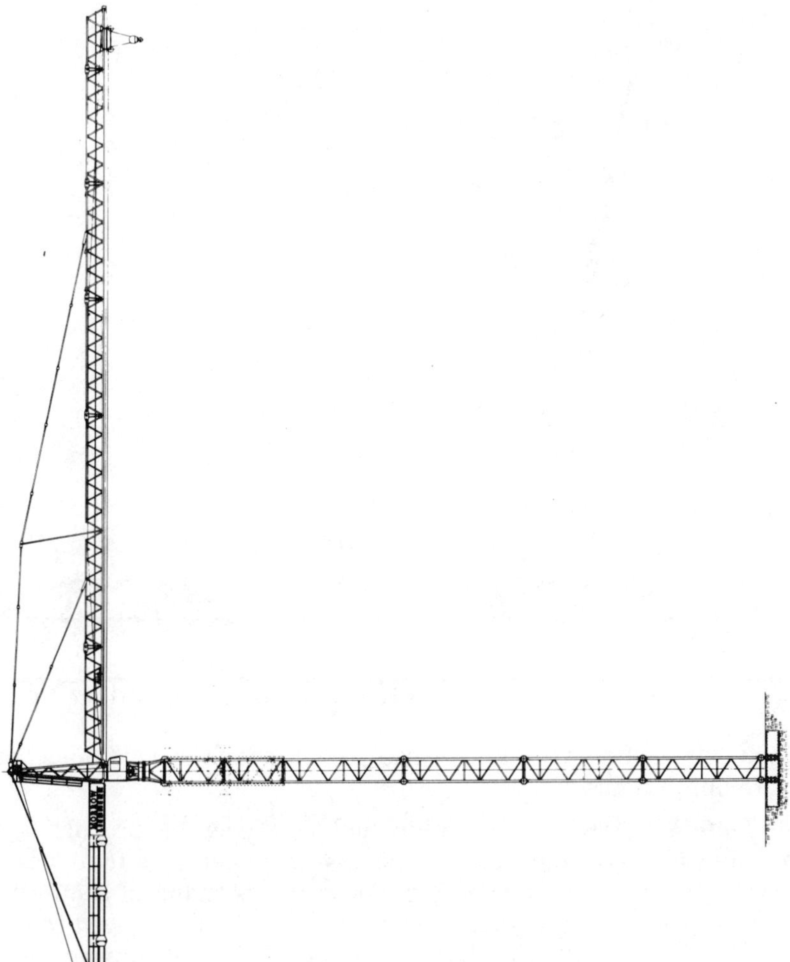

*Reprinted with permission of Morrow Crane Company, Inc., Salem, Oregon.

Exhibit 5-7
Hydraulic Cranes*

* Reprinted with permission from Grove Manufacturing Co., Shady Grove, PA.

construction. Booms can collapse under adverse conditions, or the entire unit can upset.

Boom Collapse. Booms represent a considerable proportion of the value of the crane, and collapsed booms are generally a total loss. Long booms receive a lot of handling. As they are made in sections, they must be erected at the job site and dismantled when moved to another location. If any of the boom members is bent during erection, dismantling, transit, or storage, the structural integrity of the boom will be weakened, and it may fail under a load it could normally bear.

Metal fatigue or weakened cables also contribute to boom collapse. The boom must be lowered below the horizontal to add on more sections. Constantly lifting the boom from this position can contribute to metal fatigue.

Improper operation of the crane is probably the chief cause of boom damage. Bending of the boom can result from bumping it against adjacent structures or allowing the load to swing into it. Damage may also be caused when the boom is in an almost vertical position, in contact with the boom stops, and the load is suddenly released. The suspension cables have some elasticity and will pull back sharply, causing the boom joint to jerk backward. Any sudden movement or stopping of a heavily loaded boom can twist or overload it. If the boom is operated at a high angle and the load is suddenly released, the boom may spring back and fall over the cab. The crane itself may upset, causing the boom to strike the ground. If outriggers or stabilizers are not in use under conditions that call for them, an upset can result. Lifting loads in excess of the lifting capacity of the equipment can also cause boom damage.

Periodic inspections, proper maintenance, and competent operators can minimize the exposure to boom collapse.

Probable Maximum Loss

An important feature in the evaluation of a contractors equipment risk is the determination of the probable maximum loss (PML). Some companies base their net retention on the PML, rather than on the total amount of insurance.

In estimating PML, the concentration of equipment, size of individual items, and the hazard with the potential for greatest loss should be considered. For example, road building equipment might be well spread out in an area where there is little exposure to windstorm. Damage by fire or theft of an individual item may be the key to the PML. If the insured has a storage area with a concentration of equipment, the PML might be the potential loss by fire in that area. The concentration of equipment underground is, of course, critical in the determination of PML for an underground mining risk. High valued items, such as draglines, are often the key to the PML for strip mining risks.

Insurance to Value

One of the major problems facing underwriters of contractors equipment is to determine whether there is adequate insurance to value. The cost of equipment purchased new has skyrocketed. Because new equipment is so expensive, a premium has been placed on used equipment. The value of used equipment has tended to appreciate rather than depreciate. Consequently, it has become difficult for the underwriter when examining a schedule of equipment to determine if the values shown are adequate or not. Many underwriters use the *Green Guide for Construction Equipment* to help determine value adequacy. This guide, published by Nielson/DATAQUEST, Inc., lists current values for construction equipment up to ten years old. Other underwriters also subscribe to various trade journals that publish advertisements for the sale of used equipment. Another good source of information is for the underwriter to develop a rapport with a local equipment dealer.

Many contractors depreciate the values of their equipment very rapidly on a book basis for tax purposes. In some instances, it is this book value that the contractor will give to the insurer for insurance purposes. The lower the values, of course, means the less premium to be paid. Since most contractors equipment losses are partial rather than total, the underwriter, if not careful, may find that a partial loss will result in payment of the full amount scheduled in spite of any coinsurance penalties that may apply.

Business Interruption and Extra Expense

When business interruption coverage is requested as an extension of a contractors equipment policy, the underwriter should ascertain that there are contracts in existence that support the limit of insurance requested. Without these contracts the adjuster would be at a serious disadvantage in determining how much income was lost should the contractor's covered property be damaged by a peril insured against. The contracts supporting the business interruption values should be specific as to amount and duration.

Business interruption, or loss of income as it is called in the simplified property forms, can be written on a single piece of equipment or on an entire schedule.

Single pieces of equipment selected for business interruption coverage are usually key items that are indispensable to the operation of the insured. An asphalt plant owned by a road paver could be such an item. A large dragline is essential to the operation of the strip miner. The underwriter must determine whether these items, or their parts, are readily replaceable, and the length of time it will take to replace a part or the entire machine. Big draglines are usually custom built, and take many months to replace. Apart from replacement, the underwriter must determine if there is any other equipment available to the insured which, if placed in use, could lessen the loss. A reasonable amount of investigative inquiry is necessary to determine the PML for business interruption.

Underwriting loss of income coverage on an underground coal mine requires a review of the production process. Coal is dug at the mine face, brought up through the shaft via the conveyor system, sent on to the preparation plant where it is processed, and then passed out to the loading facility. A serious loss to the conveyor system could completely suspend operations for an indefinite period of time. Coal mines could be shut down by the authorities because of an unsafe condition, or the mine may be sealed to smother a fire.

Extra expense is the additional expense required to continue operations after an insured loss. One form of extra expense, rental reimbursement, has already been mentioned under policy extensions. Extra expense may also be required for a coal company that has a contract with a public utility that would require the coal company to buy coal on the open market to fulfill the contract. There may be instances where both loss of income and extra expenses are involved. Loss of income insurance ordinarily includes coverage for extra expense to the extent that it reduces the ultimate loss.

Rating

The premium for contractors equipment may be developed by applying a rate to the limit of insurance for each individual piece of equipment, or by applying a rate to the limit of insurance for the entire schedule.

The first method is only practical when there is a limited number of items to be insured. When this is the case the underwriter will exercise his or her option to apply a higher rate to the item(s) more susceptible to loss. For example, small tools, which are subject to being lost or stolen, will probably take a substantially higher rate than a bulldozer.

When the underwriter applies one rate to an entire schedule, the type of operation in which the contractor is involved may be a key factor in rate selection. Less hazardous operations will be charged a lower rate than those more prone to loss. Road building is less hazardous than construction or mining. The road building contractor, therefore, will normally have a lower rate for equipment than the construction or mining contractor.

When applying a single rate to an entire schedule, the underwriter may select certain items for individual attention. Cranes and asphalt plants, because of their unique exposures, may be individually rated. Special surcharges may also be applied to waterborne equipment and equipment leased, loaned, or rented to others.

Deductibles play an important role in rate determination. A single deductible may be made to apply to all items. In other instances separate deductibles will be assigned to selected pieces of equipment.

When the insured has been on the insurer's books for a number of years, the loss experience of the account will also be a factor in rating.

LOSS CONTROL

Direct losses incurred for contractors equipment are estimated to be in excess of $1 billion annually. With losses of this magnitude, loss control activities assume a special importance. Contractors, insurers, and underwriters must recognize the importance of and need to establish loss control programs in the areas of management practices, fire prevention, site exposures, transportation, operator practices, and security (theft or vandalism).

Management Practices

An effective loss prevention program requires the establishment of criteria for the selection of qualified employees and the establishment of a loss prevention program involving all personnel. Such a program should involve appropriate monitoring procedures.

A designated individual should be responsible for a formal training program. The training program should establish written operation and maintenance instructions for equipment. The program should train operators in established procedures, verify qualifications of temporary employees, indoctrinate temporary employees in the company's procedures and methods, evaluate operator performance periodically, and maintain records to identify qualified personnel and those not meeting the company's requirements.

A safety program should designate an individual to establish overall safety programs including safety training sessions and emergency drills. This person should review safety procedures and inspect work practices and job site conditions and report all findings in writing to management. Operating instructions and procedures should be posted in a prominent location. The safety program should conduct accident investigations and establish preventive procedures. Methods of complying with insurance company loss control engineering recommendations should be developed. In many cases, a safety incentive award program for employees has been effective.

Equipment maintenance is another vital aspect of management practices. An effective equipment maintenance program should:

1. Designate an individual responsible for the program.
2. Establish preventive maintenance requirements and procedures for all equipment.
3. Inspect equipment regularly and maintain records to monitor compliance with procedures.

4. Establish requirements for qualifications and training of individuals responsible for maintenance.
5. Maintain a current inventory of all equipment to insure the continuation of a proper maintenance program.
6. Provide daily operator check of equipment with feedback to maintenance personnel.
7. Maintain records of equipment operating hours, breakdown, and damage repair to establish machinery history.

Fire Prevention

Fire has caused severe losses in the construction industry through the damage of valuable construction equipment. The loss of use of this equipment for extended periods, necessary to make repairs or to obtain replacements, has delayed contract completion. Often this has resulted in contracts being cancelled, or the incurring of penalties for failure to complete work on schedule.

Following some basic prevention and maintenance practices can reduce the probability of fire damage to equipment.

At the construction site, water for firefighting purposes should be made available as soon as possible. Access for emergency equipment to the site should be provided in the initial stage of site preparation.

Equipment fueling deserves careful attention. The main fuel supply should be stored in an approved, secured tank located on level ground that is remote from work areas. The fuel supply area should have an adequate size fire extinguisher and employees should be instructed to park, shut down, and secure all equipment prior to fueling. Hot engines and catalytic converters should be allowed to cool before fueling. Fuels should be transferred by approved pumps or safety cans where applicable and a continuous ground should be maintained between the pump nozzle and the equipment filler pipe. Reserve fuel should never be stored on equipment, except in an approved fuel tank. Fuel spills should be cleaned up immediately by absorbing compounds or other approved methods.

Special hazards (such as high value items with hazardous characteristics) should be protected by a suitable fixed extinguishing system. When not in use, this equipment should be stored in the open. Brush and other debris should not be allowed to accumulate under or around equipment.

Equipment repair areas should be located away from work, storage and fueling areas, and an adequate number of suitable fire extinguishers should be provided in these areas. Of course, all equipment should be inspected on a regular basis, and worn or damaged electrical wiring, cables, and fuel or hydraulic lines should be repaired or replaced.

Fixed and portable fire extinguishing equipment should be tested and serviced as recommended by the manufacturer. Welding and cutting should not be conducted in areas where combustible storage or flammable vapors are present.

Site Exposures

Contractors' knowledge of site exposure to equipment is often inadequate because of the emphasis on the other, more obvious problems of operator error, fire, theft, and vandalism. While these other problems occur more frequently, none presents greater potential for *catastrophic* loss than site exposure.

Contractors must be aware of the special climatic, geological, and topographical conditions in the areas where they will be working. These conditions vary from job site to job site and require a specific control program designed to handle the problems on each job.

The following recommendations should be considered when designing a program to control site exposures:

1. Store equipment away from flood plains, valleys, narrow passages, gorges, canyons, or other areas subject to flooding.
2. When working in an area subject to flooding, have an emergency plan to remove equipment to a safe location when a flood threatens.
3. Develop a flood salvage plan when work must be undertaken in areas with a very high flood potential.
4. Keep abreast of weather conditions and discontinue operations in weather extremes.
5. Tower cranes should be allowed to swing freely during high wind conditions. Mobile crane booms should be lowered (where possible) or tied off in accordance with manufacturer's instructions to the leeward.
6. Spread out high valued equipment. Where a large number of pieces of equipment are stored in one area, separations should be provided between small groups of equipment to prevent damage and minimize exposure.
7. Do not store equipment adjacent to high-rise buildings under construction, to prevent damage to the equipment from falling debris or materials.
8. Do not store equipment directly below or on the edge of steep cliffs or embankments.

9. Steep cliffs and embankments in work areas should be sloped back or shored up if they are unstable.
10. Determine subsurface conditions, such as quicksand, caverns, old tunnels, sewers, water mains, pipelines, and electrical conduits.
11. Evaluate overhead exposures, such as proximity to airports, powerlines, and bridges.

Transportation

Transportation of equipment is another area of potential loss. Damage in many instances is subtle and does not become apparent until the equipment is placed in operation.

The preparation for transporting equipment is important. For example, before moving a crane the boom section should be dismantled, hoisted, and secured according to the manufacturer's instructions.

A planned route should be used to move equipment. The route should be checked for defective road beds, soft ground, slopes, clearance (overhead and sides), and bridge load limits.

Operator Practices

Careless and unskilled use of equipment is a major source of personal injury, damaged machines, equipment downtime, and lost time generally. The key to loss prevention in this area is verification of skills and monitoring of operations.

Security

Contractors are aware that totally "theftproof" devices or systems cannot be designed to provide absolute protection. However, there are steps that can be taken to deter or minimize loss or damage to equipment by thieves or vandals.

The following list highlights some of the more important practices:

1. Remove keys from unattended machines and lock them in security boxes when closed for business.
2. Install alarm systems in all major pieces of equipment.
3. Attach, secure, and lock all antivandalism and antitheft devices on all machines not protected by alarms.
4. Post warning notices on machines advising that all vehicle identification numbers (VIN) and serial numbers are recorded.
5. Keep storage yards well lighted and fenced.
6. Request police to make frequent area checks when closed.

7. Employ watchmen at storage site and job sites.
8. Immobilize equipment. For example, remove rotor, lower blade or bucket, and remove battery and electric starting systems when equipment is not to be used daily. Lock up at night.
9. Use a hardened steel punch (or etching tool) to duplicate the serial number in at least two places—one obvious and one hidden.
10. Record all serial numbers and identification numbers. Take photos of equipment. Keep an accurate inventory.
11. Secure all shanties and storage buildings at home base and job site with alarm system.
12. Apply for and join the local chapter of the Associated General Contractors of America or their equivalent and request their antitheft and antivandalism literature.

SUMMARY

In terms of premium volume, contractors equipment is the largest class of commercial inland marine insurance and presents a greater diversity of exposures than any other inland marine class. To be a subject of inland marine insurance, the equipment must be "of a mobile or floating nature."

A contractors equipment policy covers the insured against loss or damage to the mobile machinery, tools, and equipment used in the insured's business. The insured equipment can be individually itemized (scheduled) or written for a single total amount of insurance (blanketed).

Contractors equipment policies are written on either an "all-risks" or a named perils basis. The equipment usually is covered wherever it is located, subject only to the territorial limits of the policy.

It is customary to insure contractors equipment on an actual cash value basis, which takes into account such factors as depreciation and obsolescence. Replacement cost is another option.

The underwriting of contractors equipment requires knowledge of the different types of operations that use mobile equipment and the principal perils that threaten the equipment used in each operation. Some of the more common types of operations that use mobile equipment include road building, ground-level open-cut quarry operations, strip mining, sub-level quarry and open-pit mining operations, stevedoring, shipyard operations, building contractors, marine contractors, logging operations, coal mining, oil and gas well exploratory rigs, and operations involving cranes.

An important factor in the evaluation of a contractors equipment risk is the determination of the probable maximum loss (PML). Some companies base their net retention on the PML, rather than on the total amount of insurance. Determining whether there is adequate insurance to value is another important consideration.

When business interruption coverage is requested as an adjunct to a contractors equipment policy, the underwriter should ascertain that there are contracts in existence that support the limit of insurance requested.

The premium for contractors equipment may be developed by applying a rate to the limit of insurance for each individual piece of equipment, or by applying a rate to the limits of insurance for the entire schedule.

Contractors, insurers, and underwriters must recognize the importance of and need to establish loss control programs in the areas of management practices, fire prevention, site exposures, transportation, operator practices, and security.

Chapter Note

1. This material is adapted from "Contractors' Equipment Guide to Loss Prevention," Loss Control Committee, Inland Marine Underwriters Association.

CHAPTER 6

Bailee and Bailor Coverages

INTRODUCTION

This chapter describes inland marine coverages that insure property while in the possession of a bailee, such as a dry cleaner or repair shop, and while in transit to and from the bailee's premises. These coverages fall into two basic categories—*bailee policies* and *bailor policies*—which represent opposite sides of the same coin.

Bailee policies are issued in the name of the bailee. One type of bailee policy is a *bailee liability policy,* which covers only if the bailee is liable for the loss. Another type of bailee policy is a *bailees customers policy,* which covers the property irrespective of the bailee's liability.

Bailor policies are issued in the name of the bailor, the person or organization that owns or otherwise has lawful possession of the property before turning it over to the bailee. Bailor policies, like bailee policies, cover the property while it is in the hands of the bailee and while in transit to and from the bailee. However, bailor policies ordinarily provide no protection for the bailee and so do not relieve the bailee of the need to carry insurance.

The 1976 Nation-Wide Marine Definition allows an inland marine policy to be written on any kind of property in transit to or from and in the custody of a bailee, provided the bailee is not owned, controlled, or operated by the bailor. Moreover, bailee and bailor policies are mostly a nonfiled class. Consequently, there are many different bailee and bailor policies in existence. This chapter examines the more common examples of these policies.

The need for these coverages is rooted in the legal liability that bailees have for property in their possession. Accordingly, this chapter begins with a discussion of that liability.

LIABILITY OF BAILEES[1]

Bailment is the delivery of property by one person to another to be held for some special purpose. The purpose may be the safekeeping of the property, or it may be the performance of some work upon the property. In bailment, title to the property does not change, and there is no intention that the title will change in the future. The parties to the act of bailment are the *bailor,* who is the owner or a person in rightful possession before the bailment, and the *bailee,* who receives the property and is to perform the service.

Bailment ordinarily is distinguished from two other similar situations in which property is turned over to someone other than the person holding legal title.

The first is a conditional sales contract in which the property is turned over to another party, but in this case it is intended that the title will pass to the other party upon the completion of certain conditions, such as the payment of the balance due.

The second situation to be distinguished from bailment is one in which the owner retains some control over the property, as in a master and servant relationship. In a bailment, the owner relinquishes control of the property, and the bailee has entire control of what is done with the property while it is in his or her custody.

Types of Bailment

There are three kinds of bailment. The first is a *gratuitous bailment for the benefit of the bailor,* such as would exist when someone agrees to keep a neighbor's cat or plants while the neighbor is away. There is no compensation involved and the benefit is entirely to the bailor—the owner of the property.

The second kind of bailment is *gratuitous for the benefit of the bailee.* An example of this would be a friend's borrowing a lawn mower. Again there is no payment, but the benefit is entirely to the bailee.

The third type of bailment is a *bailment for hire and for the mutual benefit of both bailee and bailor.* Typical examples are the laundering of clothes, the storage of furs, and the repairing of jewelry. In such cases the bailor receives the benefit of the service performed and the bailee receives the benefit of the charge made for the service. Such bailments are also called *commercial bailments.*

Degree of Care Required

The bailee has certain responsibilities to the bailor for the safety of the property. This responsibility is not clear-cut, and it may vary according to the circumstances. The responsibility of a bailee was described by one court in these words: "... the bailee thereunder was bound to exercise ordinary care of the subject matter of the bailment, and is liable for ordinary negligence. Ordinary care means such care as ordinarily prudent men, as a class, would exercise in caring for their own property under like circumstances. . . ."[2]

Ordinary care varies according to the circumstances and the nature of the property. A bailee who is storing property or performing a service gratuitously would not be required to exercise so high a degree of care as a bailee for hire. A greater degree of care would be required in the storage or handling of expensive jewelry than would be required in the care of ordinary laundry. The bailee must anticipate the hazards to which the property is subject, and exercise care commensurate with the risk. For example, the bailee must take precautions against theft when the nature of the property is such that it is a temptation to thieves.[3]

The care required of a bailee is less than that required of a common carrier. As discussed in Chapter 3, the responsibility of a common carrier is so great and it must exercise such extraordinary care that it becomes virtually an insurer of property in its possession. The bailee, in contrast, is required only to use the care an ordinarily prudent person would exercise under the circumstances in the handling of his or her own property.

The common carrier is liable for loss by fire (except in the rare instance when the carrier can prove that it was an act of God or act of the public enemy), whereas the bailee is responsible for loss by fire only if the bailee has been guilty of negligence. If the bailee can prove that it took all reasonable precautions, that its fire protection equipment was in good order, and that it was in no way responsible for the loss by fire, it is not liable for the loss. On the other hand, it has been held that a dry cleaner was negligent in leaving his truck unguarded during the time garments were stolen from the truck.[4]

Although the bailee must be guilty of negligence for the bailor to collect the value of lost or damaged property, the courts generally have taken the view that the bailor can make a prima facie case of negligence by showing that the property was not returned or that it was returned in damaged condition. This appears reasonable, because the bailor would have little chance of learning what happened to missing property that disappeared while in the hands of a bailee. The bailee is the only one who has a reasonable opportunity to determine the cause of the loss, and ordinarily must show that due care was exercised. The rule has been stated that, "Where property is in the exclusive possession of a bailee for hire and is damaged in a way that ordinarily does not occur without negligence, the burden of proof is upon the bailee to show that the injury was not occasioned by his negligence."[5]

Extension of Bailee's Liability

The liability of a bailee can be extended in several ways. The bailee may agree in an oral or written contract to assume certain additional liabilities. For example, a dry cleaner may assume responsibility for loss by fire and windstorm by so stating in the receipt the bailee gives the bailor when the clothing is received. There is almost no limit to how far the bailee can extend its liability by contract with the bailor.

The bailee may extend its liability by advertisement. It is common practice for laundries and dry cleaners to advertise that they purchase insurance for the benefit of their customers. They also may advertise that they assume certain responsibilities for the safe return of property entrusted to them. The writing of a letter to the bailor concerning the care to be given the property might result in the assumption of additional liability.

In addition to the deliberate extensions of liability just described, the bailee may inadvertently extend its liability by doing something outside or beyond the bailment contract. If the bailment contract provides for the storage of the property in a specific building or location and the bailee stores it in another place, from which it is lost, the bailee may be held strictly liable for the loss, even though the circumstances are such that a bailee ordinarily would not be held liable.

In a case involving loss of a fur coat, the owner had asked the bailee to make certain repairs, and the bailee sent the coat to a subcontractor to make them. The coat was lost while in the hands of the subcontractor. The court held that the sending of the coat to the subcontractor without the knowledge of the bailor terminated the bailment contract, and the bailee was held liable for the value of the coat.[6]

Limiting the Bailee's Liability

It is considered to be against public policy to permit a person to contract away his or her entire liability for negligence. The courts will not sustain a contract in which the bailor agrees to waive all his or her rights against the bailee for negligence.

Many garages attempt to limit their liability by posting signs to the effect that the proprietor is not liable for loss by fire or theft. Such signs are not effective in relieving the proprietor of liability for loss by fire or theft when the proprietor is guilty of negligence. Even a contract assented to by the bailor is of questionable effect when it attempts to relieve the bailee of its entire liability for negligence.

It is possible for the bailee to limit the *amount* of its liability. The one type of restriction that has stood up reasonably well is a limitation on the value of the property. It is common practice in certain types of bailment contracts for the bailor to agree that for the purposes of the contract the value of the property is limited to a specified figure. A higher charge is made when the bailor wishes to have a higher value inserted in the contract. This type of limitation has been held binding on the bailor except in some cases where gross negligence has been proved on the part of the bailee or where the bailment contract has been terminated by some act of the bailee (see the third preceding paragraph). The effect is similar to that of the released bills of lading used by common carriers to limit the amount of their liability in case of loss.

BAILEE COVERAGES

A *bailee liability* policy can be written to cover the loss exposures described above. Typically, the policy covers all sums that the insured becomes legally obligated to pay because of loss to customers' property caused by an insured peril. The costs of defending suits against the insured are also covered.

In theory, a bailee liability policy would seem to be completely adequate with respect to the bailee exposure. If the insured becomes legally obligated to pay for loss to customers' property, the policy will respond as long as loss is caused by a covered peril. If the insured is not held liable for a loss, the policy will not respond. In practice, however, many bailees want to have an additional aspect of coverage on customers' property. This is because bailees face a significant loss exposure in addition to their legal liability for customers' property.

For example, if a dry cleaning plant is destroyed by a fire originating in a neighboring building, the bailee would usually have no legal liability to the customers for loss of their clothing (unless the bailee had extended liability by contract or advertising). It might appear that no loss would be incurred by the bailee. But the public image created by a dry cleaner who failed to make good to the customers for the loss of their clothing might be so bad that the cleaner would be forced out of business.

For certain types of bailees, it has become customary to cover both the legal liability exposure and the loss-of-goodwill exposure through a single policy. This type of policy, called *bailees customers insurance,* covers customers' property while in the insured bailee's custody, whether or not the bailee is legally liable for loss. This is *dual interest insurance,* covering (1) the interest of the business operator because of potential liability for loss or damage to customers' property and (2) the interest of customers in their own property. Two common types of bailees customers policies are the laundry and dry cleaner policy and the furriers customers policy. Both are discussed in detail in this chapter.

While bailees customers coverage is in wide use, warehousemen are still insured on a legal liability basis. Accordingly, this chapter describes the warehousemen's legal liability policy as an example of bailee liability coverage.

A number of miscellaneous bailee coverages are described as well.

Laundries and Dry Cleaners

Insurance on laundries and dry cleaners is perhaps the best known bailee coverage. In fact, in some circles the term bailees customers is synonymous with insurance on laundries and dry cleaners.

The bailees customers insurance policy provides direct coverage against loss or damage from a covered peril to property the insured has accepted for the type of processing described in the policy. Payment of a loss is not dependent on the legal liability of the insured, but any loss from the perils insured against is paid up to the limit in the policy.

Covered Property The property covered is that which the insured accepts from customers for cleaning, renovating, pressing, dyeing, repairing, or laundering. Processing charges that the insured is unable to collect because of a covered loss may be insured also. Many insurance companies have separate policy forms for dry cleaning plants and exclude dry cleaning from their laundry forms. The fire hazard in a dry cleaning plant may be much greater than in a laundry. Underwriters feel that they must have an opportunity to appraise the hazards of dry cleaning on its own merits.

Property held in storage, or property for which a storage charge has been made, is generally excluded. This exclusion is often followed by a statement that property held by the insured without instructions from the owner to hold it in storage will not be considered as being held in storage. Some forms provide that such property will be considered to be in storage after the sixtieth day following the day the property was accepted from the customer.

Covered Perils Most policies insure against direct physical loss or property damage insured caused by specified perils. The covered perils vary from one insurer to another. Some typical perils are:

- fire, lightning, smoke, or explosion;
- windstorm;
- aircraft, including objects falling therefrom, or vehicles;
- vandalism or malicious mischief, strikes, riot, riot attending a strike, or civil commotion;
- burglary (meaning forcible entry of which there is visible evidence) or holdup at scheduled premises;
- collapse of bridges or culverts, or collision, overturn, or derailment of a transporting conveyance;
- theft of property in transit (another version is theft from a fully enclosed and securely locked vehicle);
- sprinkler leakage, including leakage or collapse of sprinkler tanks;
- earthquake or flood (meaning the rising of any natural body of water); and
- confusion of the property resulting from any of the above specified perils.

The explosion coverage differs from that of some inland marine policies in that it is not restricted and includes steam boiler explosion. The windstorm coverage is broad, covering damage from hail, rain, sleet, and snow whether driven by wind or not. The "confusion of goods" peril is intended to cover losses that might result from inability to identify property after it has been in the confusion resulting from a fire or other loss. Flood coverage may be eliminated or restricted if the insured premises are subject to frequent flooding.

Theft coverage (if any) is almost always restricted. Theft of individual pieces or articles is excluded from most laundry policies unless the theft is the result of burglary or robbery. This is to eliminate claims from loss of small pieces as a result of misplacing or employee dishonesty. Most dry cleaning policies and some laundry policies exclude theft of goods left on a vehicle overnight unless the vehicle is locked in the insured's private garage or some other building occupied by the insured. Policies may contain deductible clauses applying to the theft peril, or they may provide that theft from within a vehicle is covered only if the vehicle is locked at the time of the loss and there is visible evidence of forcible entry. This is considered necessary in some cities in order to encourage insureds to lock their trucks in neighborhoods where theft is prevalent.

Some dry cleaning policies and some laundry policies contain a provision that all thefts for which claims are made must be reported to the police. Occasionally an insured is reluctant to report a theft to the police because he or she suspects an employee and does not want to embarrass the employee.

Several of the exclusions in bailees customers policies are specially designed for this type of coverage. Loss or damage that occurs while goods are in the custody of any other laundry or dry cleaner is excluded unless it is specifically covered by endorsement. This exclusion is necessary in order to give the insurance company an opportunity to examine any other locations where goods might be processed.

Although this is a specified perils policy, many insurance companies put in an exclusion applying to loss resulting from misdelivery, careless destruction of goods, or other unaccountable loss when there is no evidence that the loss resulted from one of the perils insured against. This exclusion does not change the terms of the coverage, but it does help make clear to the insured the intent of the coverage, and it avoids many misunderstandings.

Some insurers offer a form covering all risks of direct physical loss of or damage to the insured property from any external cause, except as excluded. Typically, the "all-risks" form contains the following exclusions:

- Theft or pilferage of property left on vehicles overnight, unless locked in the insured's private garage or in a building occupied by the insured.
- Loss or shortage disclosed upon taking inventory.
- Mysterious or unexplained disappearance. (This exclusion and the inventory shortage exclusion are sometimes removed subject to a suitable deductible.)
- Loss, damage, or expense caused by or resulting from any processing, unless fire or explosion ensues, and then coverage applies only for loss, damage, or expense resulting from such fire or explosion.
- Employee dishonesty.
- War and nuclear hazards.
- Wear and tear, inherent vice, gradual deterioration, insects, vermin, dampness of atmosphere, or extremes of temperature.
- Delay, loss of market, loss of use, or interruption of business.

Covered Locations The insured property is covered while in the custody of the insured (1) at the insured's premises, (2) at the premises of the insured's agents or branch stores, and (3) while in the course of transportation. The locations of the insured's premises are specified in most policies. Agents' premises usually are not specified if they are not under the control of the insured. Some policies give seventy-two hours' coverage at unnamed locations owned, rented, or controlled by the insured, in order to give the insured time to report any new locations that may be established.

Limits of Insurance Traditional laundry and dry cleaners forms have a limit of insurance for each location listed in the policy, as well as a limit of insurance for property in transit. In sharp contrast, some insurance companies issue policies containing no limits, stipulating only that the amount paid will not exceed the actual cash value of the property. This is one of the few inland marine policies (and in fact one of the few insurance policies of any kind) in which insurance companies write coverage without specifying a limit in the policy.

A policy without a limit of insurance is desirable from the insured's standpoint because the insured cannot control the total value of goods in custody. A temporary breakdown in the plant may cause goods to pile up and values at risk to increase several times over the normal amount. On the other hand, such an increase in values is a problem to the insurance company and might result in a loss far beyond what the company anticipated. Many insurance companies try to compromise between the two extremes of (1) no limit of insurance and (2) rigid limits on all parts of the coverage. They set a catastrophe limit high enough to cover any loss that can be foreseen and at the same time within the limits of what the company can afford, considering its reinsurance and its own capacity.

Extensions of Coverage Extensions of coverage available through some insurers include:

- expense of debris removal;
- damage to property caused by processing (laundering, bleaching, cleaning, dyeing, or drying);
- damage (except by fire) to buildings owned and occupied by the insured caused by theft; and
- property in storage.

Insurance for property in storage is a common extension of the laundry and dry cleaners form. Usually such coverage is added by endorsement and does not apply to furs or garments trimmed with fur. Fur garments may be insured under another type of bailee policy, the furriers customers policy (discussed later in this chapter). Coverage applies only to property for which a storage charge has been made and, under some policies, to property not specifically accepted for storage but held by the insured for a period of sixty days or more. When coverage for storage is added to a stated limit policy, a separate limit usually applies to the storage feature.

Premium Payments Laundry and dry cleaners policies can be written for a flat annual premium, or on a gross receipts reporting basis. Receipts may be reported monthly, quarterly, or annually. No-limit policies are usually written on a reporting basis.

Many policies are written on a continuous basis, with the premium payable monthly. The premium is based upon the gross receipts of the insured, and the rate is expressed in cents or dollars per $100 of gross receipts. The insured is obliged to keep an accurate record of the gross receipts and report them to the company. Uncollected gross receipts must be reported because the work they represent has been done and the gross receipts are intended to serve as a measure of the amount of processing the plant has done. Many insurance companies include a full value reporting clause in their policies. A typical clause reads:

> Liability under this policy shall not in any case exceed that proportion of any loss hereunder which the last reported gross receipts bear to the actual gross receipts for the period included in the said last report.

In the absence of such a clause the insurance company would be liable for the full loss even though the insured was underreporting, unless the insurer could prove fraud in the reporting by the insured.

Rug and Carpet Cleaners Form Policies covering rug and carpet cleaners are similar in conditions to those covering laundries and dry cleaners. They do, however, differ in at least one respect. Rug and carpet cleaner policies invariably contain a limitation of value per square foot of rug or carpet. There is usually a dollar amount for domestic rugs and carpets and a separate amount for foreign rugs and carpets. These limits may be increased, when the need arises, at the underwriter's discretion.

Rating Laundry and dry cleaning policies do not contain a coinsurance clause. This omission is understandable in a no-limit policy, as it could not be applied. It is omitted in stated limit policies because of the difficulty in accurately establishing the value at risk. Underwriters, however, require a reasonable estimate of the value at risk in order to evaluate their need for obtaining reinsurance. They also need it for rating purposes.

There are many different methods for calculating a bailees customers rate, but certain basic ideas prevail in all of them. The first problem is to determine the value of the customers' goods for which the insured may be required to pay. Perhaps the easiest way to determine the value at risk is to inspect the premises to see how many garments it can hold. Another method uses the insured's gross receipts. Fortunately there seems to be a fairly constant relationship between the value of the average laundry bundle or dry cleaning package and the charge made for it. This will vary among different sections of the country, and even among sections of a city, depending upon the wealth of the community, but the relationship stays reasonably constant within these limits. Many underwriters figure that laundry and dry cleaning bundles are worth from twenty to thirty times the processing charge. The value of a dry cleaning bundle may average a little higher than that of a laundry bundle in proportion to the processing charge.

The underwriter is able to calculate the total value of the goods that go through an insured's plant in a year by multiplying the annual gross receipts by 20 or 30 (depending upon consultation with launderers and dry cleaners in that part of the country). The next step is to determine how much of this value may be in the plant at any one time. Underwriters find out from each plant operator how long it takes to process the average bundle. If the average time is 5 days, in 365 days the plant will have 73 complete turnovers of goods. The total value of the goods in a year's time should then be divided by 73 to get the average amount in the plant at any one time. The figure will fluctuate up and down with holidays and with the seasons. The longer the time for processing, the higher will be the average value in the plant at one time.

The basic factor in the rate is the fire insurance premium for the average value in the plant. To this is added a loading for burglary, theft (if covered), robbery, transportation, and any other peril covered by the policy. The ultimate measure of proper rating is whether each laundry or dry cleaning plant is producing enough premium to take care of all its regular losses plus enough to help pay for the occasional large fire loss among such plants. The premium produced by the loading must take care of the recurring losses, and the fire portion of the premium must go toward the fire losses of all insured plants of this class.

Underwriting A principal underwriting problem in connection with laundry and dry cleaning plants is the threat of a large loss by fire. Inspection by a fire protection engineer is desirable, and the amount of liability accepted should be set at a figure no higher than would be accepted for a comparable fire policy. Automatic sprinklers, fire alarms, watchman service, and fire resistive buildings are all desirable features.

The fire insurance rate is intended to measure the fire hazard, but there are many features in the management of a property that cannot be measured on schedules. Dry cleaning plants using flammable solvents are particularly susceptible to fire losses. Most dry cleaners no longer use the volatile solvents, such as naptha and benzene, which were of such concern to underwriters. Perchlorethylene and other nonflammable solvents are more common today, although Stoddard-type solvents, which have properties similar to kerosene, are still in evidence. The fire hazard may be reduced by good housekeeping, particularly with respect to laundries, which can be subject to accumulations of lint. Other precautions include placing pilot lights on electric irons (to make it easier to tell when they are on), properly grounding cleaning equipment, and maintaining cleaning equipment in a separate, fire-protected room. The degree of premises burglary protection required will depend on individual circumstances. In some areas dead-bolt locks may be sufficient. In others, bars on windows or an alarm system may be indicated.

The theft problem is examined in regard to the probability of recurrent losses from delivery trucks. In the larger cities an unattended truck is likely to have the contents stolen unless it is securely locked whenever the driver is not present. Many insurance companies recommend that their insureds equip their trucks with snap locks that lock automatically when the doors are closed. The drivers are provided with long key chains that make it easy for them to open the doors. It has been found that drivers will not use the locks on the trucks unless it is convenient for them to do so.

A comprehensive application form is desirable for the agent's use in submitting a bailees customers proposal to the company. Inspection of the plant includes a check of the insured's gross receipts to make certain they are being reported correctly. Policies usually give the insurance company the right to audit the insured's books. Many insureds do not understand that all their receipts must be reported. It is much better to have an inspector or auditor point out the correct method in advance of a loss, rather than to have the deficiency interfere with a loss settlement.

Furriers Customers Insurance

The furriers customers policy provides a special form of bailees customers coverage. The customs of the fur business and the coverages required are different from those of laundries and dry cleaning plants and require special treatment.

Furs are extremely susceptible to moth damage, and it is difficult to protect them at home. Coincidentally with the increase in the sale of furs, there developed a large business in the storage of them during the months when they are not in use. Many storage warehouses are refrigerated to a temperature too low for moths to remain active, and other warehouses are fumigated so that all moth life is killed.

The Furrier's Liability as a Bailee The furrier who accepts goods for storage and the warehouse that stores furs are bailees, and they are responsible for the safekeeping of the property in their possession to the same extent as any other bailee. As in the case of laundry and dry cleaning customers, the owners of fur garments have come to expect the furrier to make good any loss, regardless of liability. There is the same need for a bailees customers insurance policy as in other cases of bailees' servicing the personal property of their customers.

There are two important ways in which the insurance of the furrier's liability differs from the insurance of laundries and dry cleaning plants.

The first is in the breadth of the coverage. Owners of fur garments have come to expect broad coverage. Furriers are forced by the competition of the coverage furnished under individual fur coat insurance policies to provide an equally broad coverage for their customers.

The second difference is brought about by the custom in the fur storage business of issuing for each garment a receipt in which the value of the garment is stated. It is a condition of the policy that the customer be given a receipt indicating that insurance has been effected for the benefit of the customer to cover against loss by fire and theft. The receipt must list each article with its individual value and must state that the amount shown is the extent of the insured's liability for loss or damage.

Insurance Coverage Although ISO withdrew its filings for furriers customers coverage in the mid-1980s, AAIS still maintains service on this class. The discussion that follows is based largely on AAIS furriers customers filings.

Covered Property The insured may be a furrier, bank, store, laundry, cleaner, general warehouseman, fur warehouseman, cold storage warehouseman, or other bailee. Coverage is not restricted to furs in storage. The furriers customers *custody rider* attached to the policy describes the property "owned by or under contract of sale to customers" as:

a. Furs and garments trimmed with fur accepted by the named insured for storage, alterations, repairing, cleaning or remodeling;
b. Other garments, textile and similar articles customarily accepted for storage by garment stores, provided such property is accepted by the named insured for storage.

In practice, most of the articles covered are fur garments or garments trimmed with fur. However, cloth garments are covered also when the customer so desires. Only the property of customers is insured, and there is no coverage on the property of the insured. The stock of merchandise of the insured is not covered, and the furriers customers policy cannot be extended to cover it. If the insured desires a similar coverage on its stock of furs, a furriers block policy (see Chapter 9) can be purchased.

Covered Perils The policy insures against "all risks" of loss or damage to the insured property, including the insured's legal liability for such loss. The policy does not cover:

a. Against loss or damage occasioned by gradual deterioration, insect, vermin or inherent vice, or by processing or any work upon the property unless caused by fire or explosion;
b. Liability assumed by the named Insured under any agreement, express or implied, (1) to guarantee the results of processing or any work to be performed upon the property, or (2) to effect insurance upon such property in any amount except as provided herein;
c. Any amount of loss or damage on account of which the named Insured, in the absence of this insurance, would be entitled to indemnity under any applicable fidelity bond or similar undertaking.

The usual war and nuclear hazard exclusions are present as well.

Locations Covered Coverage applies while the property is at locations within, or is in transit within and between, the states of the United States, the District of Columbia, Puerto Rico, and Canada. For those insured bailees who do not have their own storage facilities, coverage applies while the property is temporarily on their premises, while in transit to the storage warehouse, and while in storage. This means that if the property has to be shipped to another location for storage, repair, cleaning, or delivery to the customer, it still is covered by the policy as long as the insured is responsible for it and it is within the territory specified.

Limits of Insurance Limits of insurance are set out carefully and clearly. The clause covering this point calls attention to the fact that premiums are to be paid on the basis of the aggregate amount of values set forth in all the receipts, but the clause also states that the limits of insurance shall apply even if the aggregate of the values stored should exceed the limits.

Specific dollar limits are set forth applying to (1) the aggregate amount for which the company shall be liable in any one casualty, (2) storage enclosures at specified premises, (3) locations outside storage enclosures at the storage premises, (4) other premises not used for storage purposes, (5) any other unnamed premises, and (6) property in transit.

The general clause on limitation of liability states that the insurer shall not be liable for more than (1) the amount stipulated in the storage receipt, (2) the actual cash value, or (3) the cost of repair with materials of like kind and quality, whichever is least. These limitations are all considered necessary because the values of fur garments are high. The total values can pyramid so rapidly that the insurer must be notified when the amount at risk goes beyond the point for which reinsurance has been arranged. It is unlikely that any insurance company would be willing to issue an unlimited policy covering furs as some insurers do for laundries and dry cleaners.

Conditions The conditions of the policy include the terms that must appear on each storage receipt. Each receipt (other than a temporary or interim receipt) given to customers shall in effect provide that:

(a) The customer accepts the receipt as correct in all respects unless the customer notifies the named Insured in writing within ten days after the date of issue thereof of any error or irregularity therein;
(b) The named Insured will have effected for the benefit of the customer insurance on each article listed in the receipt which shall, in terms usual to such insurance, cover against loss by fire and theft for the value set opposite each item, which value shall also be stated to be the limit of the named Insured's liability for any loss of or damage to said article;
(c) The provisions of the receipt shall inure to the benefit of the Company to the same extent that they inure to the benefit of the named Insured;
(d) The provisions of the receipt shall not extend in kind or amount the insurance provided by the policy;
(e) It supersedes any temporary or interim receipt given by the named Insured.

The conditions also state that the insured bailee shall use due diligence in maintaining, during the policy period, the protective safeguards which were stated in the proposal to be in effect at the inception of the policy. This is important because many fur storage premises are protected by burglar alarms, sprinkler systems, or watchman service. Rates and underwriting are based upon the presence of these devices, and the insurance company must be notified if any of them are discontinued.

The insured bailee is required to keep an accurate record of all receipts issued. The record must show the customer's name and address, a description of the property, the declared value, and the location of the property.

The insurance company reserves the right to adjust a loss with the owner of the property. If legal action is taken against the insured to enforce a claim, the company reserves the right to conduct the defense in behalf of the insured.

Certificates Rules for the class permit the insured to issue certificates of insurance to its customers. These certificates are, in effect, personal fur policies that provide "all-risks" coverage for the fur garment, whether it is in or out of storage. The term is one year. The premium for a certificate is generally less than the premium for insuring the same garment under a personal articles floater. This seems reasonable as the insured has already paid a premium for the garment while it is in storage.

Before certificates can be issued, an endorsement giving this privilege must be attached to the policy. The terms of the endorsement, as well as the conditions of the certificate, vary in accordance with the requirements of the individual state insurance departments. Some states require that the amount of insurance on the certificate not exceed the insured's estimate of the value of the article at the time of issuance. Other states require that the amount of insurance on the certificate not exceed the amount stated in the storage receipt. Requirements vary, as well, with respect to the premium shown on the certificate. Some states require that separate charges be shown for the certificate and for storage. Other states do not require this separation. The certificates must be countersigned in accordance with the state countersignature laws. Copies of each certificate issued are sent to the insurance company. In the event that a certificate is to be canceled by the company, an individual notice of cancellation must be sent to the certificate holder. Cancellation of the basic policy does not effect cancellation of certificates.

Excess Legal Liability The furriers customers policy covers the legal liability of the insured and the interest of the owner only up to the amount stipulated in the storage receipt given by the furrier to the owner. However, the furrier may be liable for the full value of the garment (in spite of the limitation in the receipt) if the owner can prove that the furrier has been grossly negligent or has performed some act that is tantamount to conversion. Even if the owner has other insurance to indemnify for the loss, the other insurance company is likely to sue for its loss if it appears that the furrier can be proved liable. This potential liability of the furrier above the values stated in the receipts is called *excess legal liability,* and it can be insured against by an endorsement to the policy.

There are two forms of this endorsement covering excess legal liability. The first (endorsement A) is issued to cover the liability in connection with garments for which the insured has issued receipts to garment owners. The other endorsement (endorsement B) is used to cover the bailee who stores garments for other bailees. For example, many cold storage warehouses, in addition to storing garments for individual fur owners, also rent out space to furriers and other storers who do not have storage facilities of their own. These bailees might be held liable for loss to the bailee, or to the owner of the garment, or to the owner's insurance company. Both endorsements might be attached to a policy that covers a storage warehouse doing both a retail and a wholesale fur storage business.

Other provisions of the two excess legal liability endorsements are the same. Both cover any loss that the insured is obligated to pay because of direct loss or damage in excess of the amount stated in the receipt to property covered by the policy. The exclusions are few and refer to liability assumed by the insured, war damage, nuclear damage, loss due to gradual deterioration, insect, vermin, inherent vice, or by processing or any work upon the property unless caused by fire or explosion. The exclusions are similar to those in the policy to which the endorsement is attached.

The insured is obligated to notify the insurance company as soon as practicable when it appears that an excess legal liability claim may be presented, and he or she must cooperate with the company in settling or defending the claim. The company has the right to defend or compromise the claim at its sole option.

Two limits of insurance appear on the excess legal liability endorsement. The first is a limit per article, and the second limits the amount the company is obliged to pay as a result of any one accident, casualty, or event.

An extra premium is charged for the excess legal liability endorsement. This premium is a percentage of the policy premium. The percentage varies with the relationship between the limit in the excess legal liability endorsement and the aggregate of declared values in the storage premises of the insured.

It is important for the insured to carry excess legal liability coverage. Many customers declare their garments for less than the actual value, either to save on storage charges or because they have other insurance. In case the insured is liable for loss above the declared values, he or she would have to pay the excess amount unless the legal liability endorsement was attached to the policy.

Accrued Storage or Service Charges The policy may be extended to cover the loss of accrued storage and service charges that are unpaid and rendered uncollectible from customers, or are prepaid but required to be refunded to customers by reason of a loss resulting in payment under the policy. A separate amount of insurance is provided for this endorsement.

Premium Payments The basic policy is a reporting form that requires the insured to report monthly the aggregate amount of values set forth in all outstanding receipts as of the last day of the preceding month. Earned premiums are then applied against an agreed upon deposit.

The policy may be amended by endorsement to apply on a

nonreporting basis. AAIS rules allow the nonreporting endorsement to be used only if the amount of coverage is not more than $500,000 and does not exceed the highest monthly value indicated by storage receipts for the past year. In addition, the endorsement may not be added to policies that allow the insured to issue certificates or that include excess legal liability coverage applying to property of customers of other furriers or bailees (endorsement B).

Accrued storage or service charges coverage may be on a reporting or nonreporting basis.

Rating and Underwriting Insurers that are members of AAIS may submit their applications for furriers customers coverage to AAIS for rating. Non-AAIS members rate their own policies.

Typically, a completed proposal is required for the rating process. The proposal requests such information as the locations used for storage, the peak values during the preceding twelve months, loss experience, limits of insurance required, and optional extensions requested. A separate form, entitled Description of Storage Enclosure and Location, must accompany the proposal. This form requests information concerning the construction of the building housing the storage enclosure, and detailed information concerning the burglary protection at the premises and the construction of the storage enclosure.

Underwriting a furriers customers policy requires an analysis of the exposures from the time the garment is first accepted from the customer until the time it is returned. The transit exposure becomes apparent if the insured has a pickup and delivery service or does not store the garments on its own premises and must transport them to the storage warehouse. Suitable locks or alarms on each vehicle will minimize the chance of loss.

Garments are exposed to loss by fire and theft while at the insured's premises awaiting delivery to the storage warehouse. Care must be taken not to mingle property accepted for storage with stock for sale. The store should be arranged so that only employees have access to the areas where the property to be stored is located.

The major concentration of value is in the storage enclosures. This may range from a nominal amount for a bailee that stores on its own premises to millions of dollars at risk in a storage warehouse.

Fur vaults that house substantial values in furs should be suitably protected against fire and burglary. With respect to the fire exposure, the vault should be constructed to maintain its integrity against fire even though the surrounding building is destroyed. Walls should be thick enough to withstand a severe fire. All openings should be equipped with fire doors. Automatic sprinklers, connected to a central station alarm, are desirable. Carbon dioxide systems, which will flood the vault in the event of fire, are an alternative to sprinklers.

Central station burglar alarms protecting all openings, as well as walls, floors and ceilings, provide substantial protection against theft. Other protective devices include electronic surveillance equipment that can detect any movement within the vault. Watchmen who record regularly on a watchman's clock can minimize or prevent both fire and burglary losses.

Warehousemen's Legal Liability

Warehousemen's legal liability was sanctioned as an inland marine class of business by the 1976 Nation-Wide Marine Definition. It is not to be confused with the storage coverage provided by motor truck cargo policies, which is normally restricted to storage incidental to transit. Some carriers maintain two policies for their warehouse exposures—a motor truck cargo policy to cover property held over during transit, and a warehousemen's legal liability policy to cover the pure warehousing risk.

The Warehouseman's Liability Unlike launderers and dry cleaners, warehousemen are insured only for loss for which they are legally liable. As a bailee, a warehouseman is liable for loss caused by its negligence. The burden of proof to show an absence of negligence is on the shoulders of the bailee. Coverage for defense costs is therefore an important part of the policy.

The warehouseman may limit the amount of its liability for negligence. Section 7-204 of the Uniform Commercial Code states:

> Damages may be limited by a term in the warehouse receipt or storage agreement limiting the amount of liability in case of loss or damage, and setting forth a specific liability per article or item, or value per unit of weight, beyond which the warehouseman shall not be liable.

The warehouseman, however, can extend this liability. The above quotation from the Uniform Commercial Code continues as follows:

> ... provided, however, that such liability may ... be increased on part or all of the goods thereunder, in which event increased rates may be charged based on such increased valuation, but that no such increase shall be permitted contrary to a lawful limitation of liability contained in the warehouseman's tariff, if any.

One agreement that limits liability, excerpted from a warehouse receipt, reads as follows:

> The liability of the warehouseman as to each package stored is limited to the actual value of each package, but not to exceed 500 times the

> amount of the base monthly storage rate per package stored unless the warehouseman is specifically notified by the storer of a higher valuation per package, in which event the base monthly storage rate will be one-fifth of one percent (1/5 of 1%) of the declared value. Such notification shall be in writing and shall be sent by registered mail or in person. The declaration of higher value and payment of extra charge shall increase the maximum liability for the warehouse per package not to exceed the actual value per package.... In no case shall the liability be extended to include any loss of profit.

This receipt limits the warehouseman's liability per package to 500 times the base rate. The amount may vary from 250 to 1,000 times the base rate. Rather than a liability per package, cold-storage warehousemen may have a limit per cubic foot in their warehouse receipts.

Agreements limiting a warehouseman's liability are not inviolate. One New York court decision nullified such an agreement for a warehouse operator following the unexplained loss of a customer's property.

Types of Warehousemen[7] Dry-storage warehousemen may store a wide variety of commodities, or specialize in a single commodity, such as furniture. Refrigerated warehouses may have facilities for cold storage under deep-freeze conditions or cold storage under cooling conditions. Moreover, there are two types of cold storage under cooling conditions: (1) storage in a normal atmosphere and (2) storage in a controlled atmosphere.

Under deep-freeze conditions, certain types of food can be preserved for long periods of time. Meat, fish, poultry, and certain kinds of fruit and vegetables are preserved mainly by freezing. The food is quick-frozen in freezing tunnels at temperatures ranging from −35°C to −50°C. This shock freezing prevents the water in the food from crystalizing as ice. Subsequent storage temperatures range from −18°C to −30°C.

Cold storage of food in a normal atmosphere is storage at temperatures near the freezing point, (0°C to 6°C), in an atmosphere that has the normal mixture of carbon dioxide, oxygen, and nitrogen. This method is used when the required storage period is relatively short, a few days, weeks, or months, until the meat, fruit, or vegetables are ready to be marketed, canned, or deep frozen. Fruits, in particular, are often preserved under these conditions. Cold-storage houses with a normal atmosphere are usually located where the fruit or vegetables are harvested, or in the principal market towns.

Cold storage in a controlled atmosphere is a means of providing storage for periods of as long as a year. The storage area is airtight and should not be entered during the entire storage period. The controlled atmosphere has reached oxygen content that must be kept within an allowable tolerance. Fruit is stored while still unripe. The reduced oxygen content permits natural fermentation, but at a slower pace.

Policy Provisions As warehousemen's legal liability is a nonfiled class of business, policy language varies considerably. The following is, therefore, a general commentary on some of the conditions found in these forms. Policies covering cold-storage warehousemen may have conditions that do not appear in policies covering warehousers of general merchandise.

Insuring Clause. In the insuring clause the insurance company agrees to pay all sums the insured becomes obligated to pay by reason of its legal liability for damage to or loss of property of others stored in the warehouse(s) described in the policy.

Defense costs are generally insured. One wording providing this coverage reads as follows:

> The Company agrees to defend any suit against the Insured seeking damages on account of loss, even if any of the allegations of the suit are groundless, false or fraudulent. It reserves the right to make any investigation, negotiation and settlement of any claim or suit as it deems expedient. But the Company is not obligated to defend any suit after the Company's liability has been exhausted by payments of judgements or settlements.

Supplementary coverage usually includes premiums on appeal bonds, premiums on bonds to release attachments for amounts not in excess of the insurer's limit of liability, interest on the judgment, and other reasonable expenses incurred by the insured at the insurer's request.

Exclusions. The property excluded and perils excluded vary from one insurer to another. Following are some of the exclusions in use. Property excluded:

- accounts, bills, currency, deeds, evidences of debt, money, bullion, notes or securities, manuscripts, plans, specifications, or other valuable papers;
- property held as "storage in transit" under the terms of a bill of lading issued by the insured (or property not under usual warehouse receipt);
- furs, manufactured tobacco, wines, liquors, or other alcoholic beverages, jewelry, watches, precious stones, gold, silver, fine arts, platinum, or other precious metals and alloys;
- animals, fish, birds, growing plants;
- property of insured's employees, or property owned or leased by the insured.

Perils excluded:

- insects, moth, vermin, rodents, inherent vice, latent defect, wear and tear, mechanical breakdown, faulty material;
- any repairing, restoration, or retouching process;
- mysterious disappearance, or loss or shortage disclosed on taking inventory;
- dampness of atmosphere, dryness of atmosphere, extremes or changes of temperature, freezing, heating, shrinkage, evaporation, loss of weight, leakage of contents, breakage of glass or similar fragile materials, marring, scratching, rust or corrosion, exposure to light, change in flavor or color or texture or finish unless such loss is caused directly by fire, lightning, windstorm, hail, explosion, strike, riot or civil commotion, aircraft, sprinkler leakage, vandalism, malicious mischief, theft, or attempted theft;
- water damage (as defined);
- willful illegal sale of property by the insured, willful conversion, or willful secretion;
- fraudulent warehouse receipts;
- liability assumed under any contract or agreement, in excess of liability imposed by law as a warehouseman;
- employee dishonesty;
- war and nuclear hazard.

Refrigerated Warehouses. When the insured is the operator of a refrigerated warehouse, the policy may be extended to cover the insured's legal liability for damage to property due to a change in temperature. The change in temperature could be the result of damage to the refrigerating or cooling apparatus or an interruption in the power supplied to the insured's premises. Such an extension of coverage might be subject to a requirement that the insured maintain the protective safeguards that were in effect at the time the policy was issued. Safeguards might typically be secondary power sources, watchmen, automatic temperature controls, or temperature alarm systems. The insured might also be required to maintain mechanical breakdown insurance covering the heating or refrigeration equipment at the insured's premises.

An exclusion sometimes found in refrigerated warehouse policies eliminates coverage for loss resulting from ammonia contacting or permeating property under refrigeration or loss caused by any process of refrigeration.

Premiums. Policies may be written for a flat annual premium, or on a gross-receipts reporting basis. Reports may be due monthly, quarterly, or annually if premium is to be adjusted at the end of the policy year. Some warehousemen make separate charges for storage and handling. The policy may have a separate rate for each of these exposures.

Rating The first step in rating is the determination of the amount at risk. The values at risk and the requested amount of insurance do not always coincide. As the policy usually does not contain a coinsurance clause, the possibility of this disparity should be recognized and compensated for in the rating process.

One way of determining the amount at risk is by an inspection. Another method involves the liability factor found in the storage receipt. This factor multiplied by the monthly average storage revenue should produce an approximation of the value at risk. (This contemplates a monthly turnover. If the turnover is twice a month, 50 percent of the liability factor is used). Some insurance companies multiply the average storage space by a factor per cubic foot. The factor varies with the type of merchandise. In the case of a cold storage warehouse the cubic footage of storage space used can be multiplied by the limit per cubic foot shown in the warehouse receipt to determine the amount at risk.

Each insurer has its own method of rating warehousemen's legal liability insurance. Under one method the fire contents rate of the warehouse is the base upon which the policy rate is built. This rate is first discounted as the form provides only legal liability coverage and the fire contents rate contemplates an exposure to fire irrespective of responsibility. The discounted fire contents rate is then applied to the limit of insurance or the amount at risk, whichever is greater, to determine the premium for the fire exposure. This premium is then debited or credited in accordance with the following:

- when the limit of insurance is less than the estimated amount at risk, a proportionate credit is usually given for the disparity;
- a loading, or debit, is then applied for the "all other perils" coverage;
- credits are then applied for protective services such as watchmen and burglar alarm systems; and
- a further credit may then be given for an increased deductible.

The rate for a reporting form is derived by dividing the premium that would be charged for a policy written on a flat annual premium basis by the annual storage revenue.

Underwriting Warehousemen's legal liability coverage must be underwritten very carefully. Under a legal liability form with no stated perils, a loss could arise from any number of causes. Many underwriters insist on inspections at the outset and periodically thereafter. The limitations of liability contained in the storage receipt will assist in determining the probable maximum loss. The insured's policy of accepting increased liability must also be considered.

Because warehousemen's is a legal liability coverage, the insurer is not obligated to pay a loss unless the insured is legally liable to the warehouse customer. Generally, the insured can avoid liability by showing an absence of negligence. Thus, a desirable account, from an underwriting standpoint, is one that is prepared to substantiate such a position by being able to show that it exercises reasonable care in the operation of its business. That degree of care would be evidenced by a well-managed operation, with properly trained personnel, keeping accurate records and showing dedication to good housekeeping and maintenance of suitable protection against fire and burglary.

Fire is the peril that presents the most potential for a catastrophic loss. The type of building construction, availability of an adequate water supply, and proximity of public fire protection are factors affecting the fire exposure. Other factors are the type of property stored and the method of storage. Property subject to water damage should be raised above the floor on skids. Adequate aisle space should be maintained, and recommended free space between sprinklers and the tops of the piles of stored property should be left unobstructed.

The presence of other tenants in the building may affect the fire exposure. Watchman service should help to prevent or provide early detection of fire. Fire detection equipment connected to a central station may serve in lieu of watchmen.

The burglary and theft exposure is in direct relationship to the type of property stored and the protection afforded. Such commodities as liquor, drugs, tobacco products, television sets, automobile accessories, and data processing equipment require more sophisticated burglary prevention equipment than other commodities less attractive to thieves.

Careless operation of forklifts, in both general merchandise and cold-storage warehouses, has been the cause of fires, sprinkler leakage, and escape of refrigerant. Improperly maintained LP gas powered lift trucks have themselves been the origin of fires.

When loss by contamination is not excluded in a policy covering a warehouser of general merchandise, the underwriter should determine whether one product can contaminate any of the others.

Deductibles play an essential role in the underwriting of warehouseman's legal liability coverage. A substantial deductible eliminates many of the breakage, marring, chipping, and scratching losses. The wording of the deductible should make it clear whether the deductible applies to defense costs.

Cold-storage warehouse policies may incorporate a waiting period, also called a no-claim period. This is a period, following damage to the refrigerating equipment, during which the required temperature will still be maintained, and in which loss due to deterioration should not normally occur. Cold storage policies may contain both a waiting period and a deductible.

A loss to a cold-storage plant may be avoided or minimized if auxiliary power generating equipment is available to keep the refrigerating plant operating during periods of public power failure. The presence of another nearby cold-storage warehouse that could be utilized in an emergency, or the availability of refrigerator trucks for the same purpose, could also improve the situation.

Bailee Coverage for Miscellaneous Situations

The bailee policies just discussed have been well established as inland marine coverages for many years. Other situations also develop under which a bailee needs coverage to protect against the liability to customers, or where bailees customers coverage is justified. In response to these situations, a number of similar bailee coverages have evolved.

Pressing or Tailor Shops A variation of the bailees customers policy is a *pressing* or *tailor shop* form. Such a policy may be written for a small shop that acts as an agent for a laundry or dry cleaner. This is usually written as a simplified bailees customers policy applying to property in the custody of the tailor shop or laundry agency. The small amount of premium involved usually requires that this be written on an annual basis. The amount of premium would not justify handling monthly payments.

Repair Shops Television, radio, and stereo repair shops have property worth many thousands of dollars in the custody of the shop for repairs. Customers expect the replacement of television sets that are destroyed in a catastrophe, whether or not the technician is legally liable for the loss. Repair shops may buy a bailees customers type of insurance policy to cover their liability and also cover for the benefit of the customer. Such a policy is written to cover the particular needs of the shop. There is no one standard form, but coverage would follow generally the pattern of the bailees customers policy for laundries and dry cleaners. Coverage is usually provided on a specified perils basis rather than on an "all-risks" basis, but either type of coverage could be written.

Department Stores and Furniture Stores Department stores and furniture stores that repair customers' property may find it advantageous to buy bailees customers insurance. The need depends primarily on the value of customers' goods in the custody of the merchant. A store with only a small amount of customers' goods on hand may consider it more advantageous to retain losses and treat them as a business expense. However, a large loss of customers' goods might seriously impair the future prospects of the merchant. The merchant would be certain to lose a great deal of future trade if payment to customers were refused. Yet the financial loss could be substantial if the merchant decides to pay for the property regardless of liability. Some of the general property insurance policies (not inland marine) provide some coverage on customers' property. This may be adequate if the amount of the customers' goods in the custody of the dealer is not large.

Property on Consignment Bailees customers insurance may also be justified when a business organization regularly accepts property on consignment for sale or distribution. Art galleries, for example, often accept the work of various artists for display and sale. These are handled on a consignment basis, and the proprietor gets a commission for any works that are sold. A large portion of an art gallery's stock, or even the entire stock, may be on consignment from artists or from other dealers. The art gallery in such a case is a bailee, with the bailee's usual liability. There may be a contract between the art gallery and the owners of the property, or the art gallery may depend upon the customs of the trade to determine liability for any property that might be lost. The determination of what exposure exists, and the decision whether to purchase bailee liability insurance or bailees customers insurance, would depend largely on the terms of any contract between the art gallery, the artist, or other dealers from whom the gallery accepts property on consignment, as well as the length of time of consignment.

Auctioneers Auctioneers conduct yet another type of business where property is accepted on consignment for sale at auctions. Here again, the need of auctioneers for insurance coverage on property in their custody will depend largely upon the terms of any contract between the auctioneers and the property owners, or upon the practices of the trade.

Cold Storage Lockers Operators of cold storage locker plants are insured under a specialized form of coverage. The 1953 Nation-Wide Marine Definition named this class specifically as in some instances there is no processing involved and the risk would not qualify. The 1976 Definition omitted mention of the category as it automatically qualifies.

Coverage applies to customers' property accepted by the insured for storage in a cold storage locker. The form may be "all-risks" or named perils, reporting or nonreporting. Reporting forms require a report of the total number of lockers occupied during the reporting period. Separate limits of insurance apply to property in any one locker, property on the insured's premises but not within a locker, and property in transit. Policies generally require immediate notice to the insurance company in the event of a failure of refrigerating equipment likely to continue for more than six hours.

Miniwarehouses Miniwarehouses, or self-storage centers, are a relatively new entry in the warehousing business. They are small adjoining structures that have the appearance of a row of private garages. The owner of the miniwarehouse merely furnishes the premises for storage purposes, and does not handle or exercise any control over the contents stored in it. Consequently it may be difficult to show that the owner was responsible for a loss, unless the loss can be attributed to a defect in the premises.

Automobile Businesses Car dealers, service stations, body shops, muffler and brake shops, and similar businesses that take custody of customers' automobiles, although they operate as bailees, are *not* an inland marine class of business. Coverage for such bailee exposures originated as a branch of automobile insurance soon after the proliferation of automobiles and has remained within the commercial auto line ever since.

The garage coverage form filed by Insurance Services Office, which provides liability coverage for garage operations and liability and physical damage coverage on the insured's autos, also contains a "garagekeepers" section for covering damage to customers' cars left with the insured. Garagekeepers coverage can be arranged on either a legal liability basis or a dual interest basis.

Other Bailees Only the more common types of bailees have been discussed in this chapter. Bailment is such a common aspect of so many businesses' operations that compiling a complete listing would perhaps be impossible. However, a partial list includes:

- film developers, enlargers, and retouchers;
- picture framers, fine arts cleaners and restorers;
- boatyards and mooring facilities (which may be insured as either inland marine or ocean marine);
- kennels, veterinarians, and horse breeders (usually insured under specialized types of *live animal floaters,* as discussed in Chapter 11); and
- bank safe deposit facilities (often insured under specialized crime forms).

The list could also include the many different types of bailees who, like the rug and carpet cleaners discussed earlier, go to the *customer's* home or business to work on property. Building, heating, plumbing, and painting contractors are common examples. Typically, such bailees do not have bailee coverage of the type discussed in this chapter. A builder who has responsibility for providing insurance on a building during the course of construction ordinarily purchases a *builders risk policy,* as described in Chapter 7 of this text. A heating contractor installing a new furnace or a plumber installing new bathroom and kitchen fixtures might obtain coverage under *installation floaters,* which are also discussed in Chapter 7.

In addition to the bailees mentioned above, there are situations generally called "rentals," but in which there is no landlord-tenant relationship and the effect is that of a bailment for hire. These include, among others:

- car, truck, and boat rentals or leases;
- furniture rental;
- computer and equipment leasing;
- telephone systems leasing.

These situations require careful reading of the rental contract or lease to determine the bailee's responsibilities for loss. If the bailee is responsible for loss to the property, there are several methods of covering the exposure.

In some cases, the bailee's homeowners, auto, or other insurance policy will provide coverage for nonowned property of the sort being rented. For example, many private passenger auto policies provide physical damage coverage for short term car rentals. In other cases, the bailee will need to buy insurance specifically to cover the rented property. *Leased property insurance* is an inland marine class of business discussed in Chapter 11 of this text.

Another coverage arrangement, although it is not technically considered to be insurance, is a *damage waiver,* whereby the contract between the lessor and the lessee relieves the lessee (bailee) of liability for damage to the leased property in return for the lessee's payment of an additional charge.

BAILOR COVERAGES

Ordinarily, a bailee is responsible for loss to its customers' property only if the loss is caused by the bailee's negligence. Because loss can result from any number of causes for which the bailee is not liable, it is desirable for bailors to have insurance on their property while in the custody of bailees or while in transit to or from bailees. Even if the bailee has, or is believed to have, bailees customers insurance covering the interests of both the bailor and the bailee, it is still prudent for bailors to carry their own insurance, particularly when large values are exposed to loss.

The most common form of such insurance is that in connection with household goods and clothing. For example, many homeowners policies provide the full amount of coverage on unscheduled personal property even while such property is away from the location named in the policy, including while in the hands of a bailee.

In contrast, commercial property forms usually provide only a limited amount of insurance on covered personal property while away from the insured's premises. The ISO building and personal property coverage form, for example, provides a $5,000 extension for covered property temporarily at a location that the insured does not own, lease, or operate. This coverage does not apply to property in or on a vehicle, nor to the insured's merchandise, raw materials, or in-process or finished goods. Consequently, there may be many bailment situations that are not covered adequately by a bailor's regular business personal property insurance.

In such situations, the coverage may be provided by an inland marine bailor policy. Two of the best known types of bailor policies are *garment contractors floaters* and *pattern and die floaters,* both of which are listed by name in the Nation-Wide Marine Definition.

In addition, bailor policies are written on many other types of property given to bailees for storage, servicing, or processing. A publishing company, for example, may buy a bailor policy to cover its plates, prints, negatives, and artwork while on the premises of typesetters, printers, and other bailees. These additional bailor policies, like bailee policies, derive their inland marine status from the provision in the Nation-Wide Marine Definition that refers to "property in transit to or from and in custody of bailees."

While many states do not impose filing requirements with respect to bailor policies, AAIS does file garment contractors forms, rules, and rates on behalf of its member insurers. The AAIS filing is discussed below as an example of bailor coverage.

Garment Contractors Insurance

Many garment manufacturers use contractors to perform some of the specialized work that must be done to complete a garment. Contractors make buttonholes, sew on embroidery and trimmings, insert shoulder pads, and perform a variety of other functions.

Originally, garment contractors policies covered garments while in transit to and from, and while in the custody of, a contractor for processing. Subsequently, coverage was extended to cover property at the insured's own premises as well.

AAIS calls the coverage *garment manufacturers* coverage, which recognizes the fact that a garment manufacturer is ordinarily the named insured whose garments are in the custody of, or en route to or from, a garment contractor's premises. Garment manufacturers coverage in accordance with the AAIS rules may be written for manufacturers of (1) women's wear (meaning cloaks, skirts, jackets, suits, and dresses only), (2) men's and boys' wear, and (3) other wearing apparel including women's wear not listed above. (These three categories are separately rated.)

AAIS files two garment manufacturers forms. One covers named perils, and the other is on an "all-risks" basis. A further difference between the two forms is the availability of coverage for a broad range of personal property as well as improvements and betterments under the "all-risks" form, a feature described in more detail below. Apart from these differences, the two forms are the same.

Covered Property The named perils form contains two coverages. Coverage A is the basic coverage that is ordinarily purchased. Coverage B is an optional extension to insure covered garments while they are on the insured's own premises. The "all-risks" form contains the same two coverages, plus Coverage C, an optional coverage for insuring contents (other than garments) and improvements and betterments at an insured location.

Coverage A. Coverage A insures property of a type described in the declarations that is owned by the insured, including raw materials, finished and unfinished garments, and their containers. Coverage A also insures similar property (1) that belongs to others and for which the insured is liable, (2) that is consigned to the insured, or (3) for which the insured has made an advance payment.

The property is covered only while:

- on the premises of the insured's contractors;
- in transit between the insured's premises and the premises of the insured's contractors; and
- in transit between the premises of the insured's contractors and the premises of the insured's suppliers.

The form defines "contractor" so as to include any party, including a subcontractor, to whom the insured sends garments or parts of garments for processing, assembly, manufacturing, or similar work. However, thread or yarn processors, printers, dyers, spongers, tanners, finishers, testing houses, or other cloth finishing works are outside the definition. So, garments of the insured located on the premises of any of these types of business are outside the scope of coverage.

Coverage B. Coverage B applies only if the declarations show a limit of insurance for that coverage. If Coverage B is purchased, property of the sort described in the declarations is covered while at the insured's location described in the policy. Coverage B also applies to the same property while in transit between the described location and the premises of the insured's suppliers.

Coverage C. Coverage C, available under the "all-risks" form only, can be arranged to insure the following types of property that belong to the insured, while at the location described in the policy:

- furniture and fixtures;
- machinery, tools, and their parts;
- patterns, molds, models, and dies; and
- office equipment and supplies.

Similar property that belongs to others and for which the insured is liable is also covered. In addition, Coverage C covers the insured's interest in tenants improvements, meaning fixtures, alterations, installations, or additions made at the insured's expense and which the insured cannot legally remove.

Coverages B and C are optional. Often, garments and other personal property on the insured's own premises are insured under regular "commercial property" policies. When that is the case, purchase of these optional coverages is unnecessary as they mainly duplicate the commercial property coverages that the insured already has.

However, an important feature of Coverage B is that it provides coverage for property in transit between the insured's premises and those of a supplier. Commercial property policies usually provide only very limited transit coverage. Consequently, if garments on the insured's premises are covered under a commercial property policy, the insured should consider the need for transit coverage under an additional policy.

Excluded Property The following types of property are excluded:

1. property that is shipped by mail.
2. leggings, spats, footwear or hosiery.
3. headwear.
4. jewelry or costume jewelry.
5. fine arts.
6. musical instruments, photographic equipment and their supplies and accessories.
7. signs or outdoor equipment.

8. air conditioners or domestic appliances.
9. carpets or cloth awnings.
10. data processing equipment and media. Media means magnetic tapes, disk packs, diskettes, paper tapes, cards and other material on which data is stored or recorded. It includes data stored on the media.

Many of the types of property excluded would not be insured under Coverage A or B even in the absence of the exclusions, as Coverages A and B apply only to *garments* of the type described in the declarations. However, many of these exclusions could come into play with respect to Coverage C, which insures a wider range of property. Coverage for most of the excluded items is available under different inland marine or commercial property forms.

Covered Perils As noted above, AAIS files an "all-risks" and a named perils version of its garment manufacturers form.

"All-Risks" Form. The "all-risks" form covers direct physical loss to covered property unless the loss is caused by an excluded peril. The insuring agreement also stipulates that loss must be due to an external cause.

One set of exclusions applies to Coverages A, B, and C. The first of these exclusions is the AAIS equivalent to the ISO dishonesty exclusion discussed in Chapter 2. Other exclusions eliminate coverage for loss by mysterious disappearance; loss evidenced only by inventory shortage; dampness of atmosphere; extremes of temperature; freezing; any process to repair, adjust, service, or maintain covered property (loss by resulting fire or explosion is covered); chaffing or rubbing; and decrease in value of a garment or part of a garment that is not physically damaged.

The last exclusion is unique to garment contractors policies. To illustrate its purpose, suppose that the insured manufacturer sends a quantity of men's suit pants to a contractor to have zippers installed, while the suit coats remain at the insured's premises. If the suit pants are destroyed in a fire at the contractor's premises, the suit coats, though they will have suffered no physical damage, may suffer a decrease in value, particularly if the insured is unable to match the fabric and reproduce the destroyed pants. Because of the exclusion under consideration, any such decrease in value is not covered. Only the physical loss to the pants will be insured.

Coverage can be arranged for this exposure through the AAIS endorsement entitled *coverage for undamaged property.* (This may be called *consequential damage coverage* in other policies.) The endorsement covers "the value of the undamaged part or parts of a garment that cannot be sold or used because of a loss caused by a covered peril." The insured's recovery is limited to the smaller of (1) the value of the undamaged property that cannot be recovered, and (2) the coverage amount shown in the endorsement. The coverage amount shown in the endorsement is in addition to the limits for Coverages A and B.

In addition to the exclusions described above, a water exclusion applies to Coverages B and C only. The exclusion eliminates coverage for loss caused by flood, surface water, waves, tidal water, or the overflow of a body of water; water that backs up through a sewer or drain; and water below the surface of the ground. However, loss caused by a resulting fire or explosion is covered. The exclusion does not apply to loss caused by water to property in transit. AAIS rules allow the exclusion to be deleted at the insurer's discretion.

Two additional exclusions apply to Coverage C only. These exclusions eliminate coverage for loss resulting from (1) mechanical breakdown or failure and (2) electrical currents, other than those caused by lightning, that damage an electrical apparatus or its wiring. Both exclusions state that loss by resulting fire or explosion is covered.

Other applicable exclusions, common to most inland marine policies, are contained in the AAIS inland marine general terms form to which the garment manufacturers form is attached. These exclusions eliminate coverage for loss due to wear and tear; gradual deterioration; intrinsic fault or weakness of covered property; insects or vermin; delay, loss of market, loss of use, or business interruption; obsolescence or depreciation; war; civil authority; and nuclear hazard.

Named Perils Form. In the named perils form, covered property *other than property in transit* is insured against certain named perils. Property in transit, however, is covered on an "all-risks basis, subject to exclusions.

Perils Applicable to Property Not in Transit. The named perils for which property not in transit is covered are:

a. fire.
b. lightning.
c. windstorm.
d. hail.
e. boiler explosion. This means an explosion or implosion that occurs inside of a boiler. Connected pipes, flywheels, engines and other machines are a part of the boiler.
f. aircraft, spacecraft or self-propelled missiles. This includes objects that fall from these items.
g. vehicles. This means the physical contact of a vehicle with covered property.
h. smoke.
i. water, except as excluded.

j. burglary. This means an illegal entry by force when the premises are not open for business. There must be visible marks that entry was forced.
k. robbery. This means the illegal taking of property from another by force or fear of force.

This named perils coverage is subject to the same exclusions as described above in connection with "all-risks" coverage. Consequently, an insured with the named perils form is not covered for decrease in value of property that has not been physically damaged. Coverage for the exposure can be arranged using the same "coverage for undamaged property" endorsement described above.

Strike, riot, vandalism, and explosion (other than boiler explosion) can be added by a single endorsement, for an additional premium charge.

Similarly, another endorsement can be used to add theft coverage. Although the basic named perils include burglary and robbery, there are other kinds of theft that those perils do not cover.

For example, the burglary peril as defined above would not cover theft of covered property resulting from burglars entering *without* leaving visible marks of forced entry. The burglary peril would also not cover theft by a thief who concealed himself during open hours and "broke out" after the premises closed for the night. Similarly, the robbery peril would not cover loss by a "sneak thief" who used neither force nor threat of violence to take property.

Theft coverage, in contrast, insures against any illegal taking of property except as excluded in the theft endorsement. The exclusions found in the theft endorsement consist of the dishonesty exclusion (see Chapter 2) and exclusions of:

- swindling, fraud, trick, or false pretense;
- the acceptance of (1) counterfeit money or fraudulent post office or express money orders, or (2) checks or promissory notes that are not paid upon presentation;
- mysterious disappearance; and
- loss evidenced only by an inventory shortage.

Perils Applicable to Property in Transit. Under the named perils form, property in transit is nevertheless covered on an "all-risks" basis, subject to the same exclusions applicable to Coverages A and B of the "all-risks" form, plus two additional exclusions. These additional exclusions eliminate coverage for (1) vandalism and (2) strike, riot, or civil commotion.

Limits of Insurance The garment manufacturers form is subject to various limits of insurance.

For purposes of Coverage A, a separate amount of insurance is scheduled for each contractor's premises. In addition, there is a limit for property at any contractor's premises that are not scheduled.

There are separate limits for property in transit by (1) air carrier, (2) private paid delivery service, (3) other common or contract carrier, (4) a vehicle operated by the insured, and (5) other means.

For purposes of Coverages B and C, each location to be covered is scheduled with an amount of insurance for that location.

Additional Provisions Five additional provisions are contained in the named perils form, relating to deductible, coinsurance, coverage territory, valuation, and subrogation. The "all-risks" form contains the same five provisions plus a sixth condition addressing how much the insurer will pay for loss to tenants improvements. The AAIS inland marine general terms form contains all other applicable provisions. These provisions are comparable in most respects to the ISO commercial inland marine conditions discussed in Chapter 2.

Deductible. The basic deductible amount under AAIS rules is $100. Larger deductible amounts may be used to obtain an appropriate rate credit. Whatever deductible is chosen applies "to each loss after all other adjustments have been made."

Coinsurance. The garment manufacturers form contains a 100 percent coinsurance clause.

Coverage Territory. Coverage applies only while the property, including property in transit, is in the United States, Canada, or Puerto Rico. However, property in transit *to or from* Alaska, Hawaii, or Puerto Rico is outside the coverage territory.

Valuation. Garments or parts of garments are valued at the cost of labor and materials. Labels, containers, and wrappers are valued at the cost to replace them with new items. All other property is valued at its actual cash value.

Subrogation. The subrogation provision differs from the usual type of subrogation clause (see Chapter 2) in that it states that the insured may only waive its right of recovery against a common carrier to the extent of a bill of lading that limits the carrier's liability to not more than $50 a shipment or $1 a garment. Any greater waiver of recovery against a common carrier enables the insurer to deny coverage for a loss subject to such greater waiver. In a situation other than with a common carrier, the insured may waive its right to recovery in writing before a loss occurs.

Tenants Improvements. Because the "all-risks" form contains an option for covering tenants improvements, the form contains a provision explaining how much the insurer will pay for loss to such property. The most that the insurer will pay is the *smallest* of these three amounts:

1. the cost to repair, replace or rebuild the property with material of like kind and quality if it is done within a reasonable time.
2. a part of the original cost if the property is not repaired, replaced or rebuilt within a reasonable time. To determine that part, we will:
   a. count the number of days from the date of the loss to the end of your lease;
   b. count the number of days from the date the improvements were installed or acquired to the end of your lease;
   c. divide step a. by step b.; and
   d. multiply the result in step c. by the original cost.
3. the coverage amount that is shown.

Reporting Endorsements The garment manufacturers form is intended to apply on a flat annual premium basis unless reporting provisions are added by endorsement. One endorsement allows for monthly, quarterly, semiannual, or annual reports of *gross sales.* Another endorsement calls for monthly reports of *values* for all covered property.

Rating Insurance companies that are members of AAIS may submit their applications for garment manufacturers coverage to AAIS for rating. Otherwise, the policy is rated by the insurance company.

The information requested by garment contractors application forms typically includes:

- the names and addresses of all contractors used for a total of thirty days or more during the twelve months preceding the date of application;
- the maximum value of property on the premises of each contractor during the last twelve months (average monthly amount for policies on a gross sales basis);
- the limit of insurance required at each location; and
- the 100 percent coinsurance fire contents rate at each location.

When insurance is to apply at the insured's premises, the application will request information concerning inventory values at the insured's premises, protective safeguards in effect at the insured's premises, and the fire contents rate at the insured's premises. The fire contents rates for the various locations covered are used as the basis for premium determination.

Underwriting The garment manufacturers policy is principally a bailor form, covering the insured bailor's property in transit and while on the premises of contractors and subcontractors. The insured may require the use of a number of contractors for the completion of the garments it manufactures. The major contractors, those that require the higher limits of insurance, are scheduled in the policy. Those with lesser exposures are grouped under the category of unnamed contractors, with a single limit applying for any one of those unnamed. The AAIS rules state that this limit may not exceed 25 percent of the largest limit for a scheduled location.

The contractors are often located some distance from the insured, and from each other. Transit may be between contractors as well as between the insured and contractors. Hence, there is a considerable transit exposure, particularly considering the nature of the property involved. Clothing has traditionally had a particular attraction for thieves. Subrogation possibilities against the carrier may be slim, as many truckers have a special tariff for clothing that releases them substantially. One dollar per garment is the extent of some carriers' liability.

While the property is on the contractor's premises the major exposures are fire, theft, and water damage. The extent of these exposures may be readily investigated for the larger contractors. This may not, however, be practical for a number of smaller contractors, named and unnamed, among which there may be some less-than-desirable fire, theft, and water damage exposures.

The major exposures at the insured's premises are fire and theft. The burglary protection there is an important feature of both the underwriting and the rating. The extent of protection an underwriter may require will depend on such factors as the amount of insurance required and the location involved.

Pattern and Die Floater

A common bailor processing policy is the pattern and die floater. Many companies send their patterns and dies to foundries where they are used in the making of castings. The policy covers loss or damage to the property while it is in transit to and from, and while on the premises of, the foundry.

While policy terms vary, an insuring agreement might cover "patterns and dies, molds and castings, the property of the insured or held by the insured in trust or on commission or on consignment, or for which the insured may be liable in the event of loss or damage."

The transit coverage may be restricted to property in the custody of railroads, public truckers, private truckers, and trucks owned or operated by the insured. Shipments by mail are excluded. The name and location of the bailee (foundry) is listed in the policy. Separate limits are set for property in transit and property at the location listed.

Insurance may be on an "all-risks" or named perils basis. Losses or damage not insured against include those arising out of wear and tear, depreciation, obsolescence, soiling, inherent vice, fading, rusting, poor workmanship, faulty manufacture, inventory shortage, warping, cracking, or splitting.

When the policy is not written on a reporting basis a coinsurance clause usually applies. Reporting forms require reports based on the values at risk.

Some patterns and dies become obsolete and their reduction in value must be accounted for in the valuation clause. One valuation clause in use values the property at replacement cost at place and date of loss, less depreciation, including depreciation for obsolescence. It is important that the insured keep a record of all patterns in use with a value for each.

Miscellaneous Coverages

Many other processing exposures are covered by bailor (and bailee) policies. Examples of these processing operations are annealing or baking metal or plastics, binding books, chroming metal, dressing fur hides, dyeing leather, heat treating metal, recapping tires, sand blasting metal parts, shrinking cloth, tanning leather, and drying lumber in kilns.

Policies written to cover these operations are nonfiled, and so may contain any conditions mutually agreed upon by the insured and the insurance company. Coverage may be "all-risks" or named perils, or a combination of "all-risks" in transit and named perils at fixed locations.

SUMMARY

This chapter describes inland marine coverages that insure property while in the possession of a bailee, such as a dry cleaner or repair shop and while in transit to and from the bailee's premises. These coverages fall into two basic categories—*bailee policies* and *bailor policies.*

There are three types of bailment—gratuitous bailment for the benefit of the bailor, gratuitous bailment for the benefit of the bailee, and bailment for hire and for the mutual benefit of both bailee and bailor. The degree of care required of a bailee is not clear-cut, and may vary according to the circumstances. The liability of a bailee can be extended in several ways. While it is considered to be against public policy to permit a person to contract away his or her entire liability, it is possible for the bailee to limit the *amount* of liability.

Types of bailee coverages include laundry and dry cleaners

insurance, furriers customers insurance, warehousemen's liability insurance, and some miscellaneous coverages, such as pressing or tailor shops, repair shops, department stores and furniture stores, property on consignment, auctioneers, cold storage lockers, and miniwarehouses.

Because loss can result from any number of causes for which the bailee is not liable, it is desirable for bailors to have insurance on their property while in the custody of bailees or while in transit to or from bailees. Types of bailor policies include garment contractors insurance, the pattern and die floater, and coverage for other miscellaneous processing exposures.

Chapter Notes

1. The discussion of bailees' legal liability is adapted with permission from William H. Rodda, *Marine Insurance: Ocean and Inland,* 3rd ed. (Englewood Cliffs, NJ: Prentice-Hall, 1970), pp. 324-28.
2. Fraam v. Grand Rapids & Indiana Rwy. Col, 161 Mich. 556, 126 N.W. 851 (1910).
3. Peet v. Roth Hotel Col, 191 Minn. 151, 253 N.W. 546 (1934).
4. More v. Fisher, 245 Ill. App. 567 (1927).
5. Braman-Johnson Flying Service, Inc. v. Thomson, 167 Misc. 167, 3 N.Y.S.(2) 602 (1938).
6. Aetna Cas. & Surety Co. v. Higbee Co., 80 Oh. App. 437 (1947).
7. The technical information on cold storage is derived from "Deterioration of Stock Insurance" (Munich: Munich Reinsurance Company, 1974).

CHAPTER 7

Builders Risks, Installation Floaters, and DIC Policies

INTRODUCTION

Most of the classes of property listed in the Nation-Wide Marine Definition are *personal property,* meaning movable property that is not attached to the ground or to a building or other structure attached to the ground. Buildings and other attached structures are *real property.* This chapter examines three types of inland marine policies that may cover personal property *and* real property.

Builders risk policies cover buildings and other structures while they are being built. The coverage extends to the real property being constructed and to personal property that is to become part of the building.

Installation floaters cover property, such as electrical, heating, or plumbing equipment, while it is being installed. Ordinarily, the property covered is in the category of personal property, but coverage may continue to apply after the property is installed (and therefore becomes real property) until the work is accepted by the owner or the insured's interest in the property ceases.

A *difference in conditions (DIC) policy* supplements a named perils property policy with "all-risks" coverage. The DIC policy covers the same property covered by the named perils policy, whether that property is buildings or personal property or both. DIC "all-risks" coverage is often broader than the "all-risks" coverage available under commercial property policies. Many DIC policies cover flood and earthquake.

Because of their many similarities, builders risk policies and installation floaters are considered in the same section of this chapter.

The type of builders risk policy described in this chapter is that which is generally written on *buildings* in the course of construction. More specialized types of builders risk policies—those on bridges and other "instrumentalities of transportation"—are described in Chapter 8, along with the forms used to insure completed instrumentalities of transportation.

BUILDERS RISK POLICIES AND INSTALLATION FLOATERS

The 1976 Nation-Wide Marine Definition made possible the addition of the words "builders risk" to the title of this chapter. Under the 1953 Definition, inland marine underwriters were confined to the issuance of installation floaters, which cover property while in transit and while being installed. Builders risk policies cover real property while it is being built, renovated, repaired, or tested, as well as personal property that will become a permanent part of the building while that property is in transit and while being installed in the building.

Under both the 1953 and the 1976 Definitions, coverage under an installation floater must cease when the interest of the insured ceases, or when the property has been accepted as satisfactory, whichever occurs first. An exception is made under the 1953 Definition for building materials. Coverage for materials such as bricks, mortar, lumber, and structural steel must cease as soon as the materials have become a part of the realty. The removal of this rule in the 1976 Definition sanctioned builders risk as an inland marine class of business in those states that have approved the 1976 Definition.

Eligibility under the 1976 Definition is limited to builders risks or installation floaters that insure against perils in addition to fire and extended coverage. This does not mean that a builders risk policy or installation floater written as inland marine must *exclude* fire and extended coverage, as must a DIC policy. It merely means that the policy must insure against additional perils.

Both the 1953 and the 1976 Definitions permit coverage on property in transit to the installation or construction site. The 1976 Definition adds "...and during temporary storage or deposit." A temporary storage site is often needed for larger construction projects.

In most states builders risks may be insured under either a commercial property policy or an inland marine policy. The rates and forms of the commercial property builders risk policy usually are filed with the state, whereas the rates and policy conditions of the inland marine builders risk policy are not subject to filing requirements. Given this flexibility, inland marine builders risk policies are often broader in coverage than their commercial property counterparts.

As an example, the ISO simplified commercial property builders risk coverage form covers property intended to become a permanent part of the building under construction while that property is "located in or on the building or structure or within 100 feet of its premises." Inland marine forms generally cover such property while at the building site, at temporary storage locations, and while in transit. Inland marine forms also usually provide broader coverage for theft. The ISO simplified causes of loss—special form does not cover theft of building materials and supplies that are not attached as part of the building or structure. Inland marine builders risk policies usually do not have this restriction.

Builders risk policies and installation floaters are a nonfiled class of business, except in a few states that require builders risk filings. As such, they can be written to provide the coverage mutually agreed upon by the insured and the insurance company. Many companies use their own standard forms. Standard forms, however, may be changed to fit individual situations. Standard forms are used principally to insure general construction, such as schools, shopping centers, apartment houses, office buildings, condominiums, dwellings, and other properties that do not require the installation and testing of very expensive and highly damageable machinery and equipment. The latter types of equipment are found in structures such as electric generating plants and oil refineries. Builders risk policies on property of these types are generally specially prepared forms that address the particular exposures involved.

The insured under an installation floater may be the owner of the property, the contractor doing the installation or the one selling the property.

The insured under a builders risk policy may be the owner of the property under construction, the contractor, or both the owner and the contractor. Subcontractors may be named as well. State statutes often define the relationship between contractor and subcontractor. In some states the contractor may be precluded by statute or case law from subrogating against a subcontractor.

Covered Property

Both builders risk policies and installation floaters cover property of the insured and property of others for which the insured is liable. The property insured under a builders risk policy is the property undergoing construction, reconstruction, alteration, or repair. When existing structures are being altered or repaired, the policy should clearly state whether coverage applies only to the alterations or repairs. The property insured consists of the machinery, equipment, materials, supplies, and fixtures that will become or have become a permanent part of the building or structure. Included as well, sometimes on an optional basis, are the forms, scaffolding, falsework, and temporary structures used in the construction. Coverage for the cost of debris removal is also generally included, either as an additional amount of insurance or as part of the policy limit.

Installation floaters are generally associated with such properties as plumbing, heating, cooling, and electrical systems, but can be written to insure any property being installed. Carpeting, tile, glass window frames, elevators, and machinery are examples of property that can be covered.

Property excluded under builders risk policies and installation floaters varies from one insurer to another. The following properties are sometimes excluded:

- trees, shrubs, grass, plants, or land values (builders risk only);
- plans, drawings, designs, blueprints, or specifications;
- property in storage, unless it has been specifically assigned to the job site;
- machinery, tools, equipment, and property of a similar nature not destined to become a permanently attached part of the building or structure; and
- existing property to which alterations or additions are being made (builders risk only).

Covered Perils

The majority of builders risk and installation floater forms provide "all-risks" coverage. In addition to the usual exclusions found in inland marine "all-risks" policies, the following are typical of the exclusions found in builders risk policies:

- error, omission, or deficiency in design, faulty workmanship, or faulty materials (unless an insured loss ensues, and then only for the ensuing loss);
- subsidence, settling, cracking, shrinking, bulging, or expansion of foundations, pavements, sidewalks, driveways, walls, patios, floors, roofs, or ceilings unless caused by specified perils;
- loss or damage caused by rain, snow, or sleet to property in the open that is not a permanent part of the structure or installation (property in the custody of carriers for hire excepted);

- loss covered under any guarantee, warranty, or other similar assumed obligation;
- order of any governmental authority, or enforcement of any state ordinance or law that requires the demolition of any part of insured property damaged by a peril insured against;
- testing of machinery or electrical appliances or devices, including wiring, unless fire ensues, and then only for the ensuing loss by fire;
- penalties for noncompletion of or delay in completion of contract or noncompliance with contract conditions;
- flood and water damage (as defined);
- earthquake (as defined); and
- employee dishonesty.

Installation floaters generally exclude wear and tear, gradual deterioration, and inherent vice. They may also exclude mechanical breakdown, electrical injury from artificial causes, errors in design, faulty workmanship or materials, and explosion or rupture of steam boilers.

Time Period Covered

Insurance under builders risk policies or installation floaters may be stated to begin when transit commences or when the insured acquires a financial interest in the property. Under the latter wording, the insured who acquires a financial interest at the supplier's premises is covered for his or her interest even though transit has not begun.

Insurance may be stated to end at the earliest of the following times (items 4, 5, and 6 do not apply to installation floaters):

1. when the financial interest of the insured ceases;
2. when the purchaser accepts the property as complete;
3. when the policy expires or is canceled;
4. when the property is put to its intended use, leased or rented to others, or occupied (although permission may be given for certain types of occupancy, such as office or habitational, while the property is still under construction);
5. thirty (or sixty, or ninety) days after construction has ceased (especially apropos for reporting forms written on an "until cancelled" basis); or
6. when the insured abandons the construction with no intention to complete.

When two or more structures are insured under a builders risk policy, it may be appropriate to include a stipulation that the provisions terminating the policy apply separately to each structure insured.

Limits of Insurance

A separate limit of insurance usually applies to property in transit and to property at the job site. Builders risk policies generally also include a limit for property at a location other than the job site. When earthquake or flood is insured, a sublimit may apply to each of these perils.

Extensions of Coverage

Builders risk policies are often extended to include coverage for loss of rents, loss of earnings, and "soft costs." Another possible extension, more common in international markets than in the United States, is coverage for damage due to the insured contractor's maintenance work after the insurance would otherwise have ceased.

Loss of Rents and Earnings Coverage for loss of rents and coverage for loss of earnings are two common extensions of the builders risk policy. These coverages come into play when the property under construction is damaged by a peril insured against, causing a delay in the completion of the structure and advancing the completion date beyond that which had been anticipated had no loss occurred. Faced with such delay, an owner of a building who planned to rent it to others would suffer a loss of rents. An owner of a building who planned to use it for his or her own business would suffer a loss of earnings. A small property damage loss could result in a substantial time element loss. Speedy replacement of damaged property is essential.

Coverage is usually on an actual loss sustained basis. Forms may have a per diem, monthly, or other periodic limit as well as an overall limit in any one loss. The insured is required to exhaust all reasonable means of recouping the lost income before recourse may be had to the insurance.

Soft Costs In addition to loss of rents or loss of earnings, other expenses may be incurred when the completion of the insured property is delayed by an insured loss. Some of these other expenses, called *soft costs,* may be insured through an optional extension to builders risk policies. Examples of soft costs are additional interest expense, advertising expense, additional taxes, and commission expense.

Additional interest expense may be incurred as a result of the renegotiation of the construction loan. Advertising expense may be incurred if it is necessary to obtain new tenants. Additional real estate taxes may become payable as a result of the longer period of construction. Additional commissions may be payable to real estate agents for their renegotiation of sales contracts and leases.

A soft costs coverage extension should delineate which soft costs are insured and provide a precise definition of each. As is the case with loss of rents and loss of earnings, soft costs may have a per diem, monthly, or other periodic limit and an overall limit for any one loss.

Maintenance Coverage It is common in international markets for the insurer to extend a builders risk policy beyond the termination or completion date of the policy to provide *maintenance coverage.* There are two basic types of maintenance coverage. *Maintenance visits coverage* extends the policy to cover a loss caused by the contractor during the maintenance period. *Extended maintenance coverage* insures the contractor for any losses occurring during the maintenance period that had their origin during the construction phase.

Losses recoverable under maintenance visits and extended maintenance coverage must be of a type that would have been covered under the builders risk policy. The duration of maintenance coverage is usually twelve to eighteen months.

Valuation

The basis of settlement for a builders risk policy is generally the cost of materials and labor involved in repairing or replacing the property with materials of like kind and quality. Other factors such as profit and overhead expenses may also be included in the valuation agreement.

Installation floaters may provide for actual cash value for property of the insured, and the amount for which the insured is liable for property of others. The latter may include additional costs expended by the insured for labor and materials.

Payment of Premium

Builders risk policies may be written on either a reporting or a nonreporting basis. Nonreporting policies are generally written on a *completed value* basis. There are several methods of writing builders risk coverage on a reporting basis.

Completed Value Form Under a completed value builders risk form, the amount of insurance is the expected completed value of the property under construction. The term of the policy is the anticipated period of construction. The premium is fixed, although some forms contain a provision that provides for an adjustment of the premium if the actual completed value is greater or less by a certain percentage—5 percent, for example—than the estimated completed value. A 100 percent coinsurance clause protects the insurer from an appreciation in the completed value that is not followed by an appropriate increase in the amount of insurance.

Value Reporting Form One type of builders risk reporting form is the value reporting form, which requires periodic (such as monthly) reports of the value at risk. Value reporting forms are practical only for larger projects, where the insured keeps records in the manner required to comply with the reporting provision.

Completed Value Reporting Forms A completed value reporting form may be used to cover an insured such as a developer who is constructing a number of private homes. There are two variations among reporting forms of this type.

The first method requires that the completed value of each structure started during the preceding month be reported, and premium be paid for the entire construction period at the time the report is made. This arrangement differs from the completed value nonreporting form in that the insured has an additional period of time before the completed value must be reported and the premium paid.

The second method requires that the completed value of each structure started be reported for each month of the construction period, and premium be paid on a monthly basis.

For example, according to the first method, a $100,000 home that has a rate of $.10 per $100 per month and will take three months to build would entail a premium of $300, which would be due at the time the first (and only) report was rendered. Using the second method the insured would report $100,000 for each of three months and pay $100 each month.

In some instances, a reporting form feature may be practical for an installation floater. Reports may be monthly, quarterly, or on any other periodic basis. The subject of the report may be property installed or gross receipts.

Rating

Each company has its own formula for rating builders risk. One method is to use the annual builders risk fire rate for the property under construction. To this is added the extended coverage rate and a load for the other perils insured against. Credit is then given for any increase in the deductible, and the resulting rate is either debited or credited in accordance with any special features affecting the underwriting of the risk.

When the policy is written on a completed value basis, a percentage—usually 55 percent—of the annual builders risk fire rate can be used as a premium base. (Completed value builders risk rates are available in conjunction with the ISO simplified commercial property program. It is not necessary to use the 55 percent factor.) Since premium is charged on the completed value during the entire construction period, the 55 percent charge produces what approximates an average rate for the policy term. When it is known that values will accelerate quickly at the outset of construction, or, conversely, build up rapidly toward the end of the construction period, the 55 percent factor may be increased in the first instance or decreased in the second. Using the annual builders risk rate produces a rate for a twelve month period. When the construction period is greater or less than twelve months, the rate is prorated accordingly.

In the event that construction is not completed during the policy term and an extension of the policy is requested, consideration should be given to an adjustment of the completed value rate for the term of the extension. Values at risk during the extension period may be higher than the average values on which the completed value rate was based.

For a risk that poses hazards greater than those present in general building construction, individual rating procedures may be in order. When a project presents serious exposures during testing, separate rates are often quoted for the erection and testing periods. The premium for the testing period, which may be no more than two or three months, may be greater than the premium for an erection period of several years. Separate, substantially higher deductibles may also apply to losses occurring during testing under these circumstances.

Rates for installation floaters may be arrived at by determining the average fire contents rate of the buildings in which the insured property will be installed, and adding a loading for theft, vandalism, transportation, and all other perils.

Two installation floaters covering the same commodity with the same limits of insurance may present quite divergent amounts of exposure. A contractor with a limit of insurance of $100,000 at any one job site may expose only one job site at any one time. Another contractor with the same limit could expose half a dozen job sites at the same time. The latter contractor obviously deserves a higher premium than the former. When there is a simultaneous exposure at one or more than one location, rates should be applied to total values at risk.

Underwriting

The builders risk and installation floater underwriter has a number of exposures to loss with which to be concerned. They are, principally, fire, theft, windstorm, vandalism, collapse, transportation, and, to a lesser degree in frequency but not necessarily in severity, flood, earthquake, strikes, and civil unrest. Certain risks, in addition, may have serious rigging and testing exposures. Each risk is unique, presenting its own vulnerabilities to loss.

Fire Fire is perhaps the most common, and most devastating, cause of loss. The degree of public fire protection is an important consideration. Operational hydrants should be within reach and the site readily accessible to the fire department. Exposures from nearby buildings must be assessed.

The height and construction type of a building affects the fire risk. One- or two-story structures offer more opportunity to control a fire than a high rise whose upper floors may be outside the ready access range of fire fighters.

Frame or wooden structures are the most susceptible to fire. Masonry buildings with wooden floors or roofs are an improvement over frame, although buildings with large areas or multiple stories present a substantial accumulation of lumber. Noncombustible or all-metal buildings have the least exposure to fire, as do fire-resistive structures. However, high-rise reinforced concrete or fire-resistive buildings require extensive use of forms for pouring concrete. Wooden forms, and wooden shoring to support these forms, not only give the appearance of a lumberyard but have the same potential for fire.

Many fires are caused by the careless use of temporary heating equipment, and cutting and welding activities. Homemade salamanders, used for heating, should not be permitted near the building. Cutting, welding, and brazing activities should be closely supervised. Temporary wiring should be replaced with permanent wiring as soon as possible. Fire extinguishers should be in sufficient supply and strategically placed. On high-rise buildings under construction, standpipes providing the water supply should progress upward with the building. When sprinklers are to be installed, they should be made operational as soon as possible.

Other Perils Loss by theft and vandalism, as well as arson, can be minimized by taking proper security precautions. These might include the installation of fencing, lighting, alarm systems on trailers and storage sheds, and the employment of security guards.

Shopping centers and mercantile structures often have large span roof areas that may be subject to collapse during construction. Sports arenas and exhibition halls have the same exposure. Prototype roof designs should be carefully investigated. Special construction procedures may be in order.

Certain areas of the country are more prone to windstorm than others. Construction that will take longer than one year may be exposed during two hurricane seasons. Tilt-up construction is particularly vulnerable to loss by windstorm, poor workmanship, and earthquake. The walls are susceptible to wind and other damage until the roof is set in place.

Coverage for flood and earthquake is usually handled as an optional coverage under a builders risk policy. When such coverage is granted, it is usually subject to a sublimit and higher deductible.

The mode of transportation (truck, rail, barge, and so on) may be an important aspect of underwriting when highly valued, loss sensitive objects such as turbines and boilers are being shipped to the construction site (see Chapter 3 for responsibility of carrier). Such may be the case when the insured project is an electric generating station, chemical plant, or similar type of industrial construction. Risks of this type are also exposed to hoisting and rigging losses, as well as possibly severe losses during "hot," or operational, testing.

Operational Testing During operational testing of a chemical plant, volatile feedstock is introduced into the system, where it is subjected to high pressures and excessive temperatures. Boilers at electric generating plants are exposed to hazardous steam conditions, and turbine generators are run at over-speed during the commissioning period. It is at this time that errors in design or construction are likely to appear, sometimes with disastrous results.

When operational testing is performed, it is essential that those performing the tests have intimate knowledge of the equipment and its capabilities. The manufacturer's representative is often present during this testing period.

Some underwriters, aware of the potential for catastrophe during testing, require a sublimit for losses occurring during the testing period.

Due to their unique nature, industrial risks are often written on a manuscript form, frequently a form prepared by the producer. Manuscript forms should be carefully reviewed to prevent a misunderstanding of the conditions of insurance. Wording continuing insurance "until formally accepted by the owner as complete..." could continue insurance indefinitely, or at least until the policy expires (some policies are written with no expiration date). Wording terminating coverage "when start-up procedures begin" is often too vague to be effective.

DIFFERENCE IN CONDITIONS COVERAGE

The term *difference in conditions* (DIC) is derived from ocean marine terminology, and so the term is not entirely descriptive of the role it plays in the inland marine field. As an inland marine coverage, DIC originated at a time when only certain named perils were covered under "fire" policies. DIC coverage bridged the gap between those perils and "all-risks" insurance.

Although "all-risks" property insurance is now widely available under standard commercial property forms, DIC policies, because they are a nonfiled inland marine class, allow greater flexibility in arranging coverage. Perils that are normally excluded in standard "all-risks" property forms, such as flood and earthquake, are often covered in DIC policies.

In its simplest form, a DIC policy is an "all-risks" insurance contract that excludes the perils insured against in a named perils policy covering the same property as the DIC. Typically, the perils excluded by the DIC policy (and covered by the other policy) are fire and the perils of extended coverage, although other perils may be excluded as well. The DIC policy may supplement a policy providing direct property damage coverage or one providing business income insurance.

An important general characteristic of DIC coverage is that the policy is intended to apply to catastrophe type losses. As these usually occur infrequently, it is considered a high-severity, low-frequency coverage. Thus, most DIC policies have a high deductible.

DIC insurance was first sanctioned as an inland marine class of business by the 1976 Marine Definition. It is described in section F.22 as "Difference in Conditions Coverage excluding fire and extended coverage perils." There is no qualification as to the type of property that can be covered or the scope of coverage that can be effected. It is a nonfiled class of business and, as is the case with nonfiled classes, there is a great variety of forms on the market, perhaps more so with DIC than other classes as most contracts are individually tailored to meet particular requirements.

Covered Property

The property insured may be real property, personal property, or both real and personal property. Each building or its contents may be specifically listed in the policy, or the policy may simply cover all real and personal property owned by the insured or for which the insured may be liable. A single limit of insurance is used with this blanket approach.

Certain properties are excluded from coverage as it is felt they can best be insured under their own customary specialized forms. Other properties are excluded if it is the company's preference not to insure that particular type of property. Some properties that have been excluded under DIC policies are:

1. currency, money, deeds, evidences of debt, notes, and securities;
2. jewelry, precious stones, precious metals or their alloys; furs or garments trimmed with fur; and fine arts;
3. animals, lawns, plants, shrubs, trees, growing crops, and standing timber;
4. data processing equipment, including component parts and processing media;
5. property in the course of construction;
6. property in transit;
7. watercraft while afloat, aircraft, motor vehicles designed for highway use, railroad rolling stock, and pipelines;
8. mines, caverns, tunnels, and all property contained therein;
9. contractors equipment;
10. valuable papers or accounts receivable;
11. property sold by the insured under conditional sale, trust agreement, installment plan, or other deferred payment plan after delivery to customers;
12. bulkheads, piers, wharves, pilings, docks, dams, or reservoirs.

Covered Perils

Most DIC policies insure against risks of direct physical loss or damage from any external cause, except as excluded.

The perils excluded under a DIC form should track with the perils covered under the basic policy. If the basic policy provides broader coverage than that excluded under the DIC, there will be duplicate insurance and the "other insurance" clause in each contract will be invoked in the event of a loss covered by both policies.

Printed forms contain exclusions that can be added to or deleted as the need arises. Some printed forms exclude such perils as fire, lightning, windstorm, hail, explosion, riot, riot attending a strike, civil commotion, aircraft, vehicles, smoke, sprinkler leakage, vandalism and malicious mischief, and any other peril that is insured by endorsement to the basic property policy.

In some instances a DIC policy will state that it excludes the perils insured against in a specified policy. When naming a specific policy, such as "policy number 12345, or its renewal, issued to the ABC

Corporation by the Secure Insurance Company," the underwriter should consider adding a provision stating that the exclusions will remain in effect in the DIC even though the specific policy is canceled or is not renewed.

Rather than name a specific policy, a DIC form may exclude the perils insured under a standard property form. Before simplification of commercial property forms, the 1943 New York standard fire policy (and extended coverage endorsement) was a benchmark. Under the simplified program, ISO now offers three causes of loss forms—a basic form, a broad form, and a special form.

Various other perils may also be excluded. Some of these relate to the following:

- consequential loss (this coverage may be added back by endorsement);
- contamination, gradual deterioration, wear and tear, moths, vermin, inherent vice;
- errors in design or processing, faulty workmanship or materials (this exclusion may relate only to the property directly affected, and not exclude the resultant loss);
- rain, snow, or sleet damage to property in the open;
- employee dishonesty;
- electrical injury;
- those perils associated with coverage under a steam boiler policy;
- shrinkage, evaporation, loss of weight, dampness of atmosphere, extremes or changes of temperature, change in flavor or color or texture or finish, smog, rust, wet or dry rot, corrosion, marring, scratching or exposure to light;
- normal settling, shrinkage or expansion of foundations, walls, floors or ceilings;
- earthquake and other earth movement (this coverage may be added back by endorsement);
- flood and other water damage (this coverage may be added back by endorsement);
- freezing of plumbing or heating or fire protection systems in vacant property;
- enforcement of any ordinance or law regulating the construction, repair, or demolition of insured property;
- solidification of the contents of molten pots, molten pot lines, and appurtenances;
- unexplained loss or mysterious disappearance;
- war and nuclear hazards.

The policy may include or be extended to cover business interruption, extra expense, rental income, contingent loss of income, or any other kind of consequential loss that the underlying contract provides.

Some DIC policies have a flood exclusion, and it may be comprehensive, excluding flood, waves, tidal water or tidal wave, overflow of streams or other bodies of water, surface water, water which backs up through sewers or drains, and water below the surface of the ground including that which exerts pressure on or flows, seeps, or leaks through sidewalks, driveways, foundations, walls, or floors.

To provide complete coverage for water damage the exclusion would have to be deleted in its entirety. In some instances, there may be a preference to cover only flood, waves, tidal water or tidal wave, overflow of streams or other bodies of water. Surface water (the unusual and rapid accumulation or runoff of surface waters from any source) might be added to this list, as well as mudslides that are caused or precipitated by accumulations of water on or under the ground.

Some DIC policies have earthquake exclusions, which may be variously worded. One version eliminates coverage for "earthquake shock, volcanic eruption, landslide, mudflow, the rising or shifting of the earth, or other earth movement." The elimination of this exclusion provides comprehensive coverage for any earth movement.

When earthquake coverage is extended, the form generally states that more than one earthquake shock or volcanic eruption occurring during a period of 168 hours shall be deemed to be a single earthquake shock or volcanic eruption. This provision impacts on the limit of insurance in any one loss, the deductible in any one loss, and the aggregate amount of insurance allowed under the policy during the policy term.

Limits of Insurance

When the type of property—real, personal, or both—is stated in the policy, and the locations of coverage specified, it is possible to assign a limit of insurance to the property at each location. It is common, however, to omit the schedule of locations and designate a single limit for all the property covered. As there is usually no coinsurance in the policy, the limit may be a fraction of the total value of the property insured, particularly if there is a spread of risk.

When business interruption coverage is included there may be a separate amount of insurance for this coverage. It is not unusual, however, to have a single limit for property and business interruption combined.

When flood or earthquake is insured, it is customary to have sublimits for these perils. There may be separate, lower sublimits at locations where the exposures are most severe. It is also usual to have an aggregate limit for earthquake losses occurring during the policy term. An aggregate may also be applied to flood losses.

Deductibles

One deductible applies to physical loss. The same deductible may also apply to a combined physical loss and business interruption loss, or a separate deductible may be made to apply to business interruption. The business interruption deductible may be either a waiting period of a specific number of days or weeks or a dollar amount.

Separate deductibles apply to flood and earthquake. Earthquake deductibles may be stated as a dollar amount or a percentage of either the property damaged (5 percent, for example) or the total value of property in a given zone (2 percent, for example). Most flood deductibles are expressed as a dollar amount.

Valuation

Separate valuation provisions may apply to finished goods, raw stock and stock in process, buildings, improvements and betterments, patterns and dies, exposed film, accounts, manuscripts, mechanical drawings, blueprints, machinery, equipment, and exhibitions. To be consistent, the DIC policy should contain the same valuation conditions as the underlying policy, whether actual cash value, replacement cost, or some other method.

Other Insurance

The other insurance clause usually provides that the policy is excess over other insurance covering the same property against the same perils. The policy may contain an excess insurance clause, which gives the insured permission to have excess insurance over the limit shown in the policy. This is appropriate, as DIC insurance for larger accounts is often written in layers.

Rating

The rate for DIC coverage is truly based on judgment. The value at risk, spread of risk, deductibles, limit of insurance, exposures, coverage afforded, and loss experience are all taken into consideration.

A rate may first be determined for the property exposure, excluding flood and earthquake. This rate is applied to the total value at risk, not the limit of insurance, which may be a fraction of the total value. Loadings for flood and earthquake are then applied to the property rate if these exposures are to be covered. A premium must be calculated for business interruption if that coverage is included. The sum of all the premiums is then divided back into the total values to arrive at the policy rate.

Policies written for a three-year term or on a continuous basis call for an adjustment of premium at each anniversary date. Property values, business interruption values, and average stock values are required to be reported. If the values reported are greater or less than a given percentage (such as 2.5 percent) of the prior values, an adjustment in premium is made.

Underwriting

DIC losses may be of a nature entirely unanticipated, such as dirt being accidentally circulated through an air conditioning system and permeating an entire plant. The most common DIC losses, however, are those caused by collapse, water damage (excluding flood), and burglary.[1]

Collapse Roof collapse is the most common of collapse losses. Roofs sometimes collapse because excessive weight has been placed on them or because their structure has been weakened over a period of time. Nature often supplies excessive weight in the form of snow drifts or water. Snow drifts can accumulate against any structure in the path of the wind. Flat-roofed buildings of different heights, which are adjacent to each other, present a configuration conducive to snow accumulations.

Ponded water may also overstress a roof. Water may pond up on a roof, particularly a parapeted one, if there is a poorly designed drainage system or the drain pipes are clogged.

Another factor in roof collapse, not necessarily connected with excessive weight, is weakened timbers. Timber loses its strength if subjected to long periods of stress or long periods of excessive heat and humidity.

Water Damage Water damage is probably the most common DIC loss. Leaking roofs, pipe ruptures, and surface runoff water are the principal causes. The age and condition of the plumbing and heating system are major factors to consider when underwriting the water damage exposure. Surface water can accumulate as a result of poor landscaping. In some cases drainage ditches or barriers should be provided to prevent water from entering a building.

Burglary The burglary exposure is directly related to the property's desirability to thieves. The quality of burglary protection—

such as locks, alarms, and watchmen—should be commensurate with the exposure.

Earthquake[2] Earthquake losses occur less frequently than the types of loss already mentioned. Their severity, however, can be much greater. The factors to consider in the earthquake exposure are the type of construction and the location of the risk. Certain types of building construction can withstand an earth tremor better than others. Buildings located near faults or in areas where seismic activity can be expected have an obviously greater exposure to earthquake than buildings located elsewhere.

There is much seismic activity outside California—the traditional focus of concern. For example, in 1985, Westchester County in New York State, and in 1986, the Cleveland, Ohio, area were subjected to relatively significant earthquake activity. There has been continuing media attention on the New Madrid fault, which touches parts of Arkansas, Illinois, Kentucky, Missouri, and Tennessee. This fault was responsible for one of the most severe earthquakes in United States history.

Exhibit 7-1 shows many areas of seismic susceptibility in the contiguous forty-eight states. These areas include: (1) Puget Sound and environs, (2) New England (including the Boston area), (3) Utah, (4) Idaho, and (5) South Carolina (including the Charleston area). Exhibit 7-2 shows seismic zones for Hawaii, Alaska, and Puerto Rico, all of which have at least modest earthquake possibilities.

Given that there are areas outside of California subject to seismic activity, DIC and other inland marine coverages may have significant exposure to earthquake shock. When a policy excludes earthquake, it typically excludes shock damage, but not damage resulting from other covered perils ensuing from quake. Today, this point is even more significant with the doctrine of concurrent causation (see Chapter 2). An underwriter, when extending earthquake coverage, must consider not only the direct shock damage, but also the ensuing losses due to covered perils and indirect concurrent causes.

Assisting underwriters in their earthquake analysis is the fire and allied lines division of the Commercial Lines Manual (CLM) of the Insurance Services Office. First, ISO identifies earthquake zones by state and county, allowing underwriters to identify earthquake susceptibility. Second, ISO promulgates building classifications, evaluating exposures to earthquake by construction material, height, design, and so on. Of particular interest to the inland marine underwriter is a "special structures" exhibit, which cross-references structures such as bridges, dams, radio and TV towers, and tanks to an equivalent building class.

Exhibit 7-1
Map for Seismic Zones — Contiguous 48 States*

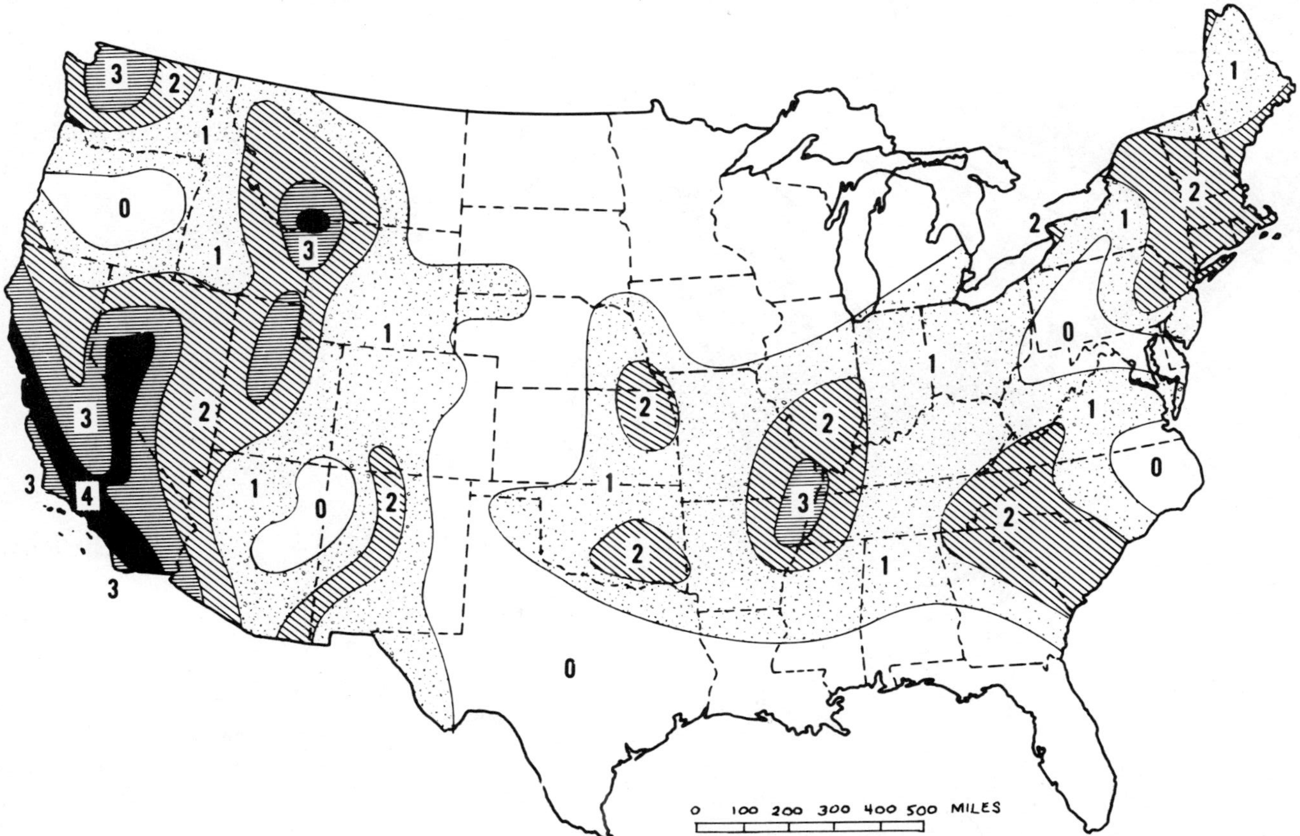

* Reproduced with permission from *American National Standard Minimum Design Loads for Buildings and Other Structures*, ANSI A58.1, copyright 1982 by the American National Standards Institute, New York, NY.

Exhibit 7-2
Map for Seismic Zones — Hawaii, Alaska, and Puerto Rico*

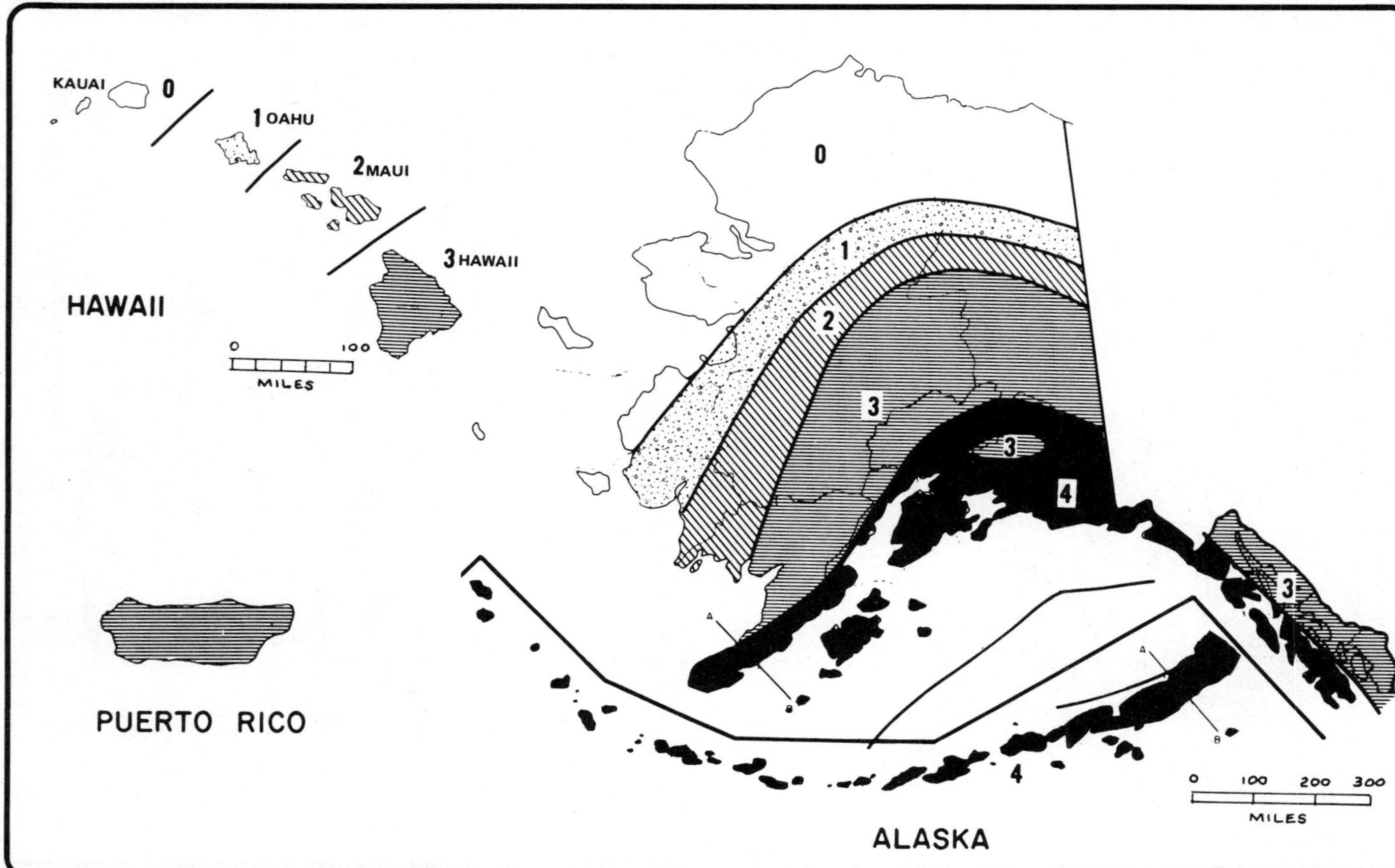

* Reproduced with permission from *American National Standard Minimum Design Loads for Buildings and Other Structures*, ANSI A58.1, copyright 1982 by the American National Standards Institute, New York, NY.

Further, contents within buildings are also graded by susceptibility to earthquake. These grades vary from state to state, or more generally, from eastern to western states, and so the CLM exception pages for each state should be consulted. In this way, an underwriter can begin to identify earthquake exposures of a risk by its location, construction, and contents.

Flood Flood, like earthquake, is a peril that occurs with relatively low frequency in comparison with other DIC perils but can result in severe losses. As with earthquake, location of the insured is a paramount concern.

Information on areas that have flooded in the past or may have a tendency to flood in the future (the so-called 100 year flood plain) may be obtained from the United States Army Corps of Engineers. The Corps will also respond to a request for such information on a specific location. Information on areas subject to flooding may also be obtained from the National Flood Insurance Program. A Community Status Book is published bimonthly by the Federal Emergency Management Agency of the Federal Insurance Administration. This book lists the communities participating in the National Flood Insurance program.

Under the National Flood Insurance Program, flood-prone communities can become eligible for federal flood insurance by making application for the program and instituting certain land use requirements. There are two programs available, the Emergency Program and the Regular Program. Qualified communities are first placed in the Emergency Program until a detailed study is made of the community and a flood insurance map is published.

Differing amounts of insurance are available under the Emergency Program and the Regular Program. "Small businesses" can buy up to $100,000 on buildings and $100,000 on contents under the Emergency Program, and $250,000 on buildings and $300,000 on contents under the Regular Program. ("Small businesses" are concerns with up to $500,000 in assets, $2,500,000 of net worth, and average net income after taxes of $250,000 for the preceding two years.) Other business concerns can buy the same limits for the Emergency Program and $200,000 on buildings and $200,000 on contents under the Regular Program. Residential properties have their own separate limits.

When insuring properties eligible for National Flood Insurance, consideration should be given to insuring only the excess over the maximum amount available under the federal program or adding a deductible for the amount of National Flood Insurance in force. It is best not to word the DIC coverage as being excess over a specific policy as that policy might be canceled or not renewed.

Inspections DIC policies may cover one specific property, several listed properties, or a number of properties too numerous to be scheduled. When a limited number of properties is insured it may be practical to make inspections to determine the exposures to collapse, water damage, burglary, flood, and other DIC type losses, such as dropping during rigging and accidental overflow of storage tanks. When numerous properties are involved it may be practical to inspect only the larger ones and rely on past loss experience to provide a gauge for the exposures at the other locations.

Information requested on applications can be most helpful. Care must be taken, however, not to ask for information concerning a type of property, such as contractors equipment, that is not covered by the policy. A court might decide that since information was solicited the property was covered.

Use of Deductibles Substantial deductibles, as indicated previously, are the norm with DIC policies. Separate deductibles usually apply to flood, earthquake, and business interruption. Manufacturing risks and high production industries are candidates for sizable business interruption deductibles. The total amount of insurance may be reduced by the deductible or remain intact after the deductible has been exhausted. The policy should clearly state which provision is in effect.

Probable Maximum Loss Two or more DIC policies are sometimes written in layers for a single insured. This becomes necessary when multi-million-dollar limits are required and the capacity of a number of insurers is needed. Participants in the upper layers are often well outside the probable maximum loss and will be called upon to respond only in the event of major catastrophe.

However, the PML is not so easily determined on a DIC risk, particularly if multiple locations are involved. When flood or earthquake is covered, the PML may well be the amount of insurance for these perils. The limit of insurance, whether it is one occurrence limit for the entire policy or a limit per occurrence at each location, will also affect the PML. When setting a "net line" above which reinsurance is required, underwriters should ascertain whether their in-house reinsurance treaties will respond to a DIC loss or if separate DIC treaties are applicable.

SUMMARY

This chapter examines three types of inland marine policies that may cover personal property *and* real property: builders risk policies, installation floaters, and difference in conditions (DIC) policies. Because of their similarities, builders risk policies and installation floaters are discussed together.

Both builders risk policies and installation floaters may cover property of the insured and property of others for which the insured is liable. The property insured under a builders risk policy is the property undergoing construction, reconstruction, alteration, or repair, and consists of the machinery, equipment, materials, supplies, and fixtures that will become or have become a permanent part of the building or structure. Installation floaters are generally associated with such properties as plumbing, heating, cooling, and electrical systems, but can be written to cover any property being installed. Property excluded under these forms varies from one insurer to another.

A separate limit of insurance usually applies to property in transit and to property at the job site. Builders risk policies are often extended to include coverage for loss of rents, loss of earnings, and "soft costs."

Each company has its own formula for rating builders risk. Rates for installation floaters may be arrived at by determining the average fire contents rate of the buildings in which the insured property will be installed, and adding a loading for theft, vandalism, transportation, and all other perils.

Difference in conditions (DIC) policies are "all-risks" insurance contracts that exclude the perils insured against in a named perils policy covering the same property as the DIC. Typically, the perils excluded by the DIC are fire and the perils of extended coverage. The policy is tailored to respond to catastrophe-type losses and is considered a high-severity, low-frequency coverage.

The property insured by a DIC may be real property, personal property, or both real and personal property. Most DIC policies insure against risks of direct physical loss or damage from any external cause, except as excluded. It is common to omit a schedule of covered locations and to designate a single limit of insurance for all property covered.

The rate for DIC coverage is truly based on judgment. The value at risk, spread of risk, deductibles, limit of insurance, exposures, coverage afforded, and loss experience are all taken into consideration.

The most common DIC losses are those caused by collapse, water damage (excluding flood), and burglary. Substantial deductibles are the norm in DIC policies. Separate deductibles usually apply to flood, earthquake, and business interruption.

Chapter Notes

1. "DIC: Difference in Conditions" (Norwood, MA: Factory Mutual System).
2. Adapted from "Earthquake," a May 1986 report of the Installation, Builders Risk and DIC Committee of the Inland Marine Underwriters Association.

Index

A

B

C

D

E

F

G

H

I

J

L

M

N

O

P

Q

R

S

T

U

V

W